I CHOSE TEACHING

*A Life Record of Self-Reliance
and
Devotion to Scholarship and Democracy*

by AMOS LEE HEROLD

Printed by

THE NAYLOR COMPANY

San Antonio, Texas

1958

Copyright, 1958

by

AMOS L. HEROLD

Printed In The United States of America

First Edition

LIBRARY OF CONGRESS CATALOG CARD NO. 58-7540

Contents

Author's Thanks

FOR permission to reprint three short poems by Mrs. Mary Erwin Overholt, I am indebted to her children — Helen, Mary, Pauline, James, John, and Richard. I quote Mary Hartshorne's "Thanksgiving Hymn" with the approval of the University of Tulsa, owner of the copyright. Gervas S. Taylor gladly gave me his consent to reprint his youthful poem, "Maid of Richmond."

For the book title, *I Chose Teaching*, I am indebted to my wife, Mrs. Virginia Smith Herold, who suggested it when the publisher requested a shorter substitute for my original, *The Adventures of an American Teacher*.

To my relatives, fellow teachers, alumni friends, former students and other friends in many States of the Union, I am deeply grateful for their generous response to the prepublication sale of the autographed edition of my recollections.

For my personal knowledge and satisfaction, most of the family data used in Part I was collected twenty to thirty years ago from the legal and historical records of the counties named in "Ancestral Land and Heritage."

1209 W. 8th Street   — A. L. H.
Austin, Texas
March 12, 1958

I CHOSE TEACHING
Part I. Ancestral Land and Heritage

CHAPTER 1

Preview

THOUGH self-analysis is difficult, and doctors have a rule against even trying to diagnose themselves, yet, everyone ought to know many things about himself much better than anyone else can know them. As a guide in this attempt at self-analysis in autobiography, I will endeavor to apply the cultural or educational principles set forth by two famous philosophers, Kilpatrick and Emerson. The first stated that everything a man does educates him, and the second asserted that the scholar is educated by nature, by books, and by activity in society.

My ancestors were a serious, independent, hard-working people of mixed Scotch-Irish, English, and German blood, who lived in the deep valleys, bluegrass hills, and timbered mountains of the two Virginias. Three lines of descent I have traced to the original immigrants of the mid-18th century, who were the first settlers in the Valley of Virginia. My study of three Virginia counties shows that these farmers of three or four generations ago were basically like the people now living. They were eager to acquire lands, own stock, and build roads and bridges, grist and lumber mills, tanneries, and harness shops, schools and churches in order that they might prosper and give their children a better chance than the parents had received. They bought and sold lands and stock, signed mortgages, quarreled, sued, and formed companies just as people still traffic for gain. In these activities my ancestors were typical examples.

The natural beauty of my native region — its clear, rippling streams of water, its corn and wheat fields, its sheep and cattle pastures, its monstrous, timbered mountains on the horizon —

1

made a deep and lasting impression on me. My mind was so filled with their beauty, mystery, and serenity that later when I read such nature poets as Bryant and Wordsworth and such naturalists as Thoreau and Burroughs, my response was immediate and appreciative. Even now, it is a pleasure to recall those lovely scenes of my youth. Yet, as I grew older, I felt confined, shut in, and imprisoned; but I found escape through books, newspapers, teaching, college, the world, and the universe. My life has been a series of rebirths, or adventurous escapes into new worlds of the mind.

During my middle teens I read the Bible from cover to cover with the intense faith and devotion of a medieval monk. I believed all that was said about the good book. Yet I observed some inconsistencies and asked some hard questions, such as where Cain got his wife. The explanation that he might have married his sister did not help at all! But this reading sharpened my taste for literature, for virtue and goodness, and my conviction that a harlot should be avoided like a rattlesnake. Many passages in the Psalms, Proverbs, and the Gospels, I voluntarily memorized; and at one time I could repeat all of the Sermon on the Mount.

In my late teens I read Franklin's *Autobiography* with lively interest and admiration for his self-reliance and resourcefulness. His mild 18th-century skepticism and rationalism were just the tonic corrective I then needed, and later I read and reread his masterpiece to satisfy an inner thirst. In high school, Steele's *Popular Astronomy* gave me a little comprehension of the infinity of space and the wonders of the stellar universe. In a college course in geology I learned more of the earth and its ways and got a little understanding of the vastness of time in creation as contrasted with the six-day story of the Bible. From biology I learned the basic laws of life — growth or evolution — with the result that some of my childish beliefs fell to pieces and were followed by better-reasoned views attained after a period of mental distress and perplexity — an experience which I later named college measles.

From the Bible I early learned that the love of money is the root of evil. Many of our sociological studies verify that ancient teaching. In spite of Jefferson's view that cities may promote evil and corruption, I have enjoyed cities, especially New York, Washington, and Austin. It is good, I reasoned, to own farms and city houses, bonds and libraries, though to attain great wealth and power is a mistaken conception of success. The true one is to seek and promote the welfare of all the people.

So, I sought neither poverty nor riches, but the wherewithal to gratify a few innocent needs and tastes. I have faith that the evils of our economic system can be alleviated, but not wholly cured, because the love of money is the root of evil.

In the First World War I served in the army to end war and to make the world safe for democracy. Later I realized that democracy is not secure in my own country and much less safe in the rest of the world. Love of property, overpopulation, and the ambitions of evil men lead to friction, conflicts, and wars. So long as men respond to the instinct to reproduce their kind, to the love of money and property, and to the fascinations of leadership and power, there are likely to be strife and war. Yet, just as dueling and human slavery in respectable nations have been outlawed and partly eradicated, so I sincerely hope that the nations of the earth may contrive some form of internationalism to settle their disputes and maintain peace and justice.

Since I have always wished to get the facts, the hard facts, and to live with them, much of my life has been an ardent search for whatever is true, good, and lovely. In college I studied Dante's *Divine Comedy* with much benefit to my grasp of the difference between virtue and vice, between evil men and good men, because if one doubts Heaven and Hell, he ought to read Dante's judgment of a thousand people rendered in the form of a great narrative and ethical poem — a timeless masterpiece of classical art.

In my lifelong pursuit of the true, the useful, the good, and the beautiful, I have sought knowledge as the highway to wisdom and prudence; courage as the highway to freedom and justice; temperance as the highway to goodness and virtue; and art as the highway to beauty.

To guide and encourage the pilgrim over the highways to his chosen goals were these treasured maxims:

1. Seek the bliss of freedom, goodness, justice, and wisdom.
2. Make vigilance the guardian of liberty and virtue.
3. Live by useful art and enjoy beauty.
4. Practice sincerity, cleanness, and industry.
5. Conserve your personal and financial resources.
6. In faith and hope refuse to be a gullible medievalist.
7. But always observe the Golden Rule.

In the course of my long teaching experience I observed three problems that still clamor for adjustment. These are neglect of American Literature in our colleges and universities, obsolete college governments, and obsolete systems of old-age retirement. In many colleges presidential dictatorships are a blight to the colleges and a menace to the American democracy; and premature, forced retirements of thousands of teachers and many thousands of other Americans are criminal violations of their civil rights under the Federal Constitution. Therefore, the importance of American Literature as a bulwark of our democracy is the subject of chapters 17 and 18; and college government and old-age retirement are the chief topics of chapters 16, 20, and 25. My trip to Europe is sketched in chapter 14, and my travels in the United States and delight in American natural beauty inspired the four chapters on "Seeing the United States."

Though I was born, passed my youth, and was educated in Eastern States, most of my mature life has been spent in the Southwest. At the age of 19 I first saw and admired the Midwest when I visited the Louisiana Purchase Exposition at St. Louis. For more than 30 years my home has been in the Southwest, where I taught college English. Influenced by friends and attracted by the mild climate, excellent libraries, and investment opportunities of Austin, Texas, I chose this progressive city for residence during my years of retired leisure.

CHAPTER 2

Happy Hunting Ground

BORN on Back Creek in Highland County, Virginia, I grew up on a Knapp's Creek farm in Pocahontas County, West Virginia, which are adjoining sections with the main Allegheny Mountain dividing them. Highland is a small upland county in the Valley of Virginia, lying between the Allegheny and Shenandoah Mountains, with three small parallel ranges intervening, where rise the headwaters of the James and South Potomac Rivers. Back Creek flows south along the eastern base of the Allegheny into the Jackson River, which joins the Cowpasture to form the famous James River. In Pocahontas County on the west slope of the Allegheny, the Greenbrier flows southwest through the center of Pocahontas toward the Ohio River. Its chief branch, Knapp's Creek, rising at the foot of Paddy's Knob in the Allegheny, meanders south and west through a beautiful valley 20 miles long to join the Greenbrier at Marlinton and to provide Indians and white men with an easy approach to a low gap across the Allegheny west of Paddy's Knob, the highest point between the two counties. Through this picturesque mountain gap passes a good modern automobile road with only one sharp curve on the Virginia side and on top of the Allegheny is another scenic highway.

Here, two centuries ago, in spring, summer, and autumn was a Happy Hunting Ground of the Indians, an earthly paradise to delight both red men and white men and to lead to strife and the bloody frontier wars for control and possession. So plentiful in this mountainous region was the game that a pioneer and his rifle were seldom separated. My great-grandfather, Samuel Ruckman, related that one day in his early life he set out on horseback on an errand a few miles away with his trusty rifle. Chancing upon a fine deer, he shot it and hung it up in a tree till he should return. Farther on, he killed a second deer. Deciding then to change his plans, he returned with two deer to his family. One old hunter in Pocahontas County, John Barlow, born in 1781, estimated that in his lifetime he had killed 1,500 deer — once six in a single day.

With deep, narrow valleys and high, oval mountains growing white pine, hemlock, and hardwood trees of several kinds, this region, at an elevation of 2,000 to 4,500 feet, is famed for its natural beauty of hills and streams, forests and bluegrass pastures. Under restrictive regulations deer are once more plentiful and hunters still find a happy hunting ground, which also is the home of many contented, hard-working Americans, who show their love for their native region by many happily chosen names of places, such as Blue Grass, Clover Creek, and Green Bank.

Monterey, the county seat of Highland, lies on a watershed between the sources of the James and Potomac Rivers at a cooling elevation of 3,000 feet; and grass-topped Paddy's Knob with grand views in all directions is nearly one mile high. How cool and refreshing are the breezes there to reward the climber! How refreshing to find there a dripping spring of clear water near the very top of the mountain!

My earliest recollections are enduringly glorified by the beauty, the majesty, and the mystery of these ancient mountains, which in the geologic ages rose up so slowly that the James, Potomac, and New Rivers succeeded in cutting gorges through them, where they continue to flow. Most remarkable is the feat of New River, which, rising near the Atlantic in North Carolina and flowing northwest in the Valley of Virginia, breaks through the Allegheny Mountain to the Ohio River on its 2,500-mile journey to the Gulf of Mexico. What natural wonders —

these imperious rivers that would not be stopped by mountains!

Perhaps the first Latin I learned was the motto of West Virginia — *Montani semper liberi* — Mountaineers are always free; and Virginia's, well fitted for the Revolution and often quoted — *Sic semper tyrannis* — Thus always to tyrants. Both mottoes impressed me deeply and soon became my own guiding principles.

Cousin Mary Erwin Overholt, the poet of my family, who was born on Back Creek and grew up in Highland, an orphan in my mother's family and her girlhood companion, wrote some lovely lines on "Father Allegheny":

> With your lofty head in cloudland,
> At your feet the rivers flow;
> Fair and clear, they travel onward,
> Scattering blessings as they go.
>
> And the men who till your valleys,
> The cattle on your thousand hills,
> Bulwarked by your stately shoulders,
> With content the prospect fills.
>
> In your sons a certain grandeur,
> A simplicity and truth,
> And a nobleness of nature
> You have nurtured from their youth.
>
> Something more of manhood sturdy,
> Of a gentle, stately grace
> Has, methought, descended on them
> From long gazing on your face.
>
> Sure it is an inspiration
> To the nobler side of man,
> To behold you pointing skyward,
> Saying, 'If you will, you can!'

In this Happy Hunting Land of the Virginia mountains, birds, game fish, and wild animals were abundant. In this region ornithologists recently identified about 300 different kinds of birds. Besides the songsters, they list ducks, herons, bobwhites, pheasants, turkeys, hawks and eagles, woodpeckers, whippoorwills, cardinals, humming birds, blue jays, sparrows, swallows, robins, and bluebirds.

Among the wild animals, now extinct, were elk and buffalo, though they are still remembered by such place names as Buffalo

Gap in Virginia and Elk River and Elk Mountain in West Virginia. Deer were plentiful then as nowadays with restricted hunting to protect the does. Rabbits were innumerable and prolific; raccoons, foxes and squirrels of several kinds, ground hogs, skunks, and o'possums abounded. Four wild animals, dangerous and destructive to man and other animals, were the bear, wolf, panther, and wildcat — all scarce now but persistent. Wolves and even panthers would sometimes hunt in packs of five to ten animals. Though panthers usually stalk their prey singly, a hunter in Pocahontas County once shot nine in succession at the same spot, and then fled to Huntersville for his life. So eager were the pioneers to get rid of wolves that Pocahontas bounties on wolf scalps rose from $5 in 1826 to $15 in 1855. All four animals along with the Indians were a dreaded menace on the Virginia frontier.

Of the many animal stories I have read or heard I will relate two about the panther, also called cougar, puma, and mountain lion, which is a long, powerful, catlike animal of a man's weight, tree-climbing, long-jumping, and deceitful; at times screaming like a terrified woman; cunning and respected by man and other beasts. It is not so large and strong as a bear, but is larger and more dangerous than a wolf or a wildcat. When I was a boy, I heard alarming stories of one or two seen or heard in our neighborhood. Like some other animals, the panther has a trick of covering up its kill for later use.

Calvin W. Price, editor of *The Pocahontas Times,* in 1939 published the story of an old-time hunter who went to sleep while waiting for deer at a stand or lick on Elk River. Toward morning he awoke hot and smothering under a pile of leaves. Recognizing at once an animal's trick or stratagem, he sprang out of the leaves and climbed a nearby tree, carrying his rifle with him. As day was breaking, he heard and then saw a great panther creeping slowly nearer and nearer, accompanied by two half-grown cubs. With a flying leap the beast soon landed on the pile of leaves, hitting and clawing with all four paws simultaneously. Keenly disappointed to find the game gone, she screamed vicious curses like the devil himself. The hunter then took careful aim and shot the brute between the eyes.

Another story told by Mr. Price shows that the Lord never intended the panther or cougar for a house pet. A sporting pioneer of Pocahontas County in his youthful ardor for novelty had tried to tame and domesticate a captured panther kitten. He and his pet were almost inseparable companions. Between this pet and the Negro servants, however, there was so much antipathy that he dared not leave it at home unless securely tied. The owner prized his pet so much and was so fearful the Negroes would kill it that he let it sleep near his bed even after it had grown to weigh more than 100 pounds. One night he was awakened by the cat's licking his throat with a sandpaper tongue. Excited, it would lick and then pinch with its teeth, each pinch becoming a little harder. When the blood was almost oozing through the skin, the man decided that its ministrations had gone far enough. So he swiftly beat off the panther and with his gun shot the blood-thirsty beast.

The Valley of Virginia

The famous Valley of Virginia, which lies between the Blue Ridge and the Allegheny Mountains, 30 to 50 miles wide, extending 300 miles from Maryland to North Carolina, and drained by the Shenandoah, James, New, and Tennessee Rivers, was first widely and favorably publicized in 1716 by Governor Spottswood's expedition across the Blue Ridge in northern Virginia. His party consisted of 50 persons — state officials, gentlemen with their retainers, a small company of rangers, and four friendly Indians, with lots of baggage and liquor carried on pack animals. After descending into the Valley and crossing the Shenandoah River, the governor with much ostentation took possession of the territory for King George I of England.

Though the governor was chiefly interested in combatting French encroachments on the northwest frontier, the glowing descriptions of the Valley spread by the party induced hunters to visit it, and within a few years German and Scotch-Irish settlers from Pennsylvania began to enter the Valley and to find homes away from persecution in Europe and annoying restrictions in the Quaker state. Joist Hite led the Germans, and the heroic John Lewis led the Scotch-Irish, who settled in and around Staunton, Virginia. By 1738 so many pioneers had entered the Valley that the Virginia colony created two new counties there — Augusta, including about five later states, and Frederick, a much smaller unit in the lower Shenandoah. By 1750 this typical melting pot of Scotch-Irish, Germans, and English was overflowing the Allegheny into the present state of West Virginia.

At this point I should like to quote a pen picture of pioneer experiences drawn by Joseph A. Waddell in his well-known *Annals of Augusta County, Virginia* (second edition, 1902, page 26):

"It is believed that all the earliest settlers came from Pennsylvania and up the Valley of the Shenandoah. It was several years before any settlers entered the Valley from the east, and through the gaps in the Blue Ridge. We may accompany, in imagination, these immigrants on their way from the settlements north of the Potomac, through the wilderness, to their future home. There was, of course, no road, and for the first comers no path to guide their steps, except, perhaps, the trail of the Indian or buffalo. They came at a venture, climbing the hills, fording the creeks and rivers, and groping through the forests. At night they rested on the ground, with no roof over them but the broad expanse of heaven. After selecting a spot for a night's bivouac, and tethering their horses, fire was kindled by means of flint and steel, and their frugal meal was prepared. Only a scanty supply of food was brought along, for, as game abounded, they mainly 'subsisted off the country.' Before lying down to rest, many of them did not omit to worship the God of their fathers, and invoke His guidance and protection. The moon and stars looked down peacefully as they slumbered, while bears, wolves, and panthers prowled around. It was impossible to bring wagons, and all their effects were transported on horseback. The list of articles was meager enough. Clothing, some bedding, guns and ammunition, a few cooking utensils, seed corn, axes, saws, etc., and the Bible, were indispensable, and were transported at whatever cost of time and labor. Houses and furniture had to be provided after the place of settlement was fixed upon. We may imagine the leaders of each band, on arriving at a well-wooded and well-watered spot, exclaiming: 'This is my rest, and here will I dwell'."

Four Heroic Pioneers

Here I will introduce a few of my own 18th-century ancestors, who thus made homes in the Allegheny woods, and of whom I am rightly and justly proud. The stories of their courage, patience, virtue, and great accomplishments in the face of numberless dangers and difficulties are thrilling. Through at least three of them I can qualify as a Son of the American Revolution. For their descendants they risked their lives and their possessions on the frontier and the battlefield in order that we may enjoy "life, liberty, and the pursuit of happiness." Should we not be forever grateful and hold their names in lasting remembrance? Let me sketch four of my ancestral heroes.

1. Sergeant David Ruckman served in a New Jersey infantry regiment in the Revolution and was twice wounded at the battle of Monmouth. Later he had charge of a battery of artillery and at Yorktown he witnessed the surrender of Cornwallis in Octo-

ber, 1781. He was the grandfather of my grandfather, David Van Meter Ruckman. The sergeant's own father, James Ruckman, though an old man of 60 years in 1776, became a color bearer in a New Jersey regiment and was killed in the fighting on Long Island.

2. Captain (later Major) Andrew Lockridge had military service on the Virginia frontier and won the praise of Washington. In 1762 he married Jane Graham, a name famous in song and story. Both were Scotch-Irish and lived in the Valley of Virginia. Captain Lockridge led a company in the decisive battle with the Indians at Point Pleasant, (West) Virginia, in 1774, in which 1,000 pioneers defeated Cornstalk's warriors in a bloody encounter. His granddaughter, Elizabeth, married Henry Simmons Herold (1800-1890), my great-grandfather. My sincerest thanks to you, dear Elizabeth, for my inheritance and for putting me in touch with George Washington.

3. John Slaven (son of Irish John), a man of powerful physique, was a noted hunter, successful trapper, and veteran of the Revolutionary War. In spite of the many bloody fights he was in and the privations he endured in the service of his country, he lived to an old age. His daughter, Margaret, became the second wife of Samuel Ruckman in 1821, who was my mother's grandfather. My sincerest thanks to you, dear Margaret, for the Slaven gift and heritage.

4. But the most famous of this ancestral group is Moses Moore, who before the Revolution settled in the woods on Knapp's Creek, (West) Virginia, a mile below my later childhood home. In 1770 he bought there about 1,000 acres of unimproved valley land for two steel traps and two pounds of English sterling, along with a fine opportunity to be killed and scalped by the Indians on this exposed frontier. He hunted, he cleared lands, he built log houses and a water mill on Mill Run, reared nine or ten children with many descendants, and lived to tell the story of an exciting experience of captivity among the Indians in his early life. When I was a boy, I knew his grandson Andrew, an old man of 80 years, who was the source of this captivity adventure as retold by William T. Price in *Historical Sketches of Pocahontas County* (1901). Moses Moore's granddaughter, Malinda, became my great-grandmother, Mrs. Samuel Harper. My sincerest thanks to you, dear Malinda, for this Moore and Harper heritage.

His Experiences in Captivity

Moses Moore's story related that in his early life in the frontier region, he spent much time hunting on Back Allegheny and along the Greenbrier River; that he was a close observer of the Indians and a cunning hunter in avoiding them. There was a certain place where the Indians were in the habit of crossing the river, using a long pole to leap over the stream and leaving it on the side where they were scouting. The Indians got wise to this interpretation and began to throw the pole back to the opposite side so as to deceive the wary white man.

This change of practice threw Moses Moore off his guard. So, one Saturday he set his traps, looked after the deer signs, and prepared his camp for a quiet and restful Sabbath spent in repose and devotional reading of the Bible. About daylight on Sunday he put a fat turkey to roast and was lying on a bear skin reading a lesson from the Scriptures, preparatory to meditation and prayer before breakfast, a practice characteristic of the Scotch-Irish of that period.

Presently he heard the breaking of a stick and looking intently in the direction of the sound, he saw five or six Indian warriors aiming their guns at him and moving cautiously toward him. Thus hemmed in without a chance to escape, he threw up his hands and signaled for them to come to him. He then put the turkey before them and made signs for them to eat. They refused until he ate some himself. Then they ate ravenously and the turkey soon disappeared with only the bones remaining.

After this breakfast they started for their home in Ohio. When they halted for any length of time, they would securely bind the prisoner with buffalo thongs and pinion him to the ground. Once they thus halted to secure and smelt ore, which they carried home with them. After a long journey through the wilderness they reached their Ohio wigwams at or near Chillicothe on the Scioto River.

The Indians were excited and elated over the capture. As a special compliment to their squaw wives and sweethearts, they decided, in a solemn council, that the captive should run the gauntlet lined with the females of the tribe. So two lines of squaws were drawn up about six or eight feet apart and armed with knives, cooking utensils, and clubs.

One captive who had preceded Moore was stabbed, bruised, and hacked to pieces. This example made clear to him that his chance to survive the ordeal was slender. It looked like death to him. However, after he had entered the line and passed a little way, a squaw struck him with a long-handled frying-pan. He succeeded in wrenching the pan from her and knocked her down with his fist. He then proceeded along the line and, striking viciously from right to left with the pan, he soon put many of the squaws to flight, to the intense amusement of the warriors.

When Moore had thus scattered his persecutors in the gauntlet line, the Indian men crowded around him, patted and praised him, saying, "good soldier, good soldier," and, admiring his skillful self-defence, decided that he should be allowed to live.

By degrees he obtained their confidence. They liked his skill in hunting and would let him have small portions of powder and shot. Slowly in secret he accumulated a surplus of ammunition, and he was eventually allowed to be away overnight, and later for two or three days, since he had the reputation of faithfully returning with game or other supplies.

With this secret supply of rations, powder, and bullets he finally escaped, getting so great a lead the Indians had little chance to recapture him. So he returned home and lived out his life without any more adventures with the red men, a timeless hero of his family and of his region.

Moses Moore and many of his descendants lie buried in the Moore graveyard on a slaty knoll beside the highway a mile below my old home. When I was a boy, one of his direct descendants, Cousin Isaac Brown Moore, father of my playmates, represented Pocahontas County in the Legislature of West Virginia.

CHAPTER 3

Honoring My Ancestors

DURING the first quarter of the 19th century both my maternal and paternal ancestors, the Ruckmans and Herolds, were living on stock and grain farms in the same neighborhood on Back Creek of James River in what is now Highland County, Virginia. They were then pioneering neighbors, facing the same problems in the woods and helping each other as need or opportunity arose. Their private homes were the only churches, and the settlers co-operated in starting the primitive elementary schools.

About 1825, however, on the restless frontier they became separated, and were not closely associated again till my father in 1884 married into the Ruckman family. The pioneers, Christopher Herold and his wife Elizabeth, sold their home and 170 acres of land on Back Creek for $3,000 and with their children removed across the Allegheny Mountain to the neighborhood of the present Minnehaha Springs in the new county of Pocahontas, (West) Virginia, where in the next 20 years Christopher purchased eight tracts of land, mostly timbered and totaling 6,000 acres, for $5,000. They reared seven sons and three daughters, lived to about 1860, and with two of their children are buried on the old farm on Douthard's Creek. When nearing the age of 90, Christopher died tragically by falling headlong into an open fire.

On the other hand, the Ruckman family remained for many years on Back Creek, increasing in numbers and acquiring more valuable lands, some of which are still occupied by their descendants, the children of Edwin A. and Lucy Ruckman Wade. But about 1890, when my grandmother, Annah Ruckman, inherited a fine farm from her father, on Long Glade, Augusta County, the Ruckmans removed there though still holding their lands in Highland County.

Maternal Ancestry

My mother's family, the Ruckmans, are said to be of Welsh stock. The original immigrant, Samuel Ruckman, was born on the border of Wales in 1643 and at the age of seventeen came to Long Island, where he married and left descendants. His son Thomas went to New Jersey, where his son James and grandson David were born and became soldiers in the American Revolution.

Sergeant David Ruckman (1747-1822) married Susannah Little (1756-1843) in New Jersey. Sergeant David had been in Virginia during the war, and he and his young wife had heard perhaps glamorous stories of life among the Virginia planters and aristocrats, and they decided to migrate to the Valley. A family tradition relates how Susannah imagined that Virginia was a land of gold and a heavenly place, where the very floors were not made of planks but either marble or fine mosaic. In light verse Cousin Mary concluded her dream with these lines:

> They went. Of Susannah
> I heard no more
> Except this item
> About the floor.
>
> These floors were really
> Not made of plank
> But of mother earth
> Well trodden, but dank!

David and Susannah Ruckman were blessed with ten children. Two of them died in infancy probably owing to the hardships of the frontier, dirt floors, and their dependence upon home remedies, because it was many years before they could get professional doctors, who usually lived at a distance with only trails or crude roads for traveling. Of these hardy pioneers one can learn little apart from legal and Bible records and the number and high quality of their offspring. We do know that four sons and four daughters reached maturity, and that by sound planning and persevering work, David and his wife became well established in Bath, later Highland County, Virginia, and gave their children a fair start in life.

Samuel Ruckman

Of these children, for our purpose, the most interesting and worthwhile is Samuel, their oldest son, the diarist, born in Somerset County, New Jersey, in 1783 and died at Mill Gap, Highland County, Virginia, in 1853. Obviously, Samuel received the elements of an education, because he kept a diary, served as a justice of the peace, and in the 1840's he was a leader in the formation of Highland County. By his first wife, Nancy Hartman, he had a brilliant son, John H., who received $20,000 for inventing or improving Gibbs' sewing machine, and two daughters, Mary and Nancy. By his second wife, Margaret Slaven (1791-1867), he had three daughters and three sons, the youngest of whom, David Van Meter, was my grandfather.

Samuel's diary, still in manuscript, is in two parts: The first, kept in three composition booklets, extends from August, 1804, to August, 1812, when he was in his 20's. The second part, on bound legal-cap paper, with one gap of three years, covers the last period of his life from December, 1839, to January, 1853. The diary reveals the author himself and supplies us with much valuable information regarding the customs and practices of his period. From it we learn that he was studious, bought books, owned a big dictionary, read and thought for himself, promoted temperance, functioned as local critic, willfully sought and succeeded like a good businessman in becoming rich in lands and stock, and left behind many colorful legends of himself and his dealings. At the age of 57 he recalls that he had been a feeble child though descended from a stout and able-bodied race. He writes of having a weak and delicate stomach and a small frame, almost dwarfish. Though his brothers weighed about 180 pounds, he varied from an early 160 to a later 145 pounds. So, he was always temperate and careful of his health. Compensatory blessings were an original intelligence and a lively sense of humor.

In his early life he read the entire Bible, Bunyan's *Pilgrim's Progress, Biographia Philosophia,* Joseph Priestly's *History of the Corruptions of Christianity,* and Pope's *Essay on Man.* Quoting Pope's thought that "Reason is here no guide but still a guard," he soundly commented, "It appears to me that we have no better guide to follow than our best reason on all occasions." In his later life he read such books as Fisk's *Travels,* Dr. Combe on *Health,* a three-volume *Encyclopaedia of Geography,* Vosé's *Astronomy,* and Irving's *Life of Columbus,* which he borrowed in Pocahontas County.

His wisdom and convictions he also applied to current problems. For example, on January 8, 1836, at a local schoolhouse, Samuel delivered a 5,000-word temperance address, so forceful and timely that on March 1, 1931, it was published in full in the *Tulsa World.* In this well-written lecture he appealed to his hearers to join a total abstinence league as the best means of staying sober and of overcoming the liquor demon. In a long introduction he asserted that man's success is ever in doubt, because "his race is weak, his mind is weak, his powers are weak, weakness and feebleness attends his progeny." Lamenting idle talk, showy dress, overeating and drinking, he advised prudence and discretion in all things needful. While defining temperance as a prudent and proper use of a thing, he advocated total abstinence from all alcoholic drinks as good, sound doctrine. To succeed, temperance societies must practice total abstinence and association. To those who objected to the pledge as too binding and too restrictive of one's freedom, he declared that a freedom to do wrong or to get drunk is a poor, miserable freedom. Abandon the useless and injurious poison of drink. Unite against it as our patriot fathers united against John Bull and won. This fight is another revolutionary struggle with patriots supporting it and tories opposing it. He also denounced the sellers, manufacturers, and providers of liquor materials and called upon them to quit their occupations. "Drink not and you will not be drunk," he declared.

In his diary on May 8, 1844, in a blast at doctors, lawyers, and clergymen, he thus let off steam: "I can hardly keep my hands off of some of our clergymen. For I think I have reason to believe that many of them are in search of the fleece instead of the flock." The next month we find this effusion on superstition, the particular one being that a scar made on a tree would kill it, which he readily disproved by a test on a young apple tree: "What vain superstitious opinions some persons have imbibed in their minds when young! And how hard to extricate them from the mind in after life! Unphilosophical and unreasonable, howsoever it may really be!"

He also tells of selling a herd of fat cattle to a distant buyer, Robert J. Glendy. At the appointed time the buyer came for the cattle, but he failed to bring the cash to pay for them according to their agreement. Samuel made this laconic record of the transaction in his diary: "No money came — no cattle went." For him mere promises to pay were not enough. When his daughter, Elizabeth, contrary to his wishes, married John P. Erwin on September 1, 1847, Samuel noted this fact and followed with a modern politician's, "No comment to make." However, from the match came the poet of the family, Mary Erwin Overholt, in whom Samuel's own taste for verse and scribbling it flowered into four volumes, in which Highland was well remembered. For example, Cousin Mary's "The Fountain" celebrates a wonderful spring near Beulah Church:

> There was a spring I knew
> Long years ago, that at the mountain's foot
> Beneath cool trees, burst pulsing from the rocks,
> Bubbling up clear as crystal, cold and sweet
> From depth unknown, unfathomed, and forever,
> Through summer's heat or winter's icy breath,
> Unfettered and unshrunk it wandered on,
> Singing a sweet song all the seasons through.
> And for the love of that sweet song the flowers,
> Tenderest and fairest, came in early spring
> And leaned above the brink and listened there
> Trembling and starry-eyed; the forget-me-not
> And cowslip came, and the purple, meditative violet.
> When flowers were gone, and all the trees were bare,
> Amid the heavy snows that constant song
> Still rippled from the surging water's heart.
>
> So will some fount of memory olden,
> All sweet and pure, untouched of time or stain,
> Lift ever in the heart, and ever sing,
> And round that memory,
> Through all life's transitory joys and griefs,
> Will bloom mind's immortelles,
> The loveliest flowers of thought.
> (From Year In, Year Out, at Echoes, 1934).

Samuel was an early riser and a methodical farmer. His family produced on the farm nearly everything needed to feed and clothe themselves. Besides his regular helpers, he sometimes engaged itinerants if they could meet his somewhat eccentric tests. For example, to determine whether a prospective worker would do as directed, he might tell him to turn a grindstone all morning idly; or, he might order him to move a pile of stones from one place to another, and when finished, he would, with inner glee, tell him to move them back where they were at first! If the prospect complained or found fault, he would get no more work though he would be paid liberally for the tryouts!

Though Samuel lived most of his life in a log house at Mill Gap, in his old days he planned and produced native lumber for the construction of a substantial 10-room house, in which I was born. When Samuel died in 1853, his son David, my grandfather, continued and finished the building, which is still standing. Truly this house was substantial, because its walls were made by nailing long, two by six-inch pieces placed flat and lengthwise on the stone foundation and on top of each other for two stories, large rooms and a broad hall with a grand stairway, and then weatherboarded without and plastered within, with three brick chimneys to service fireplaces. Such a planner and such a man was Samuel Ruckman.

Grandfather Ruckman

Samuel's youngest son, David Van Meter Ruckman (1833-1905), my grandfather, inherited an independent spirit and considerable wealth from his diarist father but with more interest in business than in scholarship. In 1858 he married Annah Herring (1837-1892), the youngest daughter of Bethuel Herring of Long Glade in Augusta County, who was probably related to Lincoln's grandmother, Bathsheba. By this marriage he had nine children, my mother being the oldest, but his second wife, Elizabeth Eagle, was without issue. During the Civil War with the rank of colonel, David bought livestock for the Confederate armies. He was an energetic man with big ideas, who in the depression of 1873-1876 failed in the shipping business with liabilities of about $250,000; but, aided somewhat by his father-in-law, he retrieved himself in late middle life and accumulated in three counties properties worth about $100,000.

A story is related how effectively he could play the possum in outwitting a cattle buyer. On one occasion he and a competitor happened to meet at the home of a man with a herd to sell. After dinner grandpa professed to be sleepy and he lay down on a couch and presently began to snore intermittently, but all the while listening to the conversation between the owner and his rival. Finally, in reply to a question, the owner named a price for which he would sell. While the rival pondered a little, grandpa rose up, saying, "I will take them at that price!" And forthwith he closed the deal to the consternation of his fellow buyer.

My grandfather was a large, heavy-set man with a short gray beard and a quick temper, but full of kindness and good deeds, especially for his kin far and near. We children were always glad to see him and do chores for him, such as rubbing his head for a little cash, for we, too, had inherited a bit of Samuel's zeal for wealth! Strangely enough he was my first correspondent, though he was busily engaged, buying and selling livestock and operating his farms. His hieroglyphic handwriting was so nearly undecipherable that only my inspired mother could read his replies to my childish letters.

When I was twelve years old, he gave me a large, one-volume *Encyclopedia of Universal Knowledge,* which I read and reread with much delight and benefit. It contained something about almost everything. It told how to study, how to write letters, how to observe good manners, and even how to conduct a courtship! It contained some history, a smattering of science, and the chief wonders of the world. It was just the book to whet a boy's appetite for knowledge. About the same time I came under the spell of another book, *How to Reach Success or Room at the Top,* which greatly stimulated my ambition to make my life useful and worthwhile, if possible.

My Cousin Mary, who spent her teenage years with the Ruckman family at Mill Gap, many years ago wrote for me her recollections of the family life. From her paper I quote short passages:

"During the years when I was a member of Uncle David's family, he was approaching middle age, and was the prominent cattle dealer of the section. His buying territory took in parts of four counties [Augusta, Highland, Bath, and Pocahontas], and he yearly shipped many hundreds of cattle to the northern markets. During the fall and early winter months he spent most of his time in these cities, making his headquarters in Baltimore. While thus forced to be absent from home he left his interests in the capable hands of Billy Ruleman, who had been with him for many years. The collecting of the different herds, the hiring of drovers, the sending off of droves of cattle to market, as well as looking after Uncle David's farms were all under the management of this efficient overseer.

"On his cattle-buying trips through his widely scattered territory Uncle David rode a mule named Peg. Her gait was a very rapid walk, a sort of amble that combined speed with the greatest amount of ease for her rider, who spent continuous days in the saddle. At a signal from him she would lay back her ears and break into a rapid, smooth lope. There seemed a sort of human understanding between these comrades, and for many years she was his sole mount, bearing his weight on their long journeys over rough roads, up and down mountains, without any apparent distress. She was always sleek and well kept." [In his later life he drove a light two-horse buggy] . . .

"He had the open-handed hospitality of his time, and his house was a free inn for all who came that way. As a host he was genial, courteous, and his manner to ladies had the courtliness of the cavalier. In his own family he was autocratic and impatient. The older children often felt the weight of his heavy hand. He never took time to whip us when we erred. His temper exploded and swept all before it. He was thunder and lightning and cloudburst, and woe to the small craft in his path. . . .

"He had quite another side to his character, however. . . . He was kind to us in many ways, magnanimous even. He always brought us nice things from Baltimore and on Christmas eve it was he who stayed up and filled our stockings. Along with the candy and nuts he had some more permanent gift, a bit of jewelry perhaps. Then he indulged his sense of humor in filling the tops of our stockings with a handful of little chips or a switch. When we came downstairs at three Christmas morning to explore our stockings, he never failed to be awake, Aunt Anna said, and lay snoring but shaking with laughter at our indignant remarks about the chips, but he enjoyed just as much our delight in our gifts. He was always deeply concerned with our welfare and training, examining into our progress at school, and during hay harvest when the girls hauled hayshocks and there would be a number of hired men helping put up hay Uncle David strictly enforced the law that there should be no coarse or profane language used in our presence — nor at any time."

Yet, Cousin Mary held two grievances against my grandfather. One was that the three older children — she, her sister Annie, and my mother Kate — grew up in an atmosphere of dread when Uncle David was at home; that he never cared who was present when he chose to correct them. In consequence, she says, it was hard for the girls to maintain any dignity in the presence of strangers or air of self-possession with them, and so they were always shy and constrained. More important still, perhaps, Cousin Mary when about 12 to 15 met a well-to-do Yankee in the South, who, I suppose, recognizing her unusual gifts of mind, offered to give her an education in northern schools, for which she was very ambitious. But her Uncle David would not consent, and, being in effect, if not actually, her guardian, his decision prevailed to the life-long disappointment of the unusually gifted girl, who soon qualified herself to teach the elementary subjects, married, came West, reared and educated her children and late in life, at my urging, she and her children privately published four volumes of good verse, some of which may well outlive more pretentious and publicized work such as that of John Gould Fletcher.

I will close this section with Cousin Mary's pen picture of my grandmother, Annah H. Ruckman, whom I remember somewhat vaguely as the embodiment of goodness and kindness: "Aunt Annah, Uncle David's wife, was ten [four] years his junior. She was quite small and delicately formed, fair with blue eyes, and light brown hair that waved naturally away from her broad forehead, small feet and hands, a typical Virginia lady with gracious, pleasing manners, a product of one of Staunton's best Girls' Finishing Schools. She was a very able manager, looking well to the way of her household, and keeping an excellent table, and well-stocked pantries. She was a devout member of the Presbyterian Church, and her home was the rendezvous of visiting Presbyterian ministers at all times, but the stopping place as well of Methodist ministers. Uncle David who never joined a church remained Methodist in his sympathies, his mother having been a Methodist."

Cousin Mary assures us that while life at Mill Gap then might seem dull to outsiders, there was excitement enough to fill every day; work and play, visiting the neighbors, attending church and Sunday school, singing and day school. There was adventure in everything — the coming of a stranger, riding spirited horses, turning saddle, the passing of a mile-long parade of cattle, apple cuttings, taffy parties, stirring of maple sugar, even the *protracted* meetings, which the Presbyterians called *distracted*.

Paternal Ancestry

My father's family was of German origin. In the 1740's three Herold pioneers emigrated from the lower Rhine Valley to Pennsylvania and settled there. But just before the Revolution one of this group, presumably George Michael Herold with his family, removed to the South Branch of the Potomac in Virginia. There, as we learn from the census of 1850, Christopher Herold was born in 1773. Son of an immigrant and without any schooling available on the frontier during the Revolution, he became a typical frontiersman, strong and ambitious but unschooled. In 1799 he married Elizabeth Cook of English origin in Pendleton County, now West Virginia, and a little later they removed to Back Creek and bought farm lands near the Ruckmans, and reared a large family, the youngest of whom, Andrew Herold, an old man, I knew as a boy, hobbling around with his cane and living with his children on a farm adjoining my father's property on Knapp's Creek.

As already related, Christopher sold his farm and home on Back Creek and about 1825 removed to Pocahontas County. He succeeded in gratifying a strong appetite for improved and timbered farms. Some of his sons moved on to Nicholas County and bought more land, some of it underlain with coal, as their offspring later found out. But Christopher, his wife, and several of their children remained in Pocahontas, lived out their days, and are buried there.

Christopher Herold and Samuel Ruckman were friends and neighbors on Back Creek for about 25 years. They were sons of the Revolution who lived to the decade before the Civil War; both reared large families, accumulated considerable property, and were highly respected and typical citizens of that early period. But a spectacular difference to a modern observer is that Samuel mastered the art of writing and kept an irregular diary for the information and amusement of his descendants, whereas Christopher, in spite of his industry and practical success without schooling, adorned his last will and testament with a simple, unpretentious crossmark duly witnessed, as I know as the owner of this early document. Almost equally I prize these ancestors of mine, because each in his way accomplished so much in spite of handicaps. In Samuel's case it was feeble health, and in Christopher's, lack of elementary schooling in a forest of wild animals and Indians.

William T. Price, Presbyterian clergyman, scholar, and historian of Pocahontas County, from personal knowledge wrote the following tribute to Christopher: "Among the prosperous citizens of Pocahontas County in its early development, Christopher Herold deserves recognition of a special character. He was of pure German parentage — his immediate ancestry came from the fatherland, settling in Pennsylania, thence removing to Virginia. Though he could not read English no one would have suspected it, so well posted he seemed to be in political matters and current affairs. His powers of memory were surprising, and his business sagacity was equal to any of his contemporaries. He was honest and enterprising."

My grandfather, Washington Lanty Herold, patriotically named, was a son of Henry S. Herold (1800-1890) of Nicholas

County and a grandson of the original progenitor, Christopher. His father and his mother, Elizabeth Lockridge, had removed from Pocahontas to Nicholas in the 1840's, rearing five sons and five daughters and living there to be 90 and 92 years old, respectively. Washington, then a teenage boy, went with them, but, returning later to Pocahontas, he met and fell in love with 16-year-old Sarah Ann Harper of Knapp's Creek and in a successful run-away match married her at Christopher Herold's in 1855. They first lived on a small farm with a grist and lumber mill in the narrow gap two miles above Huntersville, which Washington and his brother Josiah had bought for $3200. My father was born there on April 12, 1857. Besides the valuable mill property, my father used to tell us that hidden away in the woods was a liquor still that also attracted customers. Later, after selling this property at a profit and being paid largely in Confederate money, Washington saw his savings disappear with the rebel cause. The family must have had a hard time for several years in passing through the aftermath of a terrible Civil War, because not until 1871 did they become firmly established again on 654 acres of land, once part of the Moses Moore lands on upper Knapp's Creek, the home of my boyhood.

This tract was part of 100,000 acres granted to the Greenbrier Company and surveyed under British auspices in 1752, but after the Revolution the owners had to get new titles from the American government. For the 654 acres, nearly all timbered with about one-third in the valley and two-thirds in the hills and Allegheny Mountain, Washington Herold agreed to pay Lanty Lockridge $2760 with no interest for nearly two years. Credits on the debt were as follows:

Three payments in 1874 amounting to $1,122, the savings of three years apparently. Next, in 1875, $300; in 1876, two payments for $642; in 1877, $654; in 1878, two payments for a total of $330; and in 1880, $130. In 1885, the year of my birth, a calculation showed that a balance of $6.35 was still due, which was paid. That was a long hard pull for Washington and Sarah Ann, who by 1880 had a family of five sons and four daughters — my uncles and aunts, born between 1857 and 1880. In 1922 the same tract with all the improvements and 25 more acres of valley land sold for $26,850 payable in cash and three annual installments with interest. But the good parents who had struggled so hard and long to become independent did not long enjoy the farm home with a new house and a new barn and other improvements. Washington's death in 1885 from asthma and allied ailments aggravated originally by excessive exertion in curbing a forest fire that threatened to destroy logs for his home, was followed by that of his wife in 1888, and they lie side by side under the whispering pine trees of that home place.

My father, Wise Herold, who was the oldest child in Washington's large family, after his father's death became the main support of his mother and the younger children before they grew up and went West. Throughout the struggle to pay for the farm he had been his father's chief helper, since his next brother, Russell, was six years younger. My father was richly endowed with a long name, of which I first heard one day when I found the initials H. A. W. followed by Herold carved on a board fence at home. When I asked who HAW HEROLD might be, I was astonished to learn that the letters meant Henry Anderson Wise Herold, my father, who had been named for Governor Wise of Virginia and who had simplified his name just as I have always sought to simplify and make reasonable and intelligible the complexities of life.

He was a faithful and efficient farmer, who insisted that the corn rows should be straight, the weeds kept down, the fences up, and the brush cut. With him work always came before pleasure, which he found in useful activities. Most of his life was devoted to clearing, improving, and cultivating about half of the 654 acres bought by his father, the other half remaining a forest where sheep and cattle could browse in the summer months. Of the improved part about 60 acres were grain or meadow land and about 240 acres were pastures, mostly limestone hills but partly in the valley sprinkled with large pine stumps, as I knew it. The woodland, chiefly on the Allegheny side of the farm, grew tall white pine, oak, hickory, and some hemlock, which, though later removed by logging companies, linger happily in my memory.

The Herold Home

When Grandfather Herold removed to this almost wholly timbered farm in the early 1870's, he and his son Wise, using long, straight pine trees hewn flat on two sides for the interior and outside walls, built near the road a story-and-half log house about 20 feet wide and 30 feet long, with two windows below, two outside doors, a chimney with a big fireplace, and a steep stairway in one corner leading to the upper part, close under the roof and fitted with a single window. Later they built a board kitchen and dining room together on one side of the main house. For 10 years or more, while the land was being paid for, that pioneer log cabin was the home of the growing Herold family.

(Recently this log cabin was sold, dismantled, and removed to Callaghan, Virginia.)

To enlarge it, the men cut and hauled pine logs with ox teams to a primitive sawmill, then hauled the lumber 10 miles and back to a planing mill, and with the lumber added at one end of the log house two stories with six rooms, a cellar underneath, a long porch in front, and a smaller one in the rear. The log part was then camouflaged with pine boards, the new rooms finished in beautiful white pine, and the entire outside painted white with brown trimmings. A spring and well of good water were close by. That nine-room house, planned and erected from native materials by the Herolds, became my memorable boyhood home, where in one of the new rooms I had my first study, fitted out with a bed, a table, a chair, a lamp, a big closet with shelves, and later my trunk and a box bookcase.

In addition to the house there were two barns — an old one built of plain pine logs, about 20 feet square and high, with board sheds all around it for horses below and hay and other feed above; and a large frame barn, built some years later from pine lumber produced on the farm. The second barn had a central driveway for wagons and four parallel stables for feeding and sheltering cattle and sheep, and with two very large mows for hay, straw, and corn fodder, later fitted out with a track under the top of the roof for a hayfork, operated by long ropes and horses, for unloading and storing hay. Here in the winter, manure would accumulate to be removed by wagon and scattered on the grain land — an operation well designed to develop a boy's muscle and stamina and clear his head for effective study when the opportunity came without any artificial gymnastics for amusing the public.

Between the log barn and the house were a granary, two corn cribs made of pine poles, and a chicken house. To the rear of the house was a woodshed, a meathouse or smokehouse, as we called it, where father cured and pickled the meats, and an icehouse made by filling wide walls with sawdust and cutting the ice from the frozen creek in the wintertime. Also there was a large wash house and refuse place, and behind it a privy for the exclusive use of the females of the family. The men and boys were ostracized to the environs of the barns or elsewhere, and segregated solely on the basis of sex, without any pretence of providing equal and comparable facilities! The notion of installing a privy for all inside the house would then have shocked the household as the innovation of a barbarous, indecent, and lazy generation.

Though in the early days both oxen and horses were used on

the farm for motive power, before my time horses alone had taken the place of oxen, which my father knew well how to handle. Usually he would have from four to six horses and one or two colts for replacements. He would have one heavyweight team for plowing and hauling and one lighter team for riding and driving or light work. In 1914 he acquired his first automobile, keeping a private supply of gasoline since there was no filling station near us.

Besides the horses the farm carried 10 to 12 cows to produce calves and milk and butter for family use. Fifteen to 30 young cattle would be wintered, pastured through the summer, and marketed in the fall. Sheep, however, furnished the most stable source of income with the least investment, as I often heard my father remark. On an average the farm would have 150 to 200 mature sheep, which produced a crop of wool in the spring of the year and a crop of lambs in the fall, yielding a dependable cash income twice a year. Important tasks were caring for the lambs in the frosty spring time and shearing the grown sheep when the weather moderated.

How fascinating it was to watch the young lambs and young calves skipping and playing in the pastures and the long-legged colts trying to walk as if they were on stilts! And how my first-hand knowledge of sheep and lambs and herding contributed later to my appreciation and enjoyment of Wordsworth's great poem, "Michael"! As a boy, I knew an old man, Wilson Ryder, who almost perfectly impersonated the shepherd in the poem. He, like Michael, was old and patient and dependable and loyal and good beyond words to express his virtues. He, too, carrying a little salt, would range far in quest of his sheep and lambs. Because his wife was dead, he alone had to bring up a large family, aided by an older daughter who postponed her marriage for years and yet, finally, reared children of her own.

On a stock farm a boy needs no Dr. Kinsey to instruct him in the mystery and power of sex, for birds and beasts observe no Victorian inhibitions. Without any Biblical lore they know instinctively that each kind is to mate and multiply, exercising their divine prerogatives without shame or apology. So, the frogs in a pond spin a web of tadpole life, and the sparrow fags himself to satisfy his mate. In the barnyard the rooster parades his masculinity by running down and ravishing the fairest hen, which is probably thrilled to be run down and fertilized. The turkey gobbler struts and spreads his wings and feathers to flatter and entice his sweetheart. Like a four-footed Brigham Young, the big ram holds forth among his gentle ewes in the pasture.

With persevering, grunting satisfaction the boar hog creates a litter of pigs. The roaring, pawing bull renders efficient and consoling service in his cow harem. Above all, the mighty stallion, a ton of tingling passion, Shakespeare's classic example in "Venus and Adonis," braces himself and rears against the bridle in his passionate efforts to consummate his chief mission in life.

With such continuing exhibitions of sex activity among birds and beasts on a farm, is it any wonder that human creatures too should be responsive to their environment? However that may be, it is a fact that country people are more prolific than city-dwellers. In my neighborhood one could point to five families within a mile of our home where each numbered seven to ten children, making a total of 40 young people, all strong and vigorous, and propagated in due and proper form according to the accepted marriage requirements.

However, in our community were at least two Hester Prynnes, known to me years before I heard of Hawthorne's famous heroine, who reared small families in defiance of man-made restrictions but not without a certain measure of respect and obvious hardship. One named Mary brought up three husky but lazy boys, and the other named Rachel, by some called Aunt Rachel, produced a boy and a girl. Both lived in simple cabins in remote places by rigid economy and lowly services with few social advantages for the children. Mary used to wash clothes for my mother, trudging six miles a day and carrying home flour and bacon for her sons. Like Hester, too, they never revealed the name of the fathers — not so far as I ever heard! Were they secret concubines? Perhaps so! I do not know, but both appeared to find consolation in smoking a clay pipe!

Though my father grew up accustomed to all kinds of farm work, he picked up in the short-term schools a fair knowledge of the elements so that he could keep his accounts in good shape, handle his correspondence, and read considerably in the New York *Thrice-a-Week World*, *The Farm Journal* and *The National Stockman and Farmer*. He also provided us children with *The Youth's Companion* and *The Pocahontas Times,* which along with the *World* I enjoyed reading. Stories of elk, deer, and moose in the *Companion* were often so thrilling that they frightened me in my dreams.

In 1896 when William Jennings Bryan was campaigning on a free-silver platform for the presidency, I followed his travels and speeches in the *World* with so much interest and admiration that his defeat in November stunned and disappointed me painfully. Only eleven, I was fascinated by Bryan's dramatic winning of the Democratic nomination by a single speech and his conducting a vigorous campaign, as he declared, against the intrenched money power. The next year my father, as a bondsman for the Pocahontas sheriff, was forced into bankruptcy, losing most of his property. Grandpa Ruckman rescued our family by buying and largely paying for our homeplace at a depression price of $4,500.

My mother, Kate Elizabeth Ruckman, the oldest child of her parents, was born and grew up at Mill Gap, Virginia. She remembered the closing years of the Civil War and used to tell me of the starving soldiers coming along and eating the hot, doughy bread before it was baked. She was a delicate, refined girl with a love of music and literature. As she read the newspapers and magazines, it was her practice to clip choice selections of prose and poetry and paste them in a large scrapbook, which one of my sisters keeps as a family treasure. Besides going to local and home schools, at 15 she attended the Warm Springs Female Academy for one year, and then, for a second year, Wesleyan Female Institute of Staunton, Virginia, where she won honors in English, instrumental music, and conduct. Cousin Mary writes that she was a bright, healthy, lighthearted girl, with fair skin, rich color, large blue-grey eyes and bronzy-brown hair that clustered in natural curls around her high forehead and plump white neck. When she came home from Staunton, Cousin Mary wrote, "She was a picture of girlish loveliness, fresh and sweet as a newly opened pink rose. I had really never seen her before to appraise her. She had many admirers but was not a coquette."

When she was about 18, she was afflicted with a serious mental illness that required hospitalization. Her cousin, Annie E. Callison, thought the basic cause was a hard fall she received when a baby in the care of a colored girl. She struck the back of her head so violently on a stone step that it left a "saucer-like depression" for life. She recovered from this terrible blow and the later illness so fully that her health once again seemed to be normal. Among her many admirers she chose my father, and on August 26, 1884, they were married at the Ruckman residence when she was 24 and he 27 years old.

Though they made their home in Pocahontas on the Herold farm, which my father bought, paying each of his brothers $1,000 and each of his sisters $500, Grandma Ruckman insisted that my mother should return to her care at Mill Gap for the birth of her first two children — Amos Lee on August 8, 1885, and Henry Van Meter on February 25, 1888, thus making both boys natives of the Old Dominion rather than of that Yankee state, West Virginia. By 1900 a third son, Edgar Wilson, and four daughters — Annah Margie, Elizabeth Belle, Lulah Bryan, and Reta Lillian— had joined the family; seven children in 15 years. All of them are still living except Margie, a skillful teacher and a popular young woman, who died from the effects of a surgical operation in 1918 and was laid to rest beside her mother and paternal grandparents on the home place beneath whispering young pine trees.

Though my mother made a complete recovery from her mental illness and had fairly good health while bearing seven vigorous children, yet as the family responsibilities grew and my father went through a bankruptcy necessitating unusual economies, her health slowly weakened and her nerves showed the strain in spite of many medical efforts to conserve her resources. While my youngest sister Reta was still a baby, my poor mother was afflicted with a second mental collapse so that for nearly ten years she was an invalid, sometimes at home in a sad, melancholy, and nearly helpless condition but mostly in a state institution for better medical care and the safety of herself and the family. Late in her checkered life, my brother Henry and I made a train trip to see her at Spencer, West Virginia, but she never recovered. Only death in 1909 could bring her perpetual rest and peace. Her tragic illness and separation from her children long shadowed my own life and future, because such an illness is the tragedy of tragedies.

My very earliest recollections are about the fact and mystery of death. I recall clearly, though only three years old then, the illness and death of Grandma Herold in the summer of 1888, and I clearly remember attending the funeral and burial of Uncle Sammy Ruckman, a promising young student, in the fall of the next year. No small part of my life and study has been directed toward trying to find a satisfactory solution for the mystery of human life and death. For the present I cannot do better than to quote some fine lines that Cousin Mary wrote on this theme called "The Dead":

> I sleep here tranquil; let me lie
> Beneath the broad protecting sky.
> Let ages in their march go by,
> I lie here resting. Let me lie.
>
> I lie here dreaming -- let me rest.
> How sweet to me the brown earth's breast!
> Behind me legends of my best;
> I lie here dreaming — I am blest.

I lie here silent, soon forgot,
The place I filled, 'twill know me not.
Unsought, unknown my resting spot.
I lie here sleeping — long forgot,
Regretting naught. Disturb me not.

Like Bryant in "Thanatopsis," she is unconcerned with the terrors of a mythical Hell or the bliss of a mythical Heaven. She accepts death as life with calm composure and serenity, resting and dreaming, regretting nothing and leaving behind her "legends of my best." What a memorable line is that, as well as the whole poem, so fitting for a memorial inscription!

I CHOSE TEACHING
Part II. The Pursuit of Happiness

CHAPTER 4
Early Schooling

MY FORMAL schooling began at the age of five or six at Mill Gap, Virginia, where for a few months I lived with my Ruckman kinfolk and attended a nearby school with three of the younger Ruckman children who were still in their teens — Uncle Glenn and Aunts Margie and Sarah. We walked to the new schoolhouse, called the Hall, taught by a lady. I recall that the older students sometimes amused themselves by dancing in the old schoolhouse. Vividly do I remember my new copper-toed boots that I wore to school and used for wading in the little creek contrary to my grandmother's prohibitions. At school I studied a little and observed much, watching the big boys and girls flirting with each other behind their upheld, open books. Already they were attracting each other like powerful magnets. The teacher was thoughtfully kind to two of us tired little boys, because she would often in fair weather let us go outside to play during school hours. Occasionally I would be alone to gaze at the mysterious timbered hills and the floating clouds and the blue sky, and to wonder what all the mighty world meant and to glimpse the glory and the mystery of life.

Returning to Pocahontas on horseback behind my father, I rejoined the Herolds and lived in the beautiful valley of Knapp's Creek, a large branch of the Greenbrier River, with its source on the west side of Paddy's Knob about eight miles away. At our house in the valley the morning sun came up over the top of the Allegheny Mountain about two miles due east and always shone on the western hill tops for almost an hour before it reached the valley, and in the evening the sun disappeared behind the hills long before it really set.

31

Though the mountains at our home, being relatively to the valley lower or farther away, appeared less impressive than at Mill Gap in Highland, they were memorably beautiful at all seasons of the year, especially in the springtime when the dogwood and honeysuckle bloomed and in the autumn when the frosts produced a riot of colored leaves ranging through the spectrum from red to violet. There were all possible combinations — as the golden and pink yellow of maple leaves against a background of green pines or hemlock and the blue sky, deep reds and browns and pinks and greens, all changing from day to day in an ecstatic farewell to the mothering trees. How could one ever forget them in all the glory of their farewell recessional! But with late fall and winter came bare trees and snow and ice and cold. On many a morning we shivered at the daily chores and as we trudged along the roads to school. The coldest was the clear morning when the Fahrenheit thermometer dropped to 40 degrees below zero, the lowest I have ever experienced! That morning the air was perfectly still as if it, too, was frozen, and from the forest one could hear the trees cracking from the extremity of cold! On that memorable occasion we abbreviated the chores and sought the fireside till Old Sol could somewhat appease the Cold Dragon.

At the Herold home I grew up with a large family of nine to ten consisting of my parents, my brother Henry, and sister Margie, and my aunts and uncles — Nora, Lula, Nina, Homer, Bedford, and Penic, to name them in the order of birth. Aunt Lula soon met and married a singing master from the Valley of Virginia, Thomas Miller, who honeymooned to the West, became an insurance executive with headquarters in Indianapolis, lived and died there; the widow lingering for several years, but joining him there in death — a perfect love match, so far as I know, without children.

Uncle Homer, always kind and helpful, made a good mechanic's record in Uncle Russell's farm-implement department. But he never married, became restless, unsettled, and sometimes intemperate, and, like some other Herolds, he loved to ramble about the world and enjoy its variety, doing odd jobs for his livelihood. On his last visit in my home I succeeded in getting him to tell me the story of his life, which I wrote down. He had been to England and all over the United States. Once in Nevada, overtaken by night in a remote region, he was pursued for hours by a panther. Badly frightened, he continued his way on foot, expecting to be attacked and killed at any time, but to his surprise and relief the animal finally slipped away and left him unmolested. Years later, when the wanderer died in hospitable New York City, Uncle Penic had his body sent to Kiowa, Kansas, for burial beside his brother Russell.

Playmates and Work

On the farm Uncle Penic, my senior by only five years, became my playmate and buddy, and through the years we have kept in touch with each other by visits and letters. He and I have always had much in common though he turned to business and followed his brothers and sisters to Kansas in 1896. In Anthony he became a successful banker, versatile businessman, and community leader of civic projects. Considerate and generous, he is also a mainstay of his many friends and relatives. Sometimes, he laughingly recalls his boyish prank of enticing me one time into trying to eat an Indian turnip, notoriously hot and peppery, as I soon learned once and for all time!

By 1896 all my Herold aunts and uncles, except Aunt Allie Moore and her husband Newton, had gone West to settle or join Uncle Russell, the leader, in south Kansas, where he conducted a large and successful mercantile business at Kiowa and could give several of them employment. After Uncle Russell's early death in 1902, Uncle Bedford became a grain and stock farmer at Byron, Oklahoma; Aunt Nora lived and died a very good and useful woman; Aunt Nina Myrtle married Wilbur F. Dean and lived in Wichita. She had been an inspiration to me before she left our home, because she was gifted at singing and playing the organ. With ballads and songs she so well-nigh hypnotized me, that, when she began to sing, I would run from my play to enjoy the songs — some sad like "Camping on the Old Camp Ground" and "My Old Kentucky Home," but some gay and lively like "The Little Black Mustache," which she sang charmingly. Indeed, having sipped the Fountain of Youth, she has always been the personification of youth and liveliness.

Among the neighborhood children my two best friends were Roy and Peyton Moore, sons of Isaac Brown Moore, and direct descendants of the famous Moses, who lived on part of the ancestral estate. Cousin Brown was a prominent Mason, a youthful teacher, a farmer (not a very good one, my father said), a lover, and a minor politician, serving one term in the state legislature. He was a good and popular citizen, and for some years a sort of model for me. Yes, he was a successful lover in that he married three times and reared or started three sets of children, ten in all. I can never forget how grieved and broken this family was when death took his first wife, leaving eight motherless children, my friends and playmates.

On the farm I learned to do all kinds of work — planting, cultivating, and harvesting; making a garden; caring for the sheep, horses, and cattle; suckling the greedy calves and milking the cows; butchering chickens, hogs, sheep, and an occasional beef for winter meat; cutting brush in the pastures, building and repairing fences, and repainting buildings. For the table we had plenty of substantial foods, such as meat, bread, milk (though I drank little till later years), butter, eggs, fruits usually, vegetables, and berries; but few dainties, for we bought only coffee, tea, sugar, and spices. Plenty of work in the outdoors made healthy appetites and prevented insomnia at night.

For several years my brother Henry and I, ten years of age and upward, did all the milking that was not done by the calves. Each of us had certain named cows to milk. Being the older, I agreed to milk the more difficult cows. So, it fell to my lot to milk a certain husky, brindled female called Lizzie, which had sensitive teats that required strong pressure to extract the milk. One approached her with fear and trembling, because on occasion she could kick viciously, dispersing bucket and milker with hard and painful blows, as I learned from experience. She never became docile; she was ever a problem cow to be handled with care and discretion. Finally, she was fattened and much to my relief marketed. I think she taught me to be patient, cautious, and circumspect! Is not the world full of many kinds of kicking cows — employers, officials, cunning salesmen, and tricky politicians, who seem to enjoy upsetting one's bucket of milk?

Many a long hot day I spent making hay or harvesting wheat or corn, sawing wood, or cutting the immortal brush in the pastures. By the age of 12 I could do the work of a grown man, and I was so proud of this distinction that I paid little attention to friendly observers who cautioned me not to overwork. To be sure, I was thin and lean but tough and hardy. In those early days I acquired the fiber and strength and health that have sustained me through 70 years and that sustain me now with good prospects for the future. An early course in physiology and hygiene indelibly impressed upon me the unwisdom of dissipating my energies or injuring my health with liquor, beer, or tobacco in any form. Though my father used tobacco, he put a positive prohibition on it for us boys, saying that it was a filthy, expensive habit. All three of his sons followed his advice. Nor have pernicious and dissolute women ever had any appeal for me, nor can I understand why any sensible man should pay any attention to them. An early reading of the Bible warned me against the wiles of the strange woman.

Boyish Adventures

I recall an episode with wild turkeys. One time my father came home from the Allegheny with six or eight wild turkey eggs he had found in the woods. Instead of eating them, we decided to try the experiment of placing them under a setting chicken hen to hatch and bring up. In due time the eggs hatched and the hen and little turkeys were put in a coop and cared for attentively, and all went well as the turkeys grew and began to feather. In a few weeks they were released to roam the farm with the mothering hen — tall, gangling, and feathered. One afternoon I had to go to the far side of the farm to bring them to the barnyard. Already they had shown signs of skittishness and they were learning to fly upon and over fences. On this particular day I became annoyed and tried to shoo them faster along homeward. Presently, to my great surprise, one or two began to run and to get on their wings like an airplane and the others followed, leaving me and the hen deserted in the field! Those young flyers kept going straight to the woods about a quarter of a mile away, where they came down among the young pines and disappeared. That ended our attempt to domesticate wild turkeys. Once later, while hunting squirrels, I chanced upon a flock of wild turkeys and, concealing myself behind a cluster of bushes and waiting a few minutes, I shot a 10-pound hen as she stuck her head up over a fallen tree. On another occasion I succeeded in killing my second and last wild turkey.

In avoiding the dangers connected with farm life, I was quite fortunate though I received several bad scares. Beginning with a board to support myself in the water, I soon learned to swim with confidence in the creek that flowed through the farm. One time, however when my younger brother, Edgar, and I were bathing and swimming stark naked in a deep blue pool about 50 feet in diameter, Edgar, in crossing the deepest part, became confused by a false bottom and went down calling frantically for help. Since I was upstream in shallow water at the time, I ran and swam toward him. I was careful not to let him catch hold of me and by holding with one hand to a long willow branch and reaching out with the other, I succeeded in catching him by the hair and pulling him to shallow water. He took to his heels and fairly shot up over a low bank so comically that I had to laugh though a few seconds before he was in grave danger of drowning. Some time later when I was trying to improve his swimming, I accidentally let his mouth get full of water and he came up spouting it like a young whale. Again I could not refrain from laughing with the result that he became angry and threatened to rock me for purposely letting him sink, though in a few moments he accepted my explanation that his sinking was wholly accidental.

While I was a small boy living on Knapp's Creek, I acquired a wholesome respect for panthers, ghosts, and rattlesnakes. When the neighbors got together, especially on a dark night, they sometimes engaged in a kind of story-telling contest well fitted to make boys wish to stay indoors till broad daylight.

Though I myself did not then see or hear any panthers, I heard a number of trustworthy stories about them so that I had no desire to meet one. But my playmate, Roy Moore, told of seeing one in the winter when he, with two dogs, went to a remote barn to milk the cows and feed the cattle. When he had finished these chores and was leaving the barn, he noticed his dogs were greatly disturbed and fearfully whining. Looking around, about 300 feet away he saw on a bank across and above the road a giant dog, as he first supposed, about five feet long and three feet tall, with a long tail. He said it was as tall as a calf and it stood there with side to him calmly looking across the meadow and watching him and his frightened dogs; but, apparently not hungry, it moved gracefully and majestically into the white pine bushes and disappeared. Since Roy had seen wildcats, he was positive that this animal was a panther, cougar, or mountain lion. About the same time and three miles down the valley two men walking along the road one night heard and saw a similar animal, which they cunningly distracted from themselves by striking and burning matches till they reached a safe distance from the panther.

Though ghosts were always reported to be harmless, bodiless phenomena, I was then fearful of them, especially in the vicinity of graveyards, under the spell of the ghost stories I had heard. One time, aged about ten, when I was returning home at dusk from hauling hay shocks for a neighbor along the highway near where Roy had seen the panther, I was thoroughly frightened by a fearful thing ahead of me that looked like a ghostly octopus ready to seize me with its ghostly tentacles. My body shivered, my hair stood on end, and my heart nearly stopped, but I stood my ground and presently I recognized the fearful thing to be the long white roots of a large, fallen pine tree!

The most startling frights were caused by rattlesnakes, for they have a fearful rattle and a poisonous bite, sometimes killing people or frightening them nearly to death. One fine June day when I was ten years old, I was alone on a far side of the farm hunting and picking a few wild strawberries. As I was crouching along in the grass on a slight slope, eagerly picking the luscious berries, suddenly close in front of me a coiled snake rattled his warning and scared me as never before or afterward. I sprang back quickly and fled as if the Indians were on my trail and trying to scalp me. I have always felt very grateful to that rattler, because I am sure that he might have struck me directly in the face, since between his head and mine there were only four or five feet, which he easily could have jumped. On a later occasion, while picking huckleberries on the Allegheny Mountain, I crouched opposite the end of a hollow log in which lay a rattler that could probably have bitten me. Instead he acted like a good sport and gave me warning. Still again, while we were repairing a piece of fence and carrying rails back and forth under the trees, I walked directly over a rattler that warned without striking. Finally, to add one more adventure, one time when I was sitting on our low front porch and reading, I chanced to look up and saw a yellow rattler crawling toward a screened door. Though he did not endanger me, I soon put an end to his prowling and spying around the house. One of our dogs, having been bitten, developed a fierce mania for hunting and killing rattlers. Finding one in a pile of brush or logs, he would lay siege to the hideout, barking and digging furiously for hours at a time. Though he may have gotten a few scalps, in the end I think they succeeded in killing him, for he disappeared.

While escaping these and other natural dangers to life, I experienced the usual childhood maladies, such as whooping cough, two kinds of measles, and many severe colds and sore throats accompanied by hard and sometimes prolonged coughing. Once a cold grew into pneumonia and I was put to bed in the care of a local physician, who, finding the malady affected only one lung, succeeded after a week or more in restoring me to normal health.

The Moore School

Between the ages of six and seventeen, when I began to teach in the public elementary schools of West Virginia, I received a total of about 50 months of elementary instruction, which was fully 40 per cent less than the modern allotment of 80 to 100 months for the same age span. At first a term had only four months in a year and later five months. While I was small, I attended regularly, but after the age of 12 in the fall or spring I might be detained at home to help harvest or plant the crops a part or even all of one month, which by special effort I made up and continued with my classes.

The Moore schoolhouse, which was about 18 by 30 feet and built of pine lumber, had been placed originally on a suitable dry site, but a change in the public road occasioned its removal across the valley to a flat spot in a poorly drained pasture so that in wet weather teacher and pupils found water and mud all around the schoolhouse with no attempt at better drainage. Fortunately, most of the time the place was either dry or frozen. Of course, the highways were no better, and mud and water were accepted as part of the equipment for training boys and girls. The bare, lonely schoolhouse was fitted out with strong pine desks for two pupils each, one table and chair for the teacher, a large iron stove for burning wood, one door, four windows, a blackboard, two long benches, a water bucket and dipper, and a monstrous-looking Webster's *Unabridged Dictionary,* which like an oracle resolved many questions and mysteries and which I reverenced next to the Bible.

All in all, I was fortunate in my teachers, five women and one man. After my initial school experience at Mill Gap, I came under the efficient instruction of Miss Rella F. Clark for two or three terms in succession. She was strict in discipline, setting goals that must be achieved and accepting no flimsy excuses. On one occasion during school hours I became so curious to investigate a disturbance outside the open door that I left my seat to peep outside at a passerby. When she saw me out of my seat, she sharply directed me to go outside and get a good look! That reprimand completely cured my spying and peeping. Under her guidance I made good progress and received commendable grades. My Cousin Myrta Herold was almost as good, besides being young and beautiful— a perfect blonde and a lovely woman, who married Price Moore and after his untimely death reared their children, an unsung heroine. My best teacher was probably Mr. John H. Lantz, a well-qualified and energetic instructor and a former superintendent of county schools, who had me in hand for two or three terms at the end of my grade-school work. In fact, some of his instruction in arithmetic, English, and physical geography was of high-school caliber. In these advanced classes Roy Moore and I were the leaders, seeking in a friendly way to surpass each other. In particular, I recall that the teacher used to give us a little printed card about once a week with four or five arithmetical problems to be solved. How we worked to prove our solutions in order to get a perfect or nearly perfect score!

Twice later in the teacher's arithmetic examination I received perfect scores — 100 per cent!

Usually there were 10 to 30 pupils with one teacher, who taught all the needed subjects quite well, combining the closely related grades and giving much individual attention to beginners and the trailers, and thus disproving much of the later criticism directed at the one-room school. In the early morning, the children would walk one or two miles to school, carrying their noon lunches. After four o'clock they would return home, talking and playing on the way. By choice, not compulsion, the boys and girls usually played separately. The boys delighted in ball games called "roly-poly" and "antony-over," in skating on the ice without skates, sliding down the hills on boards, and in snowballing one another.

One morning before school began I remember that five or six of us carried a long wide board to the top of a sleet-covered hill with a rail fence near its base. As the engineer I got in front with the other boys behind me and we pushed off. Usually we could control the speed with our heels, but that morning our heels would not dig into the sleet. Seeing nothing but disaster before us, I shouted to the boys behind to roll off, but I stuck to the board and with uplifted feet the board and I crashed into the fence and knocked it over. The amateur engineer received several scratches but no broken bones or bad cuts, thanks to the speedy response of the other boys to his shouted orders.

When Mr. Lantz was teaching, we took spiteful pleasure in getting him in the ball games with a view to warming up his posterior anatomy, as indeed we liked to burn each other with wet balls! Halfway home and near the highway a few of us had a secret shady spot in the edge of the woods where we used to practice "speeches" and other vocal exercises — an early glimpse of later professorial practices.

I enjoyed these school days, the games, the spelling matches, and the associations with my teachers and fellow students; and I suppose that I made fair progress in my studies. Reading and orthography were easy; I enjoyed American history — especially the stories of American heroes and leaders — geography, government, physiology, hygiene, and arithmetic. At first, long division was a mystery of mysteries. How many times will 969 divide into 464,752? How should I know? My later explanation or rationalization was that I had tackled long division too early. I could not grasp it readily till I was somewhat older. Just how well or poorly I had done the elementary courses will appear when we examine the results of my first teacher's examination on 13 subjects, taken a few days after my 17th birthday in August, 1902.

Quite early I acquired a marvelous power of concentration, so that nothing disturbed me when I became interested in reading or trying to solve a problem. At home the other children's playing and talking did not disturb or distract me. The family might even call me by name without my taking notice or responding. At first my mother was inclined to be alarmed, thinking that I might be losing my hearing or might otherwise be abnormal. Well, the fact was that I could concentrate and become isolated in an imaginary or purely mental world. The gift enabled me to accomplish much more in less time than I could have done otherwise, but, as the years passed, this power waned considerably though I can still concentrate under favorable conditions. In the spring and summer of 1902 in preparation for a teacher's examination, I absorbed Myers' *General History* in this effective and enriching manner, for no novel was ever more interesting and exciting than the exploits and accomplishments of the Greeks and Romans as revealed or re-enacted before my eyes. The gaining of knowledge and wisdom was fast becoming my lifelong pursuit of happiness.

Along with this gift of mental concentration I associate rainy days when I could use the gift freely. On such days we stayed at home, and father usually exempted me from special chores about the house or barns that he might want done. In consequence, I always regarded a wet season, rainy days, as a blessing when I could indulge my taste for reading books, magazines, and newspapers, or study for a teacher's examination. My sincerest thanks to the wet seasons and the rainy days!

Juvenile Dreamer

I suppose that every child passes through a period of life when imagination is more active and potent than reason. So, it was with me. The age of ten to twenty or later was my chief period of juvenile dreaming — trying to formulate my future life, my career, in a vague, uncertain, and insecure manner.

In 1896, under the spell of William Jennings Bryan, I had visions of becoming an orator or public speaker and politician in imitation of the Great Commoner. This dream had the effect of intensifying my interest in history, government, and speeches, of leading to participation in the discussion of state and national issues, and finally, as a stunt and opportunity to speak, of my once seeking in Missouri a nomination to Congress.

In 1899, at the age of fourteen, while on a trip with Benjamin

Sharp by wagon to Hot Springs, Virginia, to get supplies from the railway there, I happened to meet a vivacious young woman somewhat older than I was, who caught my fancy, fired my imagination, and set me dreaming the dreams of an infatuated boy lover. Though I did not see this charmer again for several years, she was much in my mind and I made visionary plans of my life with her on a certain piece of farm land where I hoped to build a house and barn and proceed to the business of rearing a family. Such was the beautiful vision, which was shattered a few years later by a second view of the princess, who had become the frowzy, unglamorous wife of another man! So, farewell to that youthful dream.

My third and most persistent dream was that of becoming a Presbyterian preacher and reforming the world, like a Luther or a Moody. This boyish dream and ambition began about 1900 with my "conversion" and joining the Presbyterian Church under the evangelism of Rev. G. W. Nickell, a vigorous pastor of the Marlinton, Huntersville, and Westminster Churches for several years, succeeding my boyhood venerated pastor, Rev. William T. Price, an honor graduate of Washington and Lee, who, loving truth and goodness, always practiced what he preached. This preacher dream lasted about ten years and greatly influenced my plans, purposes, and studies while it possessed my mind.

CHAPTER 5

Teaching and Learning

HOWEVER much I might be dreaming of my future in daytime or nightly solitude, at the age of sixteen, I decided to become a public schoolteacher as the best immediate means of living and gratifying my ambition to learn. I declined the offer of a friendly merchant to clerk in his local store, which would have, perhaps, led me into a mercantile career like that of Uncle Russell, who fitted himself for this work, by taking a short course in a Baltimore business college. Already I had started as a teacher in the local Sunday School.

So, for one more term under former Superintendent Lantz I continued my schooling in the home grade school, where fully half of my studies were of high-school rank. My friend, Roy Moore, and I did advanced arithmetic, physical geography, and composition-literature in addition to courses of lower grade. Following this term I planned to read and study general history without the aid of an instructor in preparation for a county teachers' examination the next summer.

Teacher's Certificate.

To qualify as an elementary teacher, I must pass successfully in 13 subjects — 12 taught in the grades and one professional requirement, the theory and art of teaching, which for me was such a *terra incognita* that my grade in it on three examinations was uniformly low, much to my disappointment but without preventing my success. In preparation for this gauntlet adventure — this two-day written test of my knowledge of 13 subjects — I reviewed and studied diligently in spare time and at night while working on the farm. For several weeks Myers' *General History* held me spellbound as the author skillfully and for the first time revealed to me the ancient pagan world. I relived the Greek, Roman, and later European life record so truly and made such brief factual notes, hitting upon mnemonic devices such as a boy of 12 years led the Children's Crusade of 1212, that I surprised the examiners and myself by getting a grade of 98 per cent. My study of numbers yielded me 85 in arithmetic and 100 in bookkeeping. I did well in the history of the United States and of West Virginia, in civil governments, geography, physiology, hygiene, and orthography. But owing to some technical questions, I was lower in English grammar and the art of teaching, as I might have anticipated.

Though only seventeen years of age and with only grade-school training, I succeeded in passing all 13 subjects with an average grade of ~~90%~~ per cent. Accordingly, the three examiners, County Superintendent James W. Warwick, T. A. Bruffey, and T. D. Moore, on August 14, 1902, issued me a Second Grade Certificate effective for two years and affirmed that I was a "person of good moral character and competent to teach and govern a common school." Of this competency I was not so confident.

My success in running this gauntlet lined by 13 well-armed old squaws, fitted out by three scalping experts, was as gratifying and stimulating to me as was Moses Moore's adventure with ignorance or my own success many years later in passing a preliminary, oral, two-hour inquisition by four scholars for a doctoral degree at Columbia University. I had proved to myself and others that I could do the job, and I was within less than three per cent of a First Grade Teacher's Certificate! Though a Second

Grade then paid only $25 a month and a First Grade only $30, the purchasing power of a dollar was three to five times greater than in 1950.

Thus equipped with a teaching certificate and looking sober but youthful, I next sought to find and contract for a school with a local board of trustees. So I inquired about vacant schools, wishing to get away from my home community. Mounted on one of our riding horses, I set out, like a knight seeking adventure, on a little pilgrimage to a remote district of the county, but trustees were wisely wary of my youth and inexperience and I, too, was wary of big, troublesome schools. Within a week, however, I contracted to teach a five-month term at the Thorny Creek School, which was about five miles from my home by the highway, though only three miles as I used to walk the distance on week-ends by a direct route across wooded hills and fenced pastures.

By starting my school early in September and teaching a few Saturdays and holidays, I could complete the required 100 school days in less than five calendar months. Then, I could either teach a second school elsewhere or attend a high school for half a year. At that time high schools were excessively scarce in West Virginia, especially in the Happy Hunting Land. Upon inquiring, I learned that my best plan would be to seek admission for the second term at the Greenbrier Presbyterial School, just started at Lewisburg, West Virginia, about 60 miles away by hack and train.

My First School

At the appointed time I opened the grade school at Thorny Creek with five little girls and nine or ten boys in attendance. Most of the children were quite young and shy. Two boys were in the upper grades and did such good work that they later became teachers, and two others were ranked somewhat lower. I organized the various small classes, and began instruction in the manner that I had often observed my own teachers practicing. One older boy with a bad reputation for misconduct at school did not appear the first day. For several weeks I dreaded his coming and almost prayed that the Lord would deliver me from him. Fortunately for me and perhaps for him, too, he did not enroll, and his reputation slowly faded from my mind except as I now recall it.

Situated at a crossroads and the edge of a forest, the school building was a new, single-room, frame structure painted white, with one door, six windows, a large wood-burning stove, a blackboard, a teacher's chair and table, two recitation benches, about a dozen new double-seated desks for the children, and a dictionary. A conspicuous novelty was a many-leaved chart mounted on a tripod and called "The New Education" prepared by the Diamond Publishing Company and advertised to be the *sine qua non* of a modern schoolroom though in spite of all my efforts I was not able to do much with it except to show the colored leaves and figures for the amusement or puzzlement of the younger children. It seemed to me that a smooth-tongued salesman had wheedled our unprofessional school leaders into a questionable expenditure, which might much better have gone toward starting a school library.

Astonishing as this statement may be, I was able to obtain room and board with one of the trustees, Mr. H. D. Hively, a former teacher now turned farmer, for $5 a month, excluding week-ends when I usually walked home to work on Saturday and spend Sunday there, returning to my school early Monday morning. Mr. and Mrs. Hively, with five children attending my school, were living in an old two-story log house with a frame dining room and kitchen attached. It was situated on a green slope near a fine spring at the base of Michael Mountain, a few miles west of the main Allegheny and a resort for deer, bears, and panthers. Within a year a new frame house replaced the log house. Mr. Hively had picked up a few books including the *Life of David Crockett by Himself,* which, with youthful trust in the veracity of publishers and authors, I read with much pleasure. Mrs. Hively, aided by her two young daughters, provided excellent foods, mostly produced on the farm — choice meats, eggs, chickens, luscious melons, fresh corn and potatoes, fruits and berries, and dairy dishes. The family was of German descent and characteristically friendly, industrious, saving, and respected.

Thus reading and observing, I began to teach in order to save a little money from a five-month total of $125, with which to continue my high-school studies, already begun in the grade school under Mr. Lantz. From that time onward to the present, I have truly been a composite student-teacher. That is, I studied to teach and I taught to learn again, and so, learning and teaching, teaching and learning, I have, from boyhood to old age, served my pupils and have always sought knowledge and wisdom for them and myself. And in writing this book of recollections, I am eager to continue my work now and hereafter and to induce others to seek the happiness conferred by knowledge and wisdom, temperance and art.

To High School

One notable fact about my schooling experience is that under
the pressure of necessity, rather than from choice, I succeeded in
abbreviating the time usually allotted for the completion of the
various steps or stages in education. For example, I finished the
grade school or elementary subjects in about 50 months instead
of the customary 80 to 100 months, as shown by my passing an
elementary teachers' examination. Next, in doing the high-
school work, I would teach from September to January in a grade
school. Then, entering high school at midyear, I would, by
strenuous efforts, catch up with the regular classes and finish with
them by June. Of course, while teaching, I was also studying and
learning in preparation for my return to high school. This
procedure I followed for three successive years and in about 20
months I completed high-school work that usually requires 30 to
36 months. In like manner, I earned the bachelor's degree in
three nine-month sessions instead of the customary four years,
winning a Greek scholarship in my second year and working for
pay during the summer vacations.

As already mentioned, for high-school instruction I turned
to Greenbrier Presbyterial School, newly organized for boys at
Lewisburg, West Virginia, the oldest and most cultured town
in the Greenbrier Valley and named for Washington's friend,
General Andrew Lewis. While teaching, I got in touch with its
principal, Rev. Matthew L. Lacy, D. D., a retired Presbyterian
preacher and one of the best men I have ever known, to
whom I am deeply indebted for aid and encouragement in my
efforts to get an education. In response to my letter explaining
my ambition, plans, and restricted means, Dr. Lacy wrote me
with his own hand from Lewisburg, on January 13, 1903, as
follows:

Dear Sir,

Your letter came today. I make you the best offer I can
afford. You may come the four remaining months Feb.
March April and May for *fifty dollars* so far as *my charges*
are concerned. That is I will charge you no tuition and
reduce board from fifteen to about twelve dollars. You
would have to get your own books. I do not know before-
hand what they would be, and can not tell what they
would cost. You also pay for your own washing, about
1.25 a month at the highest, possibly a good deal lower.
You will have to bring your own bedclothing, one pair
of sheets two pillow cases and pair of blankets or quilts.

46

These are your own and you can take them with you. I
wish I could do more but my school is not paying expenses
this year. I am losing money, but will continue to make
this offer to you.

I hope it will suit you to come as soon as you can, and
we will do all in our power for your comfort and improvement. The first half-session ends the middle of this month,
but this makes no difference.

We are laboring very hard to build up a school for the
Presbytery and want all the help our friends can give us.
We are not sectarian at all but are more convinced of the
necessity of Christian schools.

Hoping to hear from you soon
I am yours most truly,
M. L. Lacy.

When I arrived at Lewisburg ten days after receiving this
letter, I found a school with forty boys, mostly local, well
housed on the second and third floors of the school building,
and taught by Dr. Lacy and Mr. John L. Daniel, who later
abandoned the classical languages to become a college professor
of chemistry. Both were well qualified and competent instructors.
The curriculum called for the standard four years of study, with
emphasis upon the Bible, English, Latin, mathematics, history,
elementary science including astronomy, two years each of French
and German, and a little Greek.

Being granted credit for half of the freshman course, I
registered for a repeater class in first-year Latin, English grammar, Bible, beginning algebra, psychology, general history, and
spelling. Apart from physical exercise, I set to work for 10 to 12
hours a day. I knew how to study and I could concentrate. My
retained manuscripts of themes and examinations show that
I could spell my own vocabulary and write clear, respectable
English. I knew what I wanted and why I had come to the
school. I was in good health and not concerned about any fair
lady. At the end of March, April, and May I received favorable
reports, and on final examinations my grades ranged from 92 in
algebra to 98 in English and averaged 95 per cent. In spite of
serious handicaps I had done the job and had won Dr. Lacy's
confidence and approval.

One special activity at the school was the Lacy Literary Society, which met every Friday afternoon for practice in debating,
declaiming, English composition, orations, and select readings;
the programs being prepared by the principal and announced one
week in advance. With Conrad Skaggs as my debating partner I

first appeared before the society on March 6, 1903, presenting the negative of the question, "Resolved, That the United States was right in taking possession of the Philippines." My part filled six pages of a composition book. One sentence shows a bit of original diction: "This foreign policy of our country has many drawbacks but very few go-forwards." Referring to the Philippine rebellion against us, I said, "We have stuck our fingers into a hornet's nest." Again: "Though we be the richest nation on the face of the globe, we will become the poorest of them all, unless we attend to our affairs and let the business of other people alone." Though we lost this debate, I helped to win two later.

Thus I completed my first term at the Greenbrier Presbyterial School, where I had spent four pleasant and beneficial months and made some good friends among the students, my instructors, and in town. I was no longer a stranger in Lewisburg. At the Lewisburg Female Seminary I had attended receptions and recitals of stimulating interest and value, and at the Old Stone Presbyterian Church I had heard many scholarly and helpful sermons. In town I liked the shops and stores even though I had little to spend. I loved to browse around in the local bookstore, a luxury unknown in Pocahontas County. About June the first I returned to my home.

My Diary

In my composition book following the three debates referred to previously, I began during the following summer to keep a diary, which I continued for practice in writing for nearly two years. After a few introductory pages on my parents, my birth, and my dilatoriness in starting the diary, which I promised myself to keep faithfully and honestly and to prefix to it an account of my early schooling and religious experiences, I made this record for July 13, 1903:

"I notice at once that the unlucky number 13 is before me, but as I am not the least bit superstitious I will proceed with my diary, and may the blessing of God rest upon me. Today was cold and wet, and I was laughed at by my oldest sister (Margie), because I built a big fire in the sitting room, where I desired to study Latin and read the newspapers. I received a letter from my grandpa Ruckman and from the Supt. of the Spencer Hospital for the Insane. My poor mother was not any better, but remaining in the same melancholy condition. Grandpa said that he was very busy shipping lambs. It cleared off at noon and Henry, Edgar and myself spent the evening cutting 'sprouts' — young brush. I close the day by beginning this diary and in writing the outline of an essay which I am going to read before the Teachers' Institute in the beginning of next month."

During this period of my life I had a dreadful, almost superstitious, sense of religious faith and responsibility inculcated by the preachers and my own reading of the Bible and evangelical literature. I sincerely accepted and believed all of the Presbyterian doctrines without question and on Sunday I would read only the Bible and other religious matter. I had memorized the Shorter Catechism as the last word on theology and on occasion I could rattle it off verbatim. The following passage on my mother from the preface to my diary reveals my mood and sentiments as of September 16, 1903:

"Mother! yes mother first, and mother last. She is the beginning and end of all that I am or may be. She is the Alpha and Omega of my life. My heart appears to melt within me at the mention of her sweet name.

"O Heavenly Father, wilt thou not be pleased, in thy providence, to restore her again to her children, and clothed in her natural state of mind. May this be my prayer until her health is restored or until the angel of Death shall carry her spirit to the bosom of Jesus.

"I ask it in Jesus' name.   Amen."

But the ruthless laws of nature prevailed without any divine interference or amelioration, and six years later my mother succumbed to her tragic malady.

In July, Dr. M. L. Lacy visited my home while soliciting for more students. I was hopeful that Grandpa Ruckman would be so benevolent as to send me to school the following year, and at my request Dr. Lacy wrote him in my behalf without getting a reply. That very day, July 17, I thus philosophized in my diary: "Perhaps it will be better for me, to teach and work my own way through college." Though Grandpa said or wrote nothing specific to me, I think he had a low opinion of my zealous ambition to become a preacher, for he seems to have shared some of his own father Samuel's views of this profession. Within ten years I reversed myself and returned to the rational, realistic opinions of my Ruckman ancestors for reasons to be given later in this record.

In June, I had reviewed for and taken the first state-supervised, uniform examination for teachers, trying to win a First Grade Teacher's Certificate. For several weeks I was on tenterhooks to learn the results of running this educational gauntlet sponsored by state leaders. Finally, on July 31, I was notified of receiving a Second Grade Certificate effective for three years, my average grade being slightly higher than in the earlier county examination and less than two per cent short of the 90 required for the top honor.

First Grade Certificate

A third examination was announced for September 10 and 11, and after attending the Teachers' Institute of Pocahontas County for a week in early August, I decided to review for one month and try this third of the state tests, which were so much more rigorous in content and grading than the county examinations had been that some experienced teachers failed to pass and in the autumn many schools were without teachers.

On September the first, I began my second term of the Thorny Creek School. My experiences were not nearly so trying as last year. For an introductory talk to the students I had prepared a 10-point, sentence outline, in which No. 8 was, "Write, describe, define, and tell origin of my motto, 'Do Right'. " After talking 30 minutes I read a Scripture lesson and repeated the Lord's Prayer. Then I organized the classes and began the work of instruction according to my program.

Ten days later six applicants appeared in Marlinton for the third state examination for teachers. Driving 17 miles in a buggy, I arrived on the gauntlet scene by 8:30 A.M. A three-member county board supervised the test, but sent all papers to Charleston for grading. On the first day we faced a line of six subjects and on the second seven. At the end my diary records: "It was dark before I finished this evening. I stayed with Mr. Frank Hamilton, a merchant, tonight. He directed me to my room, where I found a book entitled *The Life and Works of D. L. Moody,* which I read until nearly midnight." What tireless energy after two long, strenuous days in the examination!

Here for a 12-day period I made no record in my diary till later, so busy was I preparing for the tests and so eager to obtain a coveted First Grade effective for five years with permission to renew it for another five and carrying an automatic increase in salary. My record for Sunday, September 20, shows the nature lover: "Today was one of the calmest, serenest, clearest, and (most) awe-inspiring days that I have ever witnessed. My whole spirit within me seemed to chuckle with gladness which I have witnessed before, but never have I felt it in such a high degree. I truly felt that: 'The heavens declare the glory of God, and the firmament showeth his handiwork'."

When I next received a letter from the State Department of Education, I was expecting another Second, but to my surprise and joy I had received a First Grade with an average of nearly 92 per cent. On arithmetic I scored 100 and on book-keeping and physiology-hygiene 99 each, and my three history grades were 90, 93, and 95. This handsomely printed certificate with a small state seal at the top flanked by a one-room school-house and the State Capitol was issued on September 26, 1903, over the signature of Thomas C. Miller, State Superintendent of Free Schools, and J. B. Grimes, Superintendent of Pocahontas County. Even yet, I am almost as proud of it as I am of my doctoral sheepskin from Columbia University, because I won the top teaching certificate at the age of 18 after only one short session in high school.

Class Periods

In my first teaching I was inclined to schedule too many short class periods — 35 to 38 in one day, repeating some classes in the lower grades. In practice, however, I found that fewer and longer class periods were more satisfactory and effective, with repetitions only for beginners. So, in my fourth school, I observe that I had only 24 scheduled classes a day, which indeed seem to be enough, ranging in length from 10 to 20 minutes and averaging about 15. Sometimes we would not be able to finish in a six-hour school day and would run past 4 P.M. 10 to 15 or even 30 minutes.

At the two 10-minute recesses and the noon hour the children were encouraged to exercise outdoors in fair weather in such school games as they might choose or devise with a minimum of supervision. Once, on Arbor Day, each boy brought a small tree to school and helped to set it on the school grounds, and for the girls I provided wild honeysuckle and rhododendron plants. Occasionally we would have spelling matches, verse recitations, and other exercises, or visits by the county superintendent. I issued printed monthly report cards to each child, giving his rating and signed by the teacher. At the end of the term parents and friends would attend the closing exercises.

Return to High School

By late November, in response to the advice and encouragement of Dr. Lacy, I had decided to return to his school for a second term beginning in January. I had seriously considered teaching a whole year and then going a year to high school, visiting the St. Louis Exposition during the intervening summer. Dr. Lacy thought schooling was more needful than a big show, however, and advised me to repeat what I had done the year before since the procedure in my case was working very well. With return to high school in mind, I saved my nickels and dimes, studied Latin and mathematics, and read history and literature in order to enter at midyear with some hope of succeeding. Dr. Lacy repeated his offer of the first year. With the approval of my trustees to teach on Saturdays and holidays, I finished the term by January 14, 1904, and was off to Lewisburg by the first Greenbrier River train, though temporarily saddened at the thought of being away from home and my relatives for more than four months. But with travel and work, this mood soon passed, and in all of my schooling I was truly homesick only once when most of the boys had gone home leaving just two or three of us in the dormitory. On that occasion a good novel soon brought relief.

I was welcomed by the Lacys and the boys without incident, registered, and settled down to work. My studies were Bible, rhetoric and literature, algebra followed by geometry, second-year Latin, mental philosophy, and astronomy. The last, under Dr. Lacy, was one of my best courses whether in high school or college, giving me clear, basic knowledge on the structure of the universe and dispelling many of my childish fancies. In the Literary Society we continued to debate, once discussing the need to educate all Negroes, the affirmative rightly winning the debate. So busy was I that I made no record in my diary from February 20 to May 25.

Though we had no football or baseball games, we boys had various ways of exercising, as by running, jumping, "roly-poly," skating on ice or the frozen snow, rambling (once into a cave where our lights went out fearsomely), and doing our own room chores. One time some of the boys had a lot of mischievous fun by concealing themselves in white sheets and frightening Dr. Lacy's spirited horse grazing on the school grounds into snorting hysterics. When Dr. Lacy would come out to inspect, the boys would disappear, only to reappear when he had returned to his private home just off the campus, where we got our meals.

With $5 sent to me by my father I purchased an armful of books for summer reading — Cooper's five-volume "Leatherstocking Series," Irving's *History of New York* and *Sketch-Book,* and Shakespeare's "The Tempest." Irving's humor and flow of language I greatly enjoyed, keeping lists of unfamiliar words to learn. For story, humor, style, and characterization "The Tempest" and later "The Merchant of Venice" were truly fascinating. I loved Portia quite as much as Bassanio or the Author himself, and Prospero's love of books and learning appealed to me. Cooper's stories of the Indians and pioneers I read as if they were the pure truth, completely surrendering myself to the hypnotic power of the novelist and reliving the lives of the characters.

In looking over my more ambitious high-school themes, I notice that I frequently chose to write about rather large, abstract topics concerned with conduct or one's future: for example, such topics as "Conscience," "Good Manners," "Our Mission," "Education," and "Courage." I think I chose these topics in order to make a study of them and clarify my own thinking about them, and they were very helpful in meeting this need. In writing themes, I used a dictionary, appropriate quotations, and my own observations and reflections. My instructors liked and approved my efforts. No topic could be larger or more inclusive than "Education" and some instructors would exclude it entirely as too large. However, we should remember that at a certain stage of development boys and girls need to get an over-all view of the big subjects and learn to bound them as they do countries in geography and give the main facts about them. They are not yet ready to specialize. My paper on "Education" began as part of a debate on the topic that the pen is more potent or influential than the sword. I learned of physical, mental, and moral education; that we get two educations, one from others and one by our own efforts. Surely young people need such general or comprehensive views of many large subjects, and if they fail to get them, they become lost in details and non-essentials. My 2,000-word paper on "Education" I read in a contest at our Teachers' Institute in August, 1903, and it was later published in the county newspaper.

My Third School

After spending the summer of 1904 on the farm, working, reading, thinking, writing, and planning, as indicated above, I began on August 29 to teach my third school at Huntersville, formerly the county seat of Pocahontas County and its oldest town, having been originally a meeting place for hunters and traders and the local militia. The town was beautifully located near Knapp's Creek on a flat point of elevated land jutting out into the mile-wide valley, with narrow gaps above and below the town, and surrounded by mountains, where the people could live quietly and peacefully.

Here I boarded at a small hotel kept by Cousin Zane and Ida Moore, two of the best and most industrious people that ever lived, who let me have a room over the lobby with another boarder and my meals for $7 a month, leaving me $23 a month to finance my education and a prospective trip to St. Louis. To offset the increased living expenses in town, I had better mail facilities and better opportunities to associate with different types of people, and was only 11 miles from my home.

On the opening day two of my lovely cousins, prospective teachers, Lily and Mabel Milligan, visited the school to observe my procedures and pleased me with their praise, though I felt that the performance was just fair. These and other young women I liked to associate with and might have wholly lost my heart to them but for my dominant ambition to get an education and to put this quest first on my program. Not until I had graduated from college did Venus much affect me. In the school of 25 students, two older than myself, I found a poor state of discipline, apparently a hang-over from my predecessor, and the schoolroom was badly in need of cleaning. At once I set about improving both — a birch for a few boys and one girl, I regret to say, and soap and water for the building, applied by a squad of students with my direction and help.

After three weeks of diligent efforts my school was in fair working order, and I began to think of the big show of the year, the Louisiana Purchase Exposition in St. Louis, Missouri, which, publicized and visited by thousands of people, had been in preparation for more than three years and discussed for the last 10 or 20 years. I remember the Columbian Exposition of 1892-1893 in Chicago, attended by one of my aunts, and I had heard and read of the Centennial in Philadelphia, in 1876 — all of which filled me with a strong desire to visit something similar. So, for several weeks I schemed and planned, because my funds were limited and I needed them for education. Caught in this dilemma between schooling and travel to the exposition, I was pleased to learn that some of my friends thought that $30 to $40 spent on such a trip would be a good investment in education of its kind.

St. Louis Exposition

My first plan was to accompany some of my homefolks, but they decided not to go since my father preferred to invest the cost of a trip in a piano for my sisters and a special teacher for them after the public schools closed. Upon learning of this change in their plans, I joined a local party then being organized for the trip that grew to 14 members. They were: Dr. J. B. Lockridge and his daughter, Maude, and lawyer H. M. Lockridge and his daughter, Ethel, all four direct descendants of the hero, Captain Andrew Lockridge; Cousin Ida Moore and her son, Winfred, of the Moses Moore family; Mrs. George Ginger of pioneer stock; Miss Carrie Moore, Mr. and Mrs. James Doyle, Elmer Moore, Joe Phillips, Cousin Locke Herold, and myself. The last four were unattached young men who tended to form a team for sight-seeing and protection. We had agreed to take little baggage, to wear comfortable shoes, and to carry little money. With $10 in my purse and $15 in my round-trip railway ticket, I securely pinned $20 in an inside shirt pocket since I had not yet heard of traveler's checks.

Leaving Huntersville on the fine clear morning of October 13, and traveling about 700 miles by way of Huntington, Cincinnati, and Indianapolis, we entered the Fair Grounds in St. Louis about 10 A.M. on October 15, 1904. Our first act was to ride around the grounds in a large bus-like automobile — my first ride in such a conveyance — for 25 cents. My first and most lasting impression of the exposition grounds and buildings was their magnitude, symmetry, and fairyland beauty.

Then, breaking up into convenient smaller groups, we began to tour the various buildings and to view the extensive exhibits. Transportation probably surpassed others in interest for me. How far had we advanced in traveling facilities from the camel and canoe to the steamboat, locomotive and automobile of 1904, the airplane still being only a hazardous plaything of great potentialities! The Lincoln log cabin and 264-foot Ferris wheel had unique appeal for all visitors. One afternoon by pre-arrangement I met Aunt Margie Cook of Parkville, Missouri, whose husband was, for many years, a popular professor at Park College. Another trip was to see a reproduction of Jerusalem with its camels, narrow, winding streets, and holy places. One Sunday some of us toured St. Louis itself, then a city of 750,000 inhabitants. Along the mile-long "Pike" in the fairgrounds, lined with shows, merry-go-rounds, scenic railways, spectacular paintings, imitated Boer War battle with uniformed soldiers and thundering cannon, and so on to satiation, we spent most of our late evenings, arriving at our lodgings in a private home about 11 P.M.

After making the trip and spending five days at the fair, I would sum up my views and reactions by saying: I was powerfully impressed by the vast agricultural resources of such midwestern states as Illinois, by the magnitude and prospects of such cities as St. Louis and Cincinnati, and by the phenomenal advancement of the nations as shown by this stupendous exposition. From the trip I learned a great deal, and the outlay was a sound investment, though I felt the financial pinch for nearly a year afterward.

Desiring very much to visit my mother at Spencer, West Virginia, I left St. Louis one day ahead of our party and was accompanied by a school friend, Louis Baker, as far as Huntington, West Virginia, where I stopped intending to take a night train for Spencer. But I learned that there was no train till the next morning. So I went to a hotel, wrote a few letters, rested from my travels, and abandoned the Spencer trip regretfully for fear my ticket would expire and leave me stranded.

William Jennings Bryan

The next morning, October 21, as I walked leisurely to the postoffice, reading signs, admiring buildings, and watching people, I saw a large poster announcing that the Great Commoner, William Jennings Bryan, would speak in a Huntington theater that very night. I could scarcely trust my own eyes that thus, unexpectedly, I had a rare opportunity to see and hear this renowned speaker and noble American. In my youthful enthusiasm I regarded him as a leader and statesman to be classed with Jefferson and Lincoln. I quickly decided to spend the day in Huntington, visiting newspaper plants, the Carnegie Library, one of the public schools, and other places of interest, and then at night to hear the orator himself, many of whose speeches I had previously read.

To be certain of getting a desirable seat, I went to the theater an hour before the doors were to open. I was almost the first person to arrive there, but soon the Bryan enthusiasts began coming in such numbers that at least 600 greeted the opening of the doors. I got a seat immediately in front of the speaker's stand and about 40 feet away, where I could best hear, see, and observe the performance. As the Bryan train was somewhat late, an interval on the program was filled by state politicians eager to ride on the Bryan bandwagon, though he was not then a candidate but a supporter of the Democratic national ticket led by Alton B. Parker of New York.

Amid loud cheering and shouting, Bryan arrived at 8:20 P.M. and spoke till 9:45 on various planks of the Democratic platform — the money question, imperialism, the Filipinos, the army, the labor problem, the race question, his leadership of six million fools according to a Republican critic, and Senator Black's speech nominating Theodore Roosevelt for the presidency.

With much cheering approval as he scored telling points, Mr. Bryan held the rapt attention of his auditors in a theater packed to the doors. He impressed me as a man of pure character, much knowledge, rich sympathies, and of great courage and ability. In my diary I observed that there could be no doubt of his wonderful oratorical powers. I think that I heard, understood, and appreciated every word and sentence he uttered and delivered in a graceful, forceful manner. His language flowed easily and naturally, his inflections rising or falling to suit his theme and to delight the hearer, the music of words spoken by a sincere, handsome man, concerned about the welfare of his country. But since he was opposing no one directly and was not himself a candidate, he was hardly aggressive but calm, easy, assured, and benevolent among his friends and admirers.

About 12 years later I heard him a second time address prohibition forces in a large Cincinnati auditorium, where a lot of the "Wets" tried to break up the meeting and mar his speech by getting up noisily from their seats in small successive groups and stalking from the hall in pretended scorn and disgust. Soon Mr. Bryan began to tell humorous stories with the result that the exit stopped and many of the retreating opposition slipped into rear seats and listened to the remainder of the speech. Without any show of anger but by cunning strategy, the orator completely outwitted the organized rowdies.

After Bryan's speech I left Huntington at midnight and came to Roncevert (French for Greenbrier), a junction point for the Greenbrier Branch of the Chesapeake and Ohio Railroad. There unexpectedly for the last time I saw my Grandfather Ruckman for a few minutes before we boarded different trains that separated us forever, since a year later he died of typhoid fever at the age of 72. My brother Henry and I drove 75 miles across the mountains to his funeral at Mossy Creek, where my Ruckman grandparents are buried near the Herrings.

High-School Graduate

Back in Huntersville after this adventure to the Exposition and to hear the silver-tongued Bryan, I settled down to steady teaching, repaid a loan of $30 for the trip, and tried to save my remaining funds for a third term at Dr. Lacy's school. That $45 outlay for the Fair left quite a void. Thanksgiving and the Christmas holidays came and passed without stopping my school except for a day or so. A long vacation was ruled out completely with the approval of my considerate and helpful trustees and the kind acquiescence of my students. In January at our concluding school exercises, I was surprised and gratified to receive presents paid for by student subscriptions still listed in the principal gift — a volume of Josephus' complete works along with a few handkerchiefs — presented to me for the school children by one of the sweetest and brightest girls whose beauty and charm five years later, like Dante's Beatrice, transported me to the Heaven of Love!

To pay my expenses of $95 in Lewisburg for four months I had only $50. I had spent at the Exposition precisely enough to make up the deficit. Though I could not expect any gifts to help me, I felt confident that I could finance my schooling in some way, because my credit was good for small amounts among my friends. Soon after my arrival in Lewisburg I paid Dr. Lacy $15 on account and explained my financial circumstances to him. He graciously refrained from chiding me for the St. Louis trip and agreed to allow me ample time to pay him, since this was my third and last term in his school.

As the main school building had recently burned down, classes were meeting in an old Masonic building on the other side of town. The boarders had arranged to live in Dr. Lacy's large home, where they had been getting their meals previously. I roomed with a new teacher, Mr. R. W. Blain of Covesville, Virginia, a cultivated college graduate and a good man, who used to amuse me somewhat by his Sunday-afternoon practice of lying down on the bed to read his Bible, which always proved so quieting and consoling that he would soon be fast asleep to dream of Heaven and the angels!

In this our senior year, my roommate Leach and I conceived a plan of launching a little paper to aid the school and to show our appreciation of Dr. Lacy's good work in starting and operating this much-needed high school for boys under the sponsorship of Greenbrier Presbytery. After getting permission from the principal, we organized an editorial board with Leach and myself as editors and six other leading students as associate editors, one being secretary and another treasurer, whose financial responsibility was so slight that a bond was not required. In April the first number, named *The Outlook*, appeared, a six-page, double-column sheet about seven by ten inches with various news items, announcements, jokes, and a little charitable advertising from the local merchants, selling for five cents each. In May came a second number enlarged to eight pages without an increase in price, with news items, little essays, quoted poems, and more advertising under the same leadership. As evidence of the current value of money, the April number announced that a contract for $4,950 had been let for the construction of a new two-story, brick-veneer building with gymnasium, auditorium, bathroom, hot-water heat, and rooming accommodations for 40 boys, to be completed before the fall term. The board of editors, however, found themselves about $15 in debt, which they honorably but painfully extracted from lean purses, with a strong determination on my part to beware of the fascinations of journalism.

In January I had registered for these courses: Bible, moral philosophy, Latin III, Greek I, English history, geometry, and rhetoric with composition and literature, which at the end of the term I passed with an average grade of 94. On my Bible examination I received a grade of 99¾, which shows apparently that I then knew more of Paul's "Romans," "Corinthians," and "Hebrews," and John's "Revelation" than ever before or since. But the true explanation is simple. The instructor had previously supplied the class with 81 questions from which he assured us he would choose the test questions. I worked up the answers, planning in certain cases to quote from the Bible or the Shorter Catechism verbatim. I keep this test paper as a memorial of my high-school days.

Scholarship to College

At our commencement on May 22, 1905, preceded by four declaimers, two essayists, one orator, and four debaters, all with fixed time limits, I gave the final oration, as it was classified, on "Courage," an abstract subject, which I somehow succeeded in treating concretely. As evidence of my progress in high school, I quote two excerpts:

"Courage, as the word indicates, is a heart principle; an expression of what is in the heart; the manifestation of strong character. Although there are those who are by nature timid, yet as a rule, the absence of courage implies that the character is not genuine, that the conscience has been injured, and that the heart fears truth."

"Now, my friends," I concluded, "I have spoken to you of the two kinds of courage; I have shown how it is acquired, and I have also referred to six examples. As a final word, let me say that though disaster should snatch your fortune away and hunger visit your home; though the curse of war should come on you and the loss of friends should grieve your spirit; though the heavens above you should be dark and the earth beneath be cold; yet, if you have courage, it will carry you through the darkness of defeat and bring you out in the sunlight of victory."

The scholarship to Hampden-Sidney College was awarded to Frank Brown of Lewisburg, who later became a leading Presbyterian pastor with long service in Charleston, West Virginia, and Dallas, Texas. The scholarship to Washington and Lee University was given to me. My recollection is that the speaker's medal went to winsome and brilliant Lant Slaven, who became a lawyer. Soon after returning to my home, I received a cheering letter from Judge J. M. McWhorter of Lewisburg, who, as one of three judges, had heard my effort on the subject of "Courage." He commended my material and delivery and reported that one of them had voted to give me the speaker's medal. I was well pleased with the scholarship and happy to graduate and be prepared to enter college.

CHAPTER 6

Undergraduate Adventures

I WAS attracted to Washington and Lee University by the scholarship, by two famous names, by three alumni teachers, and by an energetic president, George H. Denny, who occasionally sent me a picture card of the college that held and stimulated my interest.

Among my ancestral stock, the Scotch-Irish had started the school near Staunton as Augusta Academy in 1749; then they renamed it Liberty Hall in 1776 and removed it to Lexington, where, by successive transformation, it became Washington Academy in 1798, Washington College in 1813, and Washington and Lee University in 1871. Since few institutions are so rich in historical and cultural associations, it would be the place for me to seek wisdom, where Americans honored Washington, great in victory, and Lee, great in defeat, and celebrated Stonewall Jackson, a native son of West Virginia.

Saving Funds for College

When I graduated from high school in May, 1905, I was eager to enter college without delay, but I did not have the necessary means. To be sure, I had received a scholarship to Washington and Lee worth $50 in tuition, which was offset, however, by a debt of $45 incurred in high school with my promise to pay it promptly. Wishing at the age of 20 to keep free of debt and to maintain my independence, I decided to teach in the public schools the following year, to save as much as possible there and in two summer vacations, and then, supported by my savings, to try the adventures of college life in the shadows of great characters. In making my plans, I was advised and encouraged by Dr. Lacy and Mr. Blain, who in August happily obtained an extension of my scholarship to the following year.

After resting at home for two weeks and looking around for remunerative work, I secured a summer job at George W. Huntley's lumber camp on Douthard's Creek near the lands cleared and improved by Christopher Herold and his sons. My task was to follow the cutting crews with a measuring stick, to make a record of the diameter and length of all logs, and then to calculate the number of board feet as evidence of work done by the lumbermen or as a basis for paying local jobbers. I worked at this worthy outdoor job, scaling several million feet, from June 18 to September 28, 1905, except for a week off to attend a county institute for teachers. The pay was $35 a month plus board and lodging at the camp with the manager, my Cousin Horace M. Lockridge, a shrewd lawyer. He was refreshing, stimulating company for me, and the outdoor work improved my health.

This camp employed 60 to 75 lumbermen, mostly Austrians imported from northern cities, who spoke English imperfectly or not at all. Of course, their bosses could use both English and German effectively. Since nearly all the white pine timber originally growing in this region had been removed several years before, Mr. Huntley's camp was taking the hemlock growing in the lower parts of the mountains. The men cut the trees into logs and peeled them, leaving them slick and much slippery bark on the ground. During the winter months the logs would be assembled on the banks of a nearby creek, and when the spring floods came, somewhat controlled by log dams, the timber would be floated in the creeks and the Greenbrier River to a big mill in Roncevert, West Virginia, to be sawed into lumber and marketed.

Before starting my work, I bought a pair of lightweight, laced, lumberman's boots with heavy soles studded with steel spikes or calks to enable me to walk on the slick bark and peeled logs. Then, taking a scaler's rod about four feet long with a steel crosspiece at one end to catch the underside of a log in determining diameter, and a wooden paddle to hold my record sheet ruled to record diameters from 8 to 50 inches and log lengths from 8 to 16 feet, I was ready to begin work. I always measured the log diameters at the small end, never guessing or estimating, but I became so expert in determining the length of logs at a glance that I seldom resorted to measuring them. Usually I could easily distinguish between logs 8, 10, 12, 14, and 16 feet long, though I would occasionally check myself for accuracy.

As a protective practice, I kept some distance behind the cut-

ting crews who were working in different parts of the forests, because I wished to stay out of the range of falling trees. On a few
occasions, however, the tops of trees came entirely too close to
me for safety or comfort. Sometimes at a remote place in the
forest where the workmen had either finished cutting and peel-
ing or were not laboring, I would be quite alone and perhaps a
little fearful that a bear or panther might come around on an
inspection tour! In the loneliness of the forest a falling limb
might startle me into an alert watchman for whatever might be
prowling. During that summer there were many heavy rains,
making glorious opportunities for reading or study if one had
the chance. In the woods, however, with large slabs of bark
placed over a log or a stump, I would shelter myself, rest from
my scaling labors, and enjoy watching the water trickle down
the bark of trees, and little birds, bugs, and worms seek shelter
like the scaler. The rainfall might quickly end and again it might
continue steadily for hours without wetting me.

Keeping Records

I made frequent reports of my scaling to the manager on the
job and direct to the company headquarters, without once being
charged with an error in calculation. I had mastered long division
and the art of simple arithmetic. My study of the subject and
practice in teaching it were paying off well. Besides, I checked
and rechecked my reports to avoid mistakes. In a small notebook
used in high school, I also began to keep detailed records of my
personal receipts and expenses, striking a balance at the end of
short periods. Here is the first part of this unrevised record:

EARNED

1905. From June 18th to September 28th at lumber camp,	$109.72
October. By month's salary teaching 22 days,	38.50
By making fires at school one month,	.80
Total income to October 31,	$149.02

SPENT

1905. June,	To one pair Lumberman's cutters (boots),	$5.00
July,	To merchandise,	3.00
July,	To paid Dr. Lacy's bill with interest (unasked)	25.50
August,	To paid Winston L. Herold's school loan,	10.00
August,	To expenses at Teachers' Institute,	7.50
August,	To outlay for books and newspapers,	2.50

September,	To merchandise,	2.00
September,	To paid for subscription to Bryan's *Commoner*,	1.20
October,	To paid for 2½ dozen eggs at 20 cents, for fever patient's family,	.50
October,	To incidental expenses,	.30
	Total spent to October 31,	$57.50

Thus, at the end of October by scaling logs during the summer and teaching through October, I had earned $149.02, paid my pressing high-school debt and other necessary expenses, and had a balance saved of $91.52. The eggs call for a note of explanation. That fall among several typhoid-fever cases in our community was that of Mr. Oscar B. Sharp, a poor feeble man with a large needy family. Hearing of their plight, I bought the eggs from my father and on horseback I carried them in a basket three miles to the grateful family. Never has a little charity from my slender resources given me so much satisfaction as this of the eggs to an afflicted family. Mr. Sharp recovered and lived for many years, though he always seemed to be on the brink of death.

After winning my top certificate, teaching three terms of school elsewhere, and graduating from high school, I did not hesitate at the fairly mature age of 20 years to make a contract for teaching the Moore School, which my own relatives and children of the neighborhood would attend. This plan enabled me to live at home, work evenings and week-ends for my board, and thus increase my savings a little. I also built the fires at school in the morning and during the day, going early on cold days to make the stove hot and the room warm before the children should arrive, sometimes chilled to the bone. I remember that once, on a very cold morning, a six-year-old girl alone walked nearly two miles safely. I protested this lack of caution to her parents and it did not recur.

On one occasion to raise funds for starting a school library, I brought in three entertainers, who could play the banjo and violin or fiddle and sing ballads, to give a concert, supplemented by student exercises, to which we charged an admission fee. In this way we raised a small fund and bought a few biographies and novels for the children to read. Webster's *Unabridged Dictionary* was still a mainstay of the school.

While I was teaching the Moore School for five months from October to February, I contracted to teach the Thorny Creek School a third time, but, owing to the late start, for only four months. Going back there after a year's absence I was welcomed like an old friend by the patrons and at Mr. Hively's home, where I continued to board. The teaching was easy and pleasant and the days passed uneventfully. By this time two of the older and best students, Newman Fertig and Walter Hively, were definitely fitting themselves to teach as soon as they could qualify. I am proud to report that they proved to be good and faithful instructors with long records to their credit.

My Reading

In 1904 in my notebook I made a list of the books I had read before December of that year, and in 1906 I made a second list of books read between these two dates. My purpose was simply to check on myself and to keep a record for possible use later. The first list shows that, apart from textbooks, I had read about 30 volumes to December, 1904, including the Bible twice and "How to Reach Success or Room at the Top" no fewer than three times, because both books were interesting and stimulating. Among the others read once were "Robinson Crusoe," Irving's "Sketch Book" and "History of New York," "Masterpieces of American Eloquence," biographies of David Crockett, Robert E. Lee, William J. Bryan, Dwight L. Moody, Theodore L. Cuyler, Abraham Lincoln, and William McKinley; "Gold Hunting in Alaska", "The Johnstown Flood," Shoup's "History of Education," White's "Art of Teaching," two of Cooper's novels, supplemented by "Josiah in New York" (a gift from an aunt), "In His Steps," "Titus: A Comrade of the Cross," and Ralph Connor's "Black Rock."

In the 18-month period between December, 1904, and August, 1906, I read 18 volumes, an average of one a month in addition to my regular assignments as a student or a teacher. This second list includes such books as Franklin's "Autobiography," Wirt's "Patrick Henry," Cooper's "Pioneers," Strong's "The New Era," Shakespeare's "Julius Caesar" and "The Merchant of Venice," Parson's "Christian Missions in Africa," Macaulay's essays on Bacon, Pitt, and Hastings, Grasty's "Faith's Trials," Bunyan's "Pilgrim's Progress" (read at lumber camp), and Kerr's "The Voice of God in History."

In all, to the age of 21, I had read 50 volumes in history, literature, philosophy, and religion, but a minimum of poetry, though I loved Longfellow, Poe, Whittier, Gray, Tennyson, and Shakespeare. I think that I had read an equal quantity in half-a-dozen newspapers and half-a-dozen magazines, and perhaps more, for I have always tried to keep up with current events as an aid in teaching and to satisfy my own wishes to know what is going on in the world. As a bit of evidence, in February, 1906, I was a subscriber for *Bryan's Commoner, The Atlanta Constitution, The West Virginia School Journal, Normal Instructor,* and *World's Events* (magazine).

During my second school of 1905-1906, I was on the lookout for remunerative summer work. I could not find a scaling job, but in my reading I saw an advertisement by the Thomas Manufacturing Company of Dayton, Ohio, for agents to sell its cutlery products. In due course I became its authorized agent in Pocahontas County. I was to receive a commission of 40 per cent on my total sales and to pay my own expenses. I obtained a sample roll of the company's products containing shears, scissors, knives of several kinds, razors, and the like. In the first five weeks my commissions amounted to $90, which, less expenses, left me about $60 — $12 a week or $2 a day! I became doubtful as to whether I was truly earning the money and one day a prospect expressed grave doubts as to whether the company's guarantees would hold good.

Astonishing as my action may seem, because of these two doubts lodged in my mind, I abruptly stopped canvassing, filled the orders already taken, went straight home, and quit the job completely and finally. I did not want any tainted money in my pockets even if I should never get an education. Yet, I myself kept a few of the articles which proved to be genuine and dependable, including a pair of shears which have now seen 50 years of continuous service. Obviously the Lord did not intend me to become a go-getter businessman. I was too conscientious for that. Even yet, I wish to earn what I get unless it is an outright gift. Of course, as a teacher I have never suffered any qualms of conscience on the score of being overpaid.

My Record for 15 Months

Thus, in my money-making ventures preparatory to college, I came to September, 1906, and struck a balance on my total earnings and expenses for the preceding 15 months as log scaler, school teacher, and cutlery salesman. The final results were:

My Earnings for 15 months,	$520.52
My Expenses for 15 months including an outlay of $40 for college clothing,	$240.97
Balance on hand for college expenses,	$279.55

My highest hope and ambition had been to stay two years in college, then to teach or work a year, and return for two more years of study and a degree, I hoped. Even that expectation seemed impossible with less than $300 in available funds. Yet, I succeeded in attending three successive years and in graduating a year ahead of my entering class of 1906. Surely such a record enables me to qualify as something of a financial expert in student economy.

My savings were reduced below $300 by a trip that my brother Henry and I made by train in August, 1906, to visit our invalid mother at the Spencer Hospital. On my return from St. Louis in 1904 I had missed a train connection in Huntington and been unable to see her then. After two years, I could wait no longer even if my college education should go overboard. That trip cost each of us about $30. We made a circular journey by train through north central West Virginia to Spencer and returned by way of Huntington, Charleston, and the Greenbrier River. Our poor mother was slowly growing weaker. We could do nothing then to improve her condition. The trip was the saddest of my life. Three years later, a few months after my graduation from college, she died and her body was returned home for burial. This tragic affliction for her and her family, Death thus terminated, and slowly the dark clouds of distress and loss faded from my mind but not the memory of them.

Dr. Lacy's Advice

After my graduation from high school, Dr. Lacy wrote me three friendly letters. In early June, 1905, he sent me a copy of my scholarship certificate to hold and present at the college when I should register as a student. He added: "I would most earnestly advise you to take good care of your health. Get rid of the cough you had when here. Stand up straight, and do not sit too closely at your books. You will not gain anything by trying to study when you are too tired." A postscript courteously reminded me of my $25 debt to him. Early in August I was able to repay him with a little voluntary interest for the aid. In recognizing receipt of my check, he gave me more good advice: "Keep your head up and keep your backbone straight, literally and figuratively." Learning that I could not go straight to college, he advised me to consult President Denny regarding the scholarship. At Mr. Blain's request, the college extended it one year to fit my plans. Again this advice: "Take a regular course and be prepared for anything to which you may be called. My highest pleasure now next to my own children is to know of the high character and success of those I have tried to help." Finally, just a few days before I left for college, he wrote to inquire about my probable needs then or later and the help he could get from the Presbyterian Church, if necessary. That led to my getting some aid or a loan in my second and third college years, totaling $150, which I later repaid. He thought my going to the woods was good for my health, as indeed it was, and that I should get outdoors and exercise more in the fresh air and sunshine.

He concluded his last letter of sincere friendship to me with the sad report that, after being four years in charge of the Presbytery's school for boys and "a great deal of trouble about it," he was being replaced as principal and feared he would be left without employment. Surely he was my true friend and benefactor. As good and useful a man and Christian as ever lived, he died January 13, 1912, and was buried in the Presbyterian cemetery at Lewisburg, West Virginia. Many years later I was able to show my gratitude to him and his family by sending occasional checks to his maiden daughter, Lena Lacy, then enfeebled by illness and old age.

Arrival at College

When I arrived at Washington and Lee, I kept in mind Dr. Lacy's sensible advice, which had much to do with my deciding to live at Major F. W. Houston's in East Lexington, a mile from the college, so that every day I would be outdoors long enough to walk to college and back to my lodgings, where living expenses were slightly lower than in town. Major Houston's large, two-story, brick house was situated among beautiful elm and locust trees on a hill sloping gently to North River, with a fine view of House Mountain on the western horizon. A small, story-and-half, stone house was also available for student roomers, where on the second floor my two friends, Harold H. Leach and Robert R. Gray, and I had a large, quiet room, heated by a stove burning wood, which we prepared. Major Houston, wearing a short gray beard and fond of jokes and stories, had an invalid wife whom we seldom saw, and a beautiful, blond daughter, Mary, who managed the household and charmed the boarders.

Besides these home-like associations, I enjoyed the companionship of ten collegians as full of life, as studious, and as manly as could be found on the campus. From Virginia were Henry R. Mahler, who became a superintendent of schools; Harry St. George Tucker, a college instructor; Robert J. Reveley, a teacher, and Forest C. Williams, a surveyor. From West Virginia besides myself came Leach and Gray, ministerial candidates; from Mississippi, Charles E. Burks and Lawrence C. Caldwell, destined for the law; from Kentucky, William L. Lord, a popular student and life-long teacher, and Stanton L. Dorsey, who left college without graduating. Ten of them won college degrees; six took two degrees, and two received three including a doctorate. Major Houston's guests consisting of six vigorous freshmen, one mature sophomore, three juniors, and one senior were a congenial and representative group of real students, not loafers and playboys at the college, though they had plenty of fun and diversion. The tallest Caldwell won the nickname of "Shorty", Williams "The Squaw", Leach "The Parson", and Herold later "Greek Shark".

In groups of varying sizes, each with his lunch, we walked to and from the college, or occasionally from the nearby railroad Y we got a train ride to town. In winter we skated on the ice and in warm weather we swam in the cool water of the river, where, during my stay in college, three boys owing to inexperience and rashness were accidentally drowned. Once eight of us made a two-day walking tour to House Mountain, spending a night under a cliff near the top and climbing next day to precipitous projections for spectacular, memento, kodak pictures.

My first visit to the college campus, always green and shady but lately modernized with cement walks, repaired and renovated buildings, was to meet President George H. Denny, Dean Henry D. Campbell, and the Treasurer and Secretary, Mr. John L. Campbell — all of whom, by their kind helpfulness, soon won my trust and admiration. At the registration on September 13, 1906, I met most of the professors, especially my prospective instructors: Dr. W. S. Currell in English, Prof. Addison Hogue in Greek, Dr. James W. Kern in Latin, Dr. L. W. Smith in mathematics, and Dr. James A. Quarles in philosophy, a white-bearded veteran of the faculty. In working out my program and advising with Dr. Quarles, I got quite a thrill by being able, from a careful study of the last catalog, to correct this genial old man on a degree requirement. When he appealed to a catalog and found that I, a freshman, was right, he graciously admitted his error, remarking that it was hard to keep up-to-date on degree requirements. Years later, as a college professor myself, I learned how hard indeed it is to keep up with changing requirements, resembling automobile numbers.

Push-Ball Contest

About 70 sophomores and 130 freshmen engaged in the customary preliminary sparring and guerrilla raids on the campus, in one of which Charles Burks and I, being older than most freshmen, evaded a sophomore posse by posing as law students, who enjoyed a neutral status.

After this interim of cold war, the college itself sponsored an original, all-out, push-ball contest between the two belligerent classes. The push-ball was a huge, inflated sphere about six feet in diameter. The rules called for placing this ball at the center of the football field and lining up the two opposing classes at a distance of about 20 yards from the ball. I think there were four short periods for the contest with brief intervals for rest. The aim was, at a given signal, to find out which side could push or roll the ball out of a neutral area and into the opponents' territory. Though the freshmen outnumbered the sophomores nearly two to one, the sophomores were better acquainted and organized.

At a pistol shot, when all were ready, the two classes rushed for the ball and collided all around and under it and under one another, pushing and shouting, tearing shirts and trousers, and sometimes engaging in personal combat. I remember clearly that I was one of those downed in the mad scramble and was scarcely able to breathe till the ball shifted elsewhere. For a while it was a close contest, with many torn or missing shirts and bruised and scratched bodies, and some students lying on the side lines, breathless or exhausted. But toward the end of the contest, the sophomores hit upon the stratagem of placing a short, heavy-set squad in front to lift the ball off the ground with a second tall squad immediately behind the short fellows to push and roll the ball over the freshmen. This ruse surprised and defeated the freshmen. In the contest several received minor injuries and one such serious punishment as to require hospitalization.

This battle between 200 students must go down in the annals of the college as the greatest ever waged there between freshmen and sophomores and the participants, whether winning or losing, must be regarded as valiant heroes. The next year the college restricted the contestants to 25 or 30 on each side and so made the annual fracas a game instead of a battle fought by massed forces. All hail to the pushballers of 1906!

The Honor System

During the registration period and later, student officials and the faculty carefully explained to all freshmen the aims and operation of the revered Honor System. It was a form of student self-government which assumed that every member of the student body was a gentleman and could be trusted to act as such. It made lying, cheating, and stealing in any phase of college work breaches of the code and it relied upon the Executive Committee of the Student Body to punish the guilty with suspension or forced withdrawal from college. During my five-year residence there the students supported and enforced the code effectively so far as I knew. I neither observed nor heard of any violations except in one literary-society election. In this spectacular case the accused stood trial and, owing to contradictory or doubtful evidence, escaped conviction.

But in June, 1954, 15 undergraduates including several athletes withdrew from the university for organized violations of the code, as discovered by the Executive Committee and admitted by the offending members. Though the college honor system is beautiful in theory and may be effective in practice, I doubt the wisdom of placing unrestricted confidence in all of any student body and the faculty's abdicating and absenting themselves from tests and examinations. The students and the faculty should cooperate to maintain honor and high standards, because eternal vigilance is the price of both liberty and honor. If they relax in their watchfulness, they invite the crooked and depraved to breach the code and disgrace the institution. One of the worst student crooks I ever knew posed as a ministerial candidate, and the worst college liar I ever knew preened himself on being the son of a college president!

My Studies

Immediately after registration I obtained my books, mostly secondhand, met all my classes, and settled down to serious, conscientious work, to determine whether a student with sufficient credits to enter college but only 20 months in high school would succeed or fail in this adventure. That was my personal problem, for I was truly uncertain as to what I could do in college. But I was determined to do my best and to accept the outcome cheerfully. So regular and dependable was I that during my first two years not a single absence from class was marked against me. I was there to learn and benefit from my hard-won opportunity.

My chief interests, I should say, were Greek, English, and mathematics, with Latin and philosophy in a secondary role. The last was comparatively easy, and Latin not too difficult. Quite early in the session I decided to try for the White Scholarship in Greek, which would be awarded to some member of the Greek class at the end of my second year and which was worth about $135. I not only studied, I mastered, every Greek lesson — vocabulary, verb parts, genders, and accents. At the same time I did not neglect my other courses; I prepared every lesson well and did all assignments promptly.

With much interest and some trepidation, therefore, I looked for my first formal report for the period ending October 27, 1906, which, signed by Secretary John L. Campbell and approved as "Excellent" by President Denny, quieted my fears and stimulated my hopes. I had received "G" on all five of my studies, indicating a grade of 85 to 100. "F" then meant passing at 75 to 85, and "D" meant a deficiency. At least I had a favorable start. In December at the end of the first of three terms, my report was a duplicate of the first, and the president commented on it: "Congratulations. Fine student. One of the very best men in his class." That praise, I confess, went to my head a little, but I did not become overconfident and relax my efforts.

Early in the session I joined the Graham-Lee Society and thus continued a valuable student activity already begun in high school. This society met every Saturday night for debate and other literary exercises. Besides debating I filled its various offices successively and represented the society in its centennial celebration on January 19, 1909, and at the following commencement. Here I met and became well acquainted with some of my best friends from other classes and departments of the university. For example, in this society the next year, I came to know and value the fine qualities of James Hubert Price, a law student, who later became a distinguished governor of Virginia.

Freshman English was perhaps my most strenuous and beneficial first-year study. Weekly themes and abstracts of selected classics and occasional outlines were an essential part of the whole year's work. During the first term we studied Genung's "Rhetoric," which summed up the standards of form, correctness, and taste, as practiced by classical English writers. The study of synonyms and antonyms cultivated a new and varied vocabulary. During the second and third terms we reviewed the rise and growth of American and English Literature, using Pancoast's introductory histories and his "English Poems." Dr. Currell gave delightful and instructive talks on famous specimens of English prose and poetry.

This course was well planned. Each student was supplied with a printed program of the textbooks, theme assignments, written reviews of Genung and Pancoast, studies of poems, special compositions, and examination instructions. The requirements were definite, strict, and enforced. Woe to the benighted freshman who neglected his work or disregarded the instructions. At that time Dr. Currell taught the whole class in one group, with three or four student assistants to grade papers. Soon afterwards the class was sectionized and assigned to instructors. Later still, most of the literary study was transferred to a sophomore course, and our own literature considerably neglected by British-minded instructors.

In mathematics I found young Dr. Smith to be a handsome and very competent instructor, who expected prompt and thorough performance from his students. In Latin Dr. Kern was both amusing and instructive, bringing dignity and scholarship to the classroom and instilling these qualities in his students. Dr. Quarles in psychology and philosophy was a gracious and stimulating veteran scholar, nearing a richly deserved retirement with high honor.

At the end of this year in college, without borrowing money or personal hardship, I had a balance of $75 in the bank from my former savings. After a month in college I ceased to keep a financial record, and I thought I had too little time for a diary. I was a busy student, automatically conserving my funds. I do have a record for September, which provides an accurate clue to my year's outlay, approximately as follows:

Nine months of room and board at $12.50 per month,	$112.50
College fees in addition to tuition,	20.00
Round-trip railroad fare over Chesapeake and Ohio,	12.00
Books for the session, mostly used,	20.00
Newspaper subscriptions,	4.00
Christmas books for my brothers and sisters,	6.00
Laundry and incidentals,	25.50
Total college expense excluding my scholarship,	$200.00

Before going to college I had invested about $40 in clothing, a new black suit ordered from Montgomery Ward, and from local stores, a pair of black shoes, gray wool trousers, several shirts, a wool hat, underwear, white collars, ties, and so on. In a kodak picture made at Major Houston's I am wearing those serviceable but baggy gray trousers, a close-fitting black coat and vest from a former suit, black shoes, a white doubled collar with a string tie, and holding two or three books tied with a leather strap. For cold weather I had a long, warm overcoat, and for rain an umbrella, like Thoreau, to protect both me and my books. The black wool suit from Ward's, costing about $15, had good material though the coat fitted very imperfectly around my neck, deserting the sides and even the back of my white collars. I was much concerned about the misfit, because the suit was intended for Sunday and all special occasions — my dress suit. There was too little time to return it for exchange and unwise to revamp it. So, a tailor suggested that I place an oval, steel stay or hoop under the collar to correct the misfit. Then, sometimes the stay would get restless and peevish and perversely show itself in order to embarrass me. Two or three years elapsed before I could replace the misfitting coat. Never again would I accept a suit untried and unseen!

At the end of the second term my grades were all good, and Dr. Denny wrote on my report and signed it in person: "Fine young man! Excellent student! He should go straight on to graduation." And in early June on my third term's report he dictated and signed this paragraph:

Dear Mr. Herold:

I am glad to hand you this report. It is one of the very best I am sending out. You have taken a very high stand in all of your classes, and your record is among the very best made here during the past session. I happen to know that you stood among the very leading men in all of your classes. I am looking forward to your taking your degree, *and of course you recognize the fact that it is of the utmost importance that you should go straightforward with your course without any interruption.* I shall be glad to help in adjusting your course for next session. If I can be of any possible help to you in any way, command me fully. I shall hope to hear from you.

Yours very truly,
George H. Denny
President

These commendations made me feel as if I had scored a home-run or a touchdown in each term. I admired the modest but memorable "Command me fully." Had I really done so, I might have won the $288 Bradford Scholarship the next year since I was in the race without knowing it. I was gunning solely for the Greek scholarship. I knew that I was near the top in Greek and English. His report on my other classes was news to me. As a fine classical scholar himself, Dr. Denny would appreciate fully my good record in Greek and Latin. He was a well-balanced, inspiring leader who could praise both scholars and athletes and win their continuing, steadfast loyalty.

Second Year in College

Upon returning home for the summer vacation, I slowly adjusted myself to the change by working at light tasks or part of the day on the farm, and at the same time I scouted around for a better-paying position, which, luckily, I found in a nearby lumber camp operated by the same company that had employed me two years before. The pay had increased to $50 a month with living expenses. This work happily solved my problem of getting back to college. By the time the session opened in September I had saved about $100, which, with the $75 balance from the previous year, and a $50 aid or loan from the Presbyterian Committee on Education (obtained later in the year), enabled me to continue my studies at Washington and Lee in the fall of 1907. In the two scaling jobs I measured seven or eight million feet of timber. What a pile that would make if stacked together! Enough to build seven to eight hundred five-room cottages.

Back at college for a second year, I obtained room and board at Lindsay's hotel or boarding house on Main Street near the college, where Mr. Leach, ten years my senior, and I were again roommates, paying the owner about $15 apiece monthly. The Houston group was scattered — some coming into town, some staying, and a few going to fraternity houses. With regular exercise in the gymnasium I sought to replace my first year's daily walking to and from college.

My course for this year was well predetermined, because I continued the second year of English, Greek, Latin, and mathematics under the same instructors. To these studies I added American history under Dr. John H. Latané, who was quite a scholar and author, physically heavy-set and much inclined to sit or lounge on his desk; and first-year geology under Dr. Henry D. Campbell, then dean, whose course was perhaps my most memorable adventure in college, though in taking it I was handicapped by having only a slight knowledge of chemistry.

Consequently, my October report on six substantial courses showed five "G's" and one "F" (passing) in geology. Yet, Dr. Denny repeated his "Excellent," and I persevered. My December report repeated the first, and the president commented: "An excellent record. Mr. Herold has continued to take high rank in his class . . . I congratulate him." Wishing to improve my geology grade, I conferred with Dr. Campbell about it, to learn where I was weak. Well, it was lack of chemistry chiefly, and geology, descriptive and historical, is a monstrously large subject with innumerable *terrae incognitae* for a beginner. The vast expanse of geological time and eras made me somewhat dizzy. By March, however, all my grades were "G," and Dr. Denny struck a new note, saying, "Excellent student. Should go on to M. A." Seeking only a degree of Bachelor of Arts, I had not even thought of the degree of Master of Arts. The president planted a seed of suggestion which bore fruit four years later.

In Greek I continued my efforts to win the $135 White Scholarship to be awarded in a class of eight or ten students. At the end of the first year Professor Hogue told me that my average grade was about 96. My chief competitor was my friend, Charles E. Burks, who entered college with two years of Greek in contrast to my half year, and who later became president of the student body and a Virginia circuit judge. Undismayed by the competition, I tried to master every detail, every irregularity in the language as well as all the regular forms. When sent to the blackboard to decline or conjugate or translate, I usually made a perfect or nearly perfect score. We read Xenophon, New Testament selections, and extracts from Herodotus and Demosthenes. For collateral in English translations, we had assignments in Greek history and literature. In my second or third year I remember reading the six extant plays of Sophocles in an English translation and was so impressed as to rate the author a wise and benevolent superman, almost a god, as his statue suggests. Well, I won the Greek scholarship, my grade for the second and more difficult year being only slightly below that of the first year.

Once while the Greek class was reading parts of the New Testament in the original language, a very amusing episode occurred. A ministerial student whose knowledge of Greek was subnormal was translating the Lord's Prayer, of which the closing words, "For thine is the kingdom and the power and the glory, forever. Amen," were omitted on the authority of the oldest manuscripts. This student, knowing the prayer perfectly, felt that he could do a first-class translation. So, he began deliberately, increased his speed, and concluded triumphantly with the part omitted from Westcott and Hort's text. At once the class burst into uncontrollable laughter to the translator's chagrin and with Professor Hogue turning alternately pale and red from embarrassment. Finally, as the class quieted, the instructor discreetly explained that the omitted words had probably been devoutly written on the margin of an old manuscript and later incorporated into the text. That theory was an eye-opener to me as to how the text could be corrupted and is a clue to other priestly fabrications.

My second-year English course, entitled "Advanced Composition and the Forms of Discourse," with considerable practice in writing exposition, argument, description, and narratives, was a large but select class under the personal direction of Dr. Currell. Toward the end of the year we reviewed the history and principles of the novel and read and studied intensively Eliot's "Romola," a great historical novel of Savonarola's Italy. We also considered the principles of literary criticism and tried our amateur pens in the art. In October I submitted a six-page negative argument on the question, "Should colleges be situated in the country?" That my effort pleased the instructor is shown by his comment: "This is refreshing and alive. Shows the real speaking instinct." My interest in Bryan and participation in the Lacy Literary Society along with my experience in teaching were paying praiseworthy dividends.

Three Illuminating Studies

Of all my studies or mental adventures in high school and college, I would spell out three of them in capital letters, because of the satisfaction and illumination they gave me then and afterwards. These three were a high-school course in astronomy under Dr. Matthew L. Lacy, using Steele's "Popular Astronomy"; a college course in general geology taught by Professor Henry D. Campbell; and a literary course in Dante and Milton under the guidance of Dr. W. S. Currell.

The introduction to astronomy gave me a comprehensive, intelligible view of the physical universe and dissipated shallow or ignorant conceptions about it. The course made me realize, as never before, the extent and wonders of the universe and my own littleness in it. The first part of Dr. Campbell's geology course explained the physical forces at work on the earth now and in the past, and prepared me for the second part, which was historical geology — a mind-shaking and earth-rocking subject with glimpses of life so long ago and so different as to be stunning and dumbfounding. These two courses in science, taught by truth-loving scholars, revolutionized my thinking about man and God, religion and philosophy, and the mystery of life in all its forms. Much that I had previously regarded as revealed truth became fiction, fairy story, or myth. The finite "I" caught a glimpse of the infinity of space and the infinity of time.

As an antidote, however, to a possible loss of faith in life or the difference between good and evil, I rate very highly a comparative study of two great epic poems, Dante's "Divine Comedy" in three parts (Hell, Purgatory, and Heaven) and Milton's "Paradise Lost" and "Regained," which I also later taught in college. Dante and Milton were two of the best scholars, thinkers, philosophers, reformers, and poets that ever lived. Dante towers over the classical and medieval worlds like a just and austere superman or god. He had absorbed all that was good in paganism and Christianity and had experienced the keenest joys and sorrows in life. He became a supreme artist. His master-piece, the "Divine Comedy," exhibits the virtues and vices of human life in a vivid, concrete story that a reader can never forget. Never was there such an imaginary journey as that taken by Virgil and Dante through Hell and Purgatory and by Beatrice and Dante up through Paradise to the Beatific Vision. Milton's "Paradise Lost" is probably a satire on the littleness and meanness of man's puny attempts to explain the mystery of life — a satire on the beliefs and speculations of Jews, Catholics, Protestants, and Pagans alike.

On my June report, which was straight "G," with official notice of the award of the Greek scholarship to me, Dr. Denny dictated this message:

Dear Mr. Herold:

I take great pleasure in handing you your report, and in expressing to you our congratulations upon your splendid record during the past session. It will not be amiss for me to tell you that your name was one of the three or four to which the faculty gave consideration in assigning the Bradford Scholarship. This is the highest compliment that could be paid, since, in the judgment of the faculty, you rank among the three or four leading men of the University. Your record and progress have been the subject of frequent favorable comment among the members of the faculty and we all feel a sense of gratification that you have achieved such fine results. You, of course, will go forward and take your *degree* with high credit, and it is a matter of very great importance to you to graduate at Washington and Lee.

Yours very truly,
George H. Denny
President

Gratified and reassured by these official reports on my first two years in college, I returned home to work, read, and rest among the serene and beautiful mountains of West Virginia. Though I was unable to get such lucrative work as I had the summer before, I felt confident that I could obtain or borrow $100 to supplement the $135 assured to me by the Greek Scholarship and that I could graduate in one more year. I was progressing far better than I had anticipated or even dreamed. Accordingly, I put aside my original plan to teach a year between my freshman-sophomore and junior-senior years as a needless delay and unnecessary financial measure.

A Family Problem at Home

But, regardless of my success and high hopes at college, I soon found myself at the age of 23 face to face with an age-old and distressing problem in my home. For several years my mother had been in a state hospital, an afflicted invalid unable to return to her home. I was the oldest child, next my brother Henry, and third my oldest sister Margie, then 16 years of age. Of four girls, Reta, aged nine, was the youngest child in the family. From the beginning of my mother's illness, getting and keeping satisfactory housekeepers had been a recurring problem. First we had a middle-aged man and his wife, providing both with work. When they left, two young women took over jointly and carried on the household for a considerable period satisfactorily. When one of these later returned to her home, only one housekeeper was left. As the years passed, this person's power and influence over my father grew beyond reasonable bounds. In firm loyalty to my mother I was deeply distressed, as were other members of the family. For most of this vacation, a civil war of conflicting emotions and impulses raged in my mind, refusing to be pacified or quieted.

Confidentially, I consulted with my older brother and sister about the problem, and I learned that they shared my views, though less intensely, and that they looked to me for a solution and leadership. At the end of the summer, just before returning to college, I reached a decision. Without preliminaries or further delay, I called together the principal parties, along with my older brother and oldest sister, to witness what I said and did. In the dramatic meeting I reviewed the situation at some length and in detail and I concluded with an emphatic demand that the housekeeper leave the home at once, and I suggested that my sister take over the management of the household for a while. The principals were so abashed and mortified that they had little or nothing to say in reply. Either that day or the next the housekeeper did depart, and within a few days I returned to college, uncertain as to what might happen at home but hoping for the best. I had not flinched from doing what I conceived to be my plain duty, come hell or high water.

In my first year I had cautiously registered for five introductory college courses, meeting 17 hours a week. The second year I registered for six advanced courses, meeting 20 hours a week. With an excellent grade record in these courses, I was allowed by the faculty to register in my third or senior year for eight courses. My weekly total of recitation periods was 23, almost four a day for six days. What ambition on my part and what faculty confidence in me! Sixty points or hours, with twice the value of the later 120-hour plan, were then required for graduation. In my last two years I also picked up two surplus points in physical culture.

I have always been attentive to my physical, mental, and moral health, living simply, avoiding tobacco and intoxicants, and getting regular exercise. After college I continued to walk much, swim, play tennis till recently, and in bad weather to do chores or calisthenics at home. In fifty years I estimate that I have walked at least 25,000 miles — around the earth. To these practices I attribute my good health and vigor early and late in my life.

The first reports to me from the home front were favorable, but about the first day of October I received a distressing letter from my 12-year-old sister saying, "Dear Brother: We did not go to Sunday School today. Papa came home from Marlinton yesterday evening drunk with three gallons of whiskey. He was falling around in the room and talking. Lula got scared and Edgar and I walked to Cousin Brown's (it was dark) and brought him up. Papa behaved all right after Cousin Brown came. Margie wrote a long letter to Henry [then at Long Glade, Virginia] telling how mean Papa has been to us. She is afraid to send it — don't know if we will get it mailed or not. Excuse bad writing.

"Your true Sister"

Immediately after receiving notice of this unusual misconduct, inspired by wine and woman, I obtained permission to be absent from college for several days or possibly longer and arranged to meet my brother, Henry, in Staunton for a conference. We decided to drive 60 miles in a buggy across the mountains to Mill Gap, Virginia, where we had a second conference with our relatives, the Wades, who had heard nothing of the affair at home. Soon we persuaded Uncle Edwin, a genial and wise man, to mount a horse and cross the Allegheny to the Herold farm about 12 miles away, to spy out the land, to deliver a message, and the next day to bring one back from my oldest sister, without revealing except to her that Henry and I were nearby, ready to do whatever seemed best and wisest. Uncle Ed performed perfectly.

He brought to us a pitiful five-page letter from Margie, recounting their hardships and distresses for the past two weeks, the abuse directed at me especially, the drinking with threats and dares to us boys, the change when visitors came in, and her daily crying for a week, scarcely knowing what to do. She concluded: "Now is the time to do something decisive. Oh! how it grieves me."

Never before in my time or at all had liquor thus affected my father or the Herold home in this way. Heretofore he had always been sober and dependable, though not averse to an occasional toddy as an appetizer. I never knew more than a pint of medicinal whiskey to be around the house at any time. Now it was rampaging and stirring the meanest passions. What were we to do? It was clear that my return home at this juncture would only make matters worse. After repeated conferences and a day's meditation, we agreed that the best immediate action would be to let Henry return home as if on a visit but to stay there to protect the younger children, because he was resourceful and abundantly able, strong and vigorous, weighing 180 pounds, to try to mend matters as much as possible, and to keep in touch with me. Then, I returned to Staunton and back to college to await further developments.

Though for two years my class attendance had been perfect, this necessary and unavoidable trip resulted in my getting 19 absences, and during the winter a slight illness added four more, in all 23, a whole week, which I feared would affect my grades adversely. A heavy load of courses, a week's absence, and my continued concern and uncertainty about home affairs made the going difficult and discomforting. Within a month I received three letters from Henry. The first was quieting, because Henry, my father, and seven neighbors had just returned from a trip to Roncevert to hear Bryan speak in his third campaign for the presidency. The next, on November 1, was disturbing, for there was more drinking. Henry was on the job and determined to carry on to the best of his ability in spite of much idle talking and bluffing to contend with. On November 8, though home conditions were still bad, Henry advised me to finish college and he would await further developments. The situation slowly improved.

Receive B. A. Degree

As quickly and efficiently as possible, I picked up the loose ends of my college work and proceeded on my way, though considerably saddened and bewildered at the ways of mankind. I had lost spirit and resiliency and only slowly regained them, thanks to the patient and long-suffering service of my brother Henry at home in trying circumstances. Though my first report was a straight "G," the second revealed a slight drop in two courses.

In some measure, perhaps, I was coasting along on the reputation built up previously. By March and June, however, I was receiving a perfect "G" record.

Some time during the autumn I was chosen one of four debaters to represent Graham-Lee Society at its Centennial Celebration on January 19, 1909, which was also General Lee's birthday. My recollection is that the question was, "That local option is preferable to or more effective than state prohibition." I was the first speaker on the negative and was completely minded to speak in stern denunciation of the liquor demon. "Local option," I declared, "ties its hands, but state prohibition binds it hand and foot." In my commencement address for Graham-Lee in June, 1909, I chose to make an appeal for greater energy and activity in combatting the national menace of tuberculosis, which I named "The Great White Plague." My home newspaper thought so well of it as to publish it in full, 2,250 words, during the following summer, and my hopeful conclusion that the malady "will soon be subject to the indomitable will of wide-ruling men" has in part been realized in the last half century. My thesis for the bachelor's degree was done in the philosophy department under Dr. James R. Howerton on the subject, "The Three Systems of Ethics Explained and Criticized," which in about 4,000 words enabled me to synthesize and digest much that I had heard or read in my four courses in philosophy. Having thus met all requirements, I received the degree of Bachelor of Arts at the commencement in June, 1909.

In the course of this chapter I have been unable to name and pay my respects to many students who were my friends and companions in the classroom and on the campus. I will mention two from seven types of student activity, fourteen, who during my undergraduate days seemed to be outstanding student leaders:

John W. Addison and John Laurence Daniel in scholarship;

Robert S. Keebler and James H. Larrick in public speaking;

Thornton W. Allen (author of "Washington and Lee Swing") and Paul A. Rockwell (journalist) in authorship;

Noble D. Smithson and Charles E. Burks in student publications;

Cleon S. Osbourn and John Izard in athletics;

James Hubert Price and James R. Caskie in law; and among the alumni,

Newton D. Baker and John W. Davis in national leadership.

I CHOSE TEACHING
Part III. Various Hazards

CHAPTER 7
Choosing a Vocation

MOST young people must choose or accept a vocation in life. When a girl or woman marries, she accepts homemaking as her chief vocation. When a boy or man agrees to succeed his father in a business or a profession, he accepts that way to earn a living. Relatively few people can live without working and should be ashamed to be idlers or drones in society. Most young people, however, may choose their vocations in life. This choice is such a momentous decision for each one that schools and parents should supply the young with data on the vocations — their requirements, opportunities, and rewards.

If the choice is wise, certain conditions must be met. The most important, I think, are these: 1. One should like the vocation chosen. 2. One should be fitted for it. 3. One should be able to live by it. If all three conditions are fullfilled, one should be happily placed in life. A first choice may well be tentative and subject to change in the light of fuller knowledge of oneself and the vocations, but the sooner adjustments are made the better. Misfits are people who made the wrong choice.

Teaching in Richmond

In my senior year at college I sought a high-school teaching position as a temporary expedient for making a living and paying a few small debts incurred during my last two years in college. In March, 1909, President George H. Denny sent me a letter he had just received from John P. McGuire of Richmond, Virginia, regarding a position to teach Greek and English in the well-known McGuire's University School. Though there were other applicants, Dr. Denny's commendation of my college record and teaching experience enabled me to secure this desirable position, paying $700 with room and board, or about $1,000 a year.

For summer employment in 1909, being a candidate for the Presbyterian ministry, I arranged to serve experimentally, at Olivet Chapel on the outskirts of Staunton, a small congregation of average Americans. I lived in Staunton with one of the church officers, visited among the members, helped with the Sunday School, and "preached" once every Sunday except when Dr. A. M. Fraser of the First Presbyterian Church of Staunton administered the Lord's Supper. For my "sermons" I made careful outlines and spoke from them extemporaneously for about 30 minutes. Specimen topics were "Christ as a Preacher," "Christ as a Teacher," "What Christ Taught," "Duties to God" (repeated in a Staunton Baptist Church), "Duties to our Fellowmen," "Immortality," "Pure Character," and "The Dignity of Labor."

In reading for and planning these talks, I had the use of Dr. Fraser's library and my own books, and, for the most part, I followed the customary reasoning and methods. But, while preparing some of them, I ran into serious difficulties in trying to present only what I myself fully and conscientiously accepted as the truth. I did not wish to practice deception or pretend to believe and teach what I myself did not fully believe and accept. On Daniel and Paul as subjects, pure character, and the dignity of labor, I could proceed easily and happily; but when I got into some matters of theological dogma, I felt insecure and unhappy. Some of the conventional explanations and reasoning seemed to me faulty and misleading in the light of my college training and personal convictions. I decided that whatever else I might be I must be an honest and sincere man. I would teach and preach truth, as I saw it, or I would teach and preach nothing at all. Throughout my life that principle has been my guiding conviction. In this uncertain and perplexed state of mind I left Staunton in September, 1909, for Richmond to begin work at McGuire's School for boys.

McGuire's University School

In Mr. John P. McGuire I met a genial, cultivated, middle-aged gentleman, who had inherited this preparatory school from his father. With him lived his charming wife and a small girl and a boy in a two-story brick residence at 7 North Belvidere Street on the border of a high-class residential district, from which came about 150 boys. Four of the unmarried teachers lived in the McGuire home, where a colored cook treated us to the more famous Virginia dishes such as corn "dodgers," sweet potatoes, choice ham and chicken. Two young ladies taught the lower grades, and four men assisted Mr. McGuire in the upper grades.

The schoolrooms and study hall, without library and laboratory, were located on the second floor of a nearby business building at the corner of Belvidere and Main Streets, with a small playground between these rooms and the McGuire residence. West of Belvidere Street was beautiful Monroe Park, but, unfortunately, along Belvidere was a railroad over which trains passed from time to time. During my first night there I was so frightened in my sleep by reverberating shocks and rattling windows that I almost jumped from my bed, supposing that I was the victim of an earthquake. Quickly I realized that the rumbling and noise were made by a passing train. In a short time, however, I became accustomed to the disturbance and scarcely noticed the passing trains by day or night.

The school prided itself upon having small classes of three to ten students each taught by well-qualified instructors and upon the fine records made by its graduates at Virginia colleges. Maxwell G. Wallace, an alumnus of this school and the University of Virginia, and later a Richmond lawyer and bank official, taught Latin and German. Angus B. Echols, young son of a mathematics professor at the University of Virginia and later a top-ranking Du Pont official at a salary of $234,000 in 1947, taught mathematics. Dr. Ben M. Rosebro had chemistry and physics, and I was instructor of Greek and English. Each of us had twelve 30-minute classes a day from 9-12 A.M. and 1-4 P.M. Mr. McGuire, known among the boys as "Jolly John P.," supervised the study hall and taught a few special and trailer courses. The various sports and games were played in the late afternoons and on Saturdays.

One could hardly find a choicer lot of boys anywhere — healthy, courteous, ambitious, gifted above the average, and eager to maintain the reputation of McGuire's School in both academic and athletic activities. In 1911 the baseball team was the champion in its group. Among the students were the sons of a former governor, judges, lawyers, physicians, preachers, bankers, and merchants — the privileged, the elite of Richmond.

In particular, I recall a gifted boy, Gervas S. Taylor, voted the smartest student and editor of the 1910 annual, "The Prep," a perfect little gentleman, and the delight of his teachers. In his English class I introduced him to Byron's lovely lyric, "Maid of

Athens," the Greek refrain of which Gervas happily translated "Life of me, I love you so." In addition the poem inspired him to compose a humorous imitation called "Maid of Richmond," which is so refreshing that I quote it:

> Maid of Richmond! ere I go,
> Give! oh give me back my dough;
> Or since that has left my purse,
> Keep it now, and take this verse;
> Hear my vow before I pack,
> Would I had my money back!
>
> By that purse whose empty pouch
> Yields so sadly to my touch;
> By its loosely flapping strings
> Which have lent my dollars wings;
> By those coins which I lack;
> Would I had my money back!
>
> By those bills which I have paid;
> By those presents I have made;
> By every luxury supplied
> Which better far had been denied;
> By every costly, plush-lined hack;
> Would I had my money back!
>
> Maid of Richmond! I am gone —
> Think of me, sweet! when alone;
> Though I flee to Istanbul
> Richmond holds you and my gold.
> Can I cease to mourn, alack!
> Would I had my money back!

The funniest boy in school was James J. Redmond, who wrote the best humorous matter in "The Prep" for 1910 and 1911. He was a walking collection of smiles and witticisms, a young Mark Twain. His questions and wisecracks contributed much amusement to every class he attended though he himself studied very little. He refused to believe in atoms or germs, because he could not see them! They must be merely imaginary! In a humorous account of a baseball trip, he described sixteen kinds of cats at Charlottesville, such as Toms and Mary Anns, long and bob tails, one-eyed, wall-eyed, and cross-eyed, striped and spotted, and the like — single, companies, and regiments of cats, all fat, sly, and sleek!

Richmond itself, founded by William Byrd at the falls of the

James River, is a notable city, with memories of and monuments to Virginia's famous leaders — Henry, Washington, Jefferson, Madison, Marshall, Davis, Lee, and Poe. Capital of Virginia and formerly of the Southern Confederacy, it has handsome capitols, libraries, churches, hotels, and business and professional buildings. In this cultural center we young teachers continued our own education and mingled in the social life of the city. We could visit the nearby battlefields or in long walks ramble about the city and its environs. My college friend, Lawrence C. Caldwell, came up from Mississippi to teach history and English at McGuire's, to marry Miss Mary McFaden, daughter of a prominent pastor, and to settle there permanently as a lawyer and state official. Fred W. Blackburn succeeded "Reddy" Echols in mathematics. My old friend, Harold H. Leach, was at the Presbyterian Seminary. James H. Price came there from Staunton to practice law, to enter the state legislature, and later to fill the chair of governor with distinction. With these and other friends, my two years in Richmond were among the happiest of my life; my pictures made then in my first tailor-made suit show a smiling, contented face, because I enjoyed my work at McGuire's School and my pleasant associations in the city of Richmond.

During this period I became a supporter of woman suffrage, then a lively political issue, in response to an appeal by Dr. Anna Howard Shaw, who spoke at the Jefferson Hotel. She was then a vigorous, keenwitted advocate of women's rights and a leader in the national campaign for the suffrage granted to colored men 40 years earlier. Retelling the story of Eve's creation, she humorously claimed that the Lord used not only Adam's rib but a piece of his backbone, which men still lack in dealing with the rights of women. She climaxed her argument with the assertion that multitudes of women were paying taxes without any voice in the way the money should be spent. This state of affairs, she declared convincingly, is taxation without representation, echoing the American Revolutionary charge against the British rulers.

Changing Vocations

During this time I also reached a firm and fortunate decision as to what my vocation should be. I had gone through high school and college with a sincere intention of becoming a Presbyterian clergyman and helping to convert the world. It was my purpose to study theology at Union Theological Seminary then on the outskirts of Richmond. I had thought of my teaching as only a temporary expedient to meet a present need and to lead on to a larger field — a more important activity. I was then filled with zeal for the work of the Lord, though my views and purposes underwent a slow transformation in college and in Richmond. After my college studies in science, literature, and philosophy had caused many a blinding scale to fall from my eyes, I saw, what was to me, truly a New Earth and a New Universe.

The childlike faith and explanations instilled into me in my youth and potent for several years no longer satisfied my mind. I realized that much of this faith and teaching would not bear close scrutiny, was merely traditional, dogmatic, unsound, unworthy of credence. The thinkers and scientists of the 19th century had exposed the weakness or futility of many a cherished fiction, myth, or dogma, and had taught the thinking part of the world to seek facts and to build on facts in shaping a philosophy of life. Before their massed and persistent impact many false, camouflaged towers of dogma came tumbling down like the walls of Jericho, never to be restored to the power they had wielded for more than 1,000 years. Or, to change the figure of speech, through the strata of accumulated errors and superstitions the Waters of Fact had cut a free outlet to the Oceans of Truth.

In this frame of mind and keenly aware of the difficulties I had encountered at Olivet Church, early in February of 1910 I called in succession upon President William W. Moore and Dr. Thomas C. Johnson of Union Theological Seminary to learn what aid and comfort I could get from them. In each conference I identified myself in some detail and then with a brief explanation I asked each of them to tell me what effect the conclusions of modern science, especially biology and geology, were having on theology or were likely to have. This question grew out of the fact that at college I had done a year's work in historical geology and two years' in biology. To my utter amazement both men replied that they knew little or nothing of the teachings of modern science, were not interested in it, and thought that science would not influence or modify the teaching of theology. After perceiving the incredible limitations and indifference of these reputedly learned professors of Presbyterian doctrine, I chatted a few minutes with each, thanked him for the conference, and departed, never to return to them or to the seminary.

The next day, however, Dr. Moore mailed me a long editorial clipping from *The Richmond Virginian* of February 5, 1910, entitled "Science and Religion," which began with Herbert Spencer's technical definition of evolution and in humorous vein went on to belittle science and to support traditional dogmas.

The editor made this amazing statement: "The truest religion is scientific and the highest science is reverent and devout," which is equivalent to the nonsense of saying that religion is scientific and science is religious! He also asserted that the geologist's hammer had not shaken the first chapter of Genesis, and that the conflict between science and religion "exists only among imperfectly informed members of each camp." Obviously the two theologians knew too little of science to realize that any conflict existed, and this editorial carried no weight with me.

On February 14, 1910, Dr. Moore, evidently concluding that I had raised serious and important questions, wrote me the following letter:

Dear Mr. Herold:

The same afternoon that you spoke to me about the possible effect of the evolutionary hypothesis on the Christian faith there appeared in the 'Richmond Virginian' an editorial which, though of course too slight to serve the purpose you had in mind, I nevertheless clipped and sent to you as an illustration of the manner in which the matter strikes the mind of a layman who has no professional interest in it, and as a further illustration of the fact that there is a vast number of Christian men who accept this hypothesis without any disturbance of their faith. Not only so, but Professor George J. Romanes, after having abandoned his Christian faith because of the findings of evolution, actually wrote another book to show the defects of the argument of the one in which he had renounced his faith and to point out that the essentials of the Christian faith were a logical necessity. You are doubtless familiar with his history. It occurred to me on thinking of our conversation that you probably needed to undertake a somewhat wider study of Christian evidences, including the question of evolution but not being restricted to that; and, if you are not already familiar with it, I would like to suggest to you a careful reading of a recent book entitled, 'Why is Christianity True?' by E. Y. Mullins, President of the Baptist Theological Seminary at Louisville, which is an up-to-date discussion of the whole subject in a quite readable form. He has one short chapter on evolution. Then I think you would do well to procure from the Presbyterian Committee of Publication a copy of 'Scientific Faith' by Howard Agnew Johnston. Two other books which do not bear directly on the question of evolution but which every man who has been in any measure unsettled would do well to read are 'The Fact of Christ' by P. Carnegie Simpson, and 'The Originality of Jesus' by G. Johnston Ross. I believe it would be a good plan for you to read a few books of this kind before proceeding to the more careful examination of the evolutionary hypothesis and its effects on faith, which I suggested when we were speaking of it.

I trust these suggestions will not be unacceptable. They are made not specifically with any reference to the question of what your life work is to be but with a view to the relief of your personal misgivings and the confirmation of your personal faith.

Cordially yours,
W. W. Moore

In a short letter I think I thanked Dr. Moore for the clipping and the courteous letter with his suggestions, though I am not certain. I may have been too shocked and dumbfounded to be courteous, because my confidence in these theologians, though refined and polished gentlemen, was shattered beyond repair or revival. Under no circumstances would I consent to study under them. That was settled. Even now, after 45 years, I am surprised at the promptness and decisiveness of my reaction to the original conferences rather than to the later friendly letter from Dr. Moore. My recollection is that the responses of the two men in conference were virtually identical though I may be mistaken about that. As for the fact of Jesus, I had not questioned that nor his originality. What troubled me was the additions and distortions made by theologians in erecting their systems of theology.

I did buy a copy of H. A. Johnston's "Scientific Faith," which had probably inspired the editorial and supplied Dr. Moore with examples for his letter. I then examined this book, and my distinct recollection is that I was much more impressed by the arguments or contentions that the author sought to refute than by his attempts at refutation, which I regarded as ineffective quibbling designed to gloss over and support all the discredited old dogmas. A re-examination of the book shows that the term "scientific" was loosely and irresponsibly applied throughout, as in "Scientific Faith," "Scientific Belief in Miracles," and "Scientific Belief in Christ." However, in asserting that Jesus was a specialist in character analysis and scientific in his own factual observations as in the parable of the sower, the author was on sure ground. But, for the most part, he would solve the problems of faith by calling them "scientific" and by branding all objectors "unscientific."

For my part I have always regarded the "Sermon on the Mount" as the basic Christian document, so important that in my youth I memorized it and could recite it from start to finish. This sermon shows a discriminating knowledge of the Old Testament and sets forth principles on which men may build structures to withstand storms and cyclones. But in it the speaker did not say a word about virgin birth, blood atonement, inspired writing, his deity, miracles, and other contentions of followers then and later. Long ago Thomas Jefferson, whose democratic principles were thoroughly Christian, observed the vast difference between what Jesus probably taught and claimed for himself and what later theologians taught and claimed for him, and Jefferson also prepared his own version of "The Life and Morals of Jesus of Nazareth Extracted Textually from the Gospels of Matthew, Mark, Luke, and John," omitting "every verse or paragraph that to his mind was ambiguous or controversial, and every statement of fact that would not have been admitted as evidence in a court of justice."

My Fortunate Choice

In the spring of 1910, therefore, I decided finally to give up the pursuit of theology and to follow the vocation of teaching, in which I was already happily engaged. I have always enjoyed teaching and never more so than when I reached the age of 65 with retirement too near to please me. That very spring, I arranged to return to Washington and Lee University for the master's degree, but being cordially invited to teach another year at McGuire's, I accepted the offer and postponed for one year my return to *alma mater*. After that decision I felt no uncertainty as to what my vocation would be. It was teaching English in high school or college.

This choice I regard as one of the wisest I ever made. In the church I would probably have encountered many difficulties if I had held to my determination to be an honest man and preach no false doctrine. Of course, I might have turned reformer and spent my life advocating radical changes in theology, but I prized peace and the consolation of great literature so much that I refused to engage in controversy of this kind. I would let the Lord reform the church in his own time and way. I would not deliberately seek persecution and burning at the stake for my convictions. I could live by teaching untheological grammar, composition, and literature, whether English or American, Greek or Italian, with a clear, easy conscience about what I taught. Indeed, I could teach the Bible itself as the literature of the Hebrews without accusing God of dictating any part of it!

At no time have I had any reason to regret my decision. The mild protests of preacher friends carried no weight, and I refused to argue with them at length, just as I did not revisit nor correspond with the gracious Dr. Moore. *I deliberately refused to be a medievalist in the modern world.* I would face all the facts and try to live with them without surrendering my right and freedom to think and believe for myself.

In my later studies I was gratified and reassured to learn that a great American author, Ralph W. Emerson, and a great British thinker and poet, John Milton, had passed through similar experiences to similar conclusions.

CHAPTER 8

Losing Sweethearts

THROUGHOUT my high-school and college years my primary ambition was to get a bachelor's degree in arts. With the achievement of this goal I refused to let anything else interfere. All secondary matters like making love and getting married I put aside firmly. Of course, I had young sisters to help and to love, charming cousins, and other feminine friends with whom to associate without any serious commitments. Throughout this early period, to the age of 24, my head ruled my heart, whose normal outflow of feeling was somewhat impounded like flowing waters by a dam. Love energy accumulated to be released by a fitting and effective spark plug of the feminine gender.

From my observation and reading I fully realized that choosing or rather winning a wife was an important adventure to be undertaken with foresight and circumspection. A mistaken match could mean a distressing divorce or a lifetime of needless misery, whereas a wise marriage could contribute greatly to one's happiness and success. I would not act hastily and I would avoid a marriage of mere convenience. I wanted my head and heart to agree on the venture, because it would be a long commitment, and I had no illusion that marriages were arranged and sanctioned by the Lord.

Many difficulties arose on the amorous adventure. A man could choose a vocation without much opposition or back talk;

but one could only partly choose a life partner, for the lady had to be like-minded. She could object, delay, or baffle. Then her family and tribe must be agreeable, and your own family in all its ramifications could favor or oppose your ambition. In countless ways a hopeful love affair could be thwarted. It was like running a long gauntlet with old squaws from both tribes lining the runway and brandishing social clubs and scalping knives. So real and true could this be that a disinterested observer might well conclude that the ancient practice of letting parents mate their children had the merit of reason without the blind unreason of youthful passion or tribal taboos.

However, when I graduated from college in June, 1909, I began to feel that the time had come to look around for a life partner. That summer at Olivet and Staunton my heart fluttered a little at the fair ones. Just a little. I began to feel like a lone Adam in his Garden of Eden, hoping and trusting the Lord would help him find his Eve. In Richmond, my love scouting continued so obviously that the McGuire boys observed it, and in June, 1910, they mischievously awarded " A most Loving-hearted Herold a Certificate of Improvement in the Studies of the Calico School during the Session of 1909 -1910."

My Beatrice

In Shakespeare's plays we read of love at first sight as in "Romeo and Juliet" and "As You Like it." I had always been somewhat doubtful of such sudden love until Cupid demonstrated with and for me. Casually I returned home to Pocahontas for the Christmas holidays and I functioned normally until New Year's Eve when the young people attended a party at Dr. J. B. Lockridge's new home at Minnehaha Springs. There it happened! There I met my Beatrice though that was not her name. Cupid hit me with a bolt of love lightning! I saw my Eve — a beautiful, spirited, magical young woman! She caught my eyes, she aroused my fancy, she touched my heart. Five years before she had been my gifted, winsome pupil; now she was a glamorous young woman with magical attraction. She was It! I knew that she was It! With her Cupid had performed a miracle. The world for me was transformed. She and the world were fascinating! I was in love!

But at the time I could do or say nothing to the purpose. Within a day or two I left for Richmond with the firm intention of writing to Beatrice. Within a week I did write my first of many letters to her and here it is exactly as I then composed it:

7 North Belvidere St.,
Richmond, Va.,
January 8, 1910.

My dear Lynette,

I have been writing a few letters this evening, and just to surprise you, I decided to write one to you. Now I hope that this will be an acceptable New Year's gift and that, to please me, you will send a short letter in return, for I remember very distinctly that you used to write sweet little letters when you were my pupil, and they were composed merely for practice. Yes, I have always had a peculiar interest in you and your advancement, and have never had a doubt that you will succeed in measuring up to my expectations.

How rapidly you have grown! Why, I could scarcely believe my eyes, when I saw you at Dr. Lockridge's New Year party. You told me you were sixteen, and I could scarcely believe you, but I think it would be in keeping with truth and the old idea to say that you are "sweet sixteen." To be sure, you are budding forth into young womanhood, and soon your blood will tingle with the joys and hopes of a beautiful life. Lynette, I am proud of you.

Here at the McGuire University School, I am well pleased. I live with Mr. McGuire's family, and I receive a good salary. There are seven teachers and one hundred and sixty boys in the school.

I may return to college next year for my master's degree. I have just received an offer to instruct a class of thirty in English at the University next year, with good pay.

Wishing you a happy New Year,
I remain, yours sincerely,
A. L. Herold.

In this initial letter to the little magician, my head succeeded in holding the reins and choosing the language. I remember well that when I wrote, "Lynette, I am proud of you," my heart was saying, "I love you," but my head said such language is premature and unwise. My hope that her blood would tingle erelong was evidence that my own blood was tingling. Some girls would have sent me a speedy, gushing reply, but not Lynette. She was deliberate and circumspect and kept me waiting about two weeks for her response, which told me of her schoolwork, her music, her plan to take a teacher's examination, her nickname "Little Nette," which I at once adopted, and so on — not too long but just right, as I infer from my reply on January 29, when I addressed her as "Dear Little Nette," with a "spiel" about my own nicknames at McGuire's and in college. My reply, three times as long as my first letter, thus recorded my response to her neatly penned, artistic letter:

"I was greatly pleased to receive your letter and I have read it with the keenest interest and enjoyment, for in truth you can write a delightfully sweet letter. I can account for its sweetness in no other way than by thinking that one of your kisses accidentally got into the letter, and before reaching me, had diffused itself throughout the whole letter, which was perfumed like a rose and sweetened like a sugar cake. Now, I am passionately fond of roses and I was never known to refuse a sugar cake, and your letter, as it appears to me, had the qualities of both roses and sugar cakes." In concluding, I requested a continued correspondence with her, since I prized both her and her letters with the diffused kisses. "Be pleased, then, to grant my request at an early date." Thus, I prayed to my earthly goddess.

Still testing the faith of her worshiper, she let me wait and get thirsty for her response, which pleased me even more than the first answer to my longing. On February 16, I wrote, "Your letter was simply delightful, and, if it were possible, I should like to receive one from you every week. It seems to me that some of your own sweetness and loveliness creeps into your composition, and charms me. Well, to begin with, you are an exceptionally sweet and high-minded girl, whose heart is pure, and whose lips are messengers of truth and goodness. Besides,_____(I'll tell the rest at some other time)." I was then reading Scott's "Kenilworth" and Mark Twain's "Innocents Abroad," which I cordially recommended to her. Of an alumni dinner I wrote her:

"Just one week ago tonight, in a palatial room in the magnificent Jefferson Hotel, which is perhaps the best in the South, a college friend, 'Dick' Larrick, of Winchester, Virginia, and I, fitted out in newly pressed Tuxedo suits, attended a banquet of the Richmond Alumni of Washington and Lee University. We, big fellows, eh? 'Heap much' big time! About 40 members were present, including President Denny of W. and L., Dr. Strickler of the Seminary, Col. James, who is secretary of the Commonwealth of Virginia, and a number of lesser lights and satellites. We were entertained by several reminiscent, jocular, and witty speeches." In reply to a question regarding the identity of a young lady I had taken to see the "Merry Widow" show, I could say that she was one of our lower-school teachers. I concluded with an affectionate good night, leaving much unsaid.

In early March I was writing again to her and sending a copy of a poem "In Virginia," the first stanza of which well depicted my feeling at that time:

> The roses nowhere bloom so white
>   As in Virginia.
> The sunshine nowhere shines so bright
>   As in Virginia.
> The birds sing nowhere quite so sweet,
> And nowhere hearts so lightly beat
> For heaven and earth both seem to meet,
>   Down in Virginia.

Beginning my reply, "I was delighted to receive your good letter a few days ago. I had just come from the schoolroom when I got it, and knowing how interestingly you write, I went out into Monroe Park to read your missive. 'Attractive', I say, on the outside, on the inside, and in between. With a light gay heart in the sunshine I opened the letter and read it, and as I sat reading, groups of boys and girls passed by and cast enquiring glances at me in my pleasant retreat, and seemed to say, 'Why are you, stranger, so contented, and what do you read?' Of course I didn't stop to tell them."

Then I quote from her letter as follows: " 'The girl for whom the most votes were cast received the cake, though she was not the prettiest girl present. I will leave you to guess who the girl is.' How characteristic of you, Lynette! Pretty, yet not proud or assuming; frank but not boastful; gentle, intelligent, delicate, and generous altogether. I know that you are the sweet-faced girl that received the beauty cake, and, had I been there, I should have added one more vote to your majority. I am more anxious now than ever before to have one of your pictures to look at and to show to my friends, and, just as soon as I can send you one of mine, I am going to ask you to mail me your photograph." Later I told her the finest compliment I ever received was spoken by a flaxen-haired girl in Lewisburg, who told a friend of mine that she thought from my appearance it would be impossible for me to tell a lie.

After telling of a cordial invitation to return to McGuire's next year and the likelihood of my accepting, I concluded thus: "I heard a beautiful song a few nights ago entitled 'Pet Names', and it was so rich that I have been inspired to write these lines on your name.

> A pretty sweet girl is gay Lynette,
> Fair is she and not a brunette;
> She'll never be a suffragette;
> Nor stoop to play the vain coquette;
> Somebody's darling she'll be I'll bet,
> Somebody's turtledove to love and pet,
> For pretty and sweet is gay Lynette.

On March 30, in a long letter bubbling with emotion, my head lost control of my heart, and pent-up feeling expressed itself in prose and in extempore verse. It was springtime and I was thoroughly in love and far enough along in our correspondence to let the current flow. My joy was something that sprang up within me and transformed the appearance of the world. Casting formality and inhibitions aside, I began and continued in ardent language:

> My Sweetheart, —
> Let me call you that, for I like it best of all. It expresses my thought and feeling better than any other term I know of. 'Dear Little Nette' is very pretty and sweet, but I really think that 'Sweetheart' is prettier and sweeter still. Don't you think so too? And if your own warm throbbing heart prompts you to do so, you may call me 'Sweetheart' in turn, and then you'll be my sweetheart, and I'll be yours, and we shall both each other's sweetheart be.
>
>> No longer call me Mister,
>> Be dearer than a sister;
>> Just listen to my loving breast
>> And call me Sweetheart best;
>>
>> For long, indeed, I've loved you,
>> I've found you good and true,
>> And now, Sweetheart, I love you more
>> Than ever yet before.
>
> Yes, I began to love you long ago. I was your unworthy teacher, and you were my bright, attractive, good-natured, beautiful pupil. Then Cupid besieged my heart but I could not tell you so, for you were so very young, and I, your teacher, was young. I was scarcely nineteen and you twelve. Don't you remember the night on which my school closed? The grateful, kind-hearted school-children brought several nice presents for me — among them a beautiful book, Josephus' History of the Jews, which I now have with me, my name inscribed in it by your own angelic hand. And on that night, you recited most charmingly a beautiful

poem, in which the ringing refrain was, 'Lips that touch liquor shall never touch mine!' How I would like to hear you recite it once more. I think I have a claim to the kisses, for liquor has not touched my lips and I have ever tried to keep my heart fresh and pure — a noble heart worthy of a maiden's love.

Her reply to my ardent letter was, of course, awaited with happy anticipations, which were not disappointed. Though she said that she scarcely knew what love is, yet she admired and liked me and signed herself "Fondly yours." I was very well satisfied, for her letters to me were delicious love letters, delighting and stirring me deeply. "Your last one caused my heart to leap with joy and bubble over with affection for you, the delight of my eye and the charm of my soul," even though she had postponed replying to my unexpected questions.

"Here is a big surprise for you, perhaps," I wrote. "You wonder why I should care for you. I have an ideal of what my bride shall be — lovable, fair, intelligent, sympathetic, young, happy, fond of music, of books, of home, of nature. Such a one I seek, and to her I shall give my whole heart with its wealth of affection. Her I will love and protect; with her divide my sorrows and multiply my joys."

In an April letter of 12 pages, Lynette covered a number of important topics. Among them she played with the idea that my love for her was only a passing fancy, an imaginary affection, which would vanish when I should see her again and learn to know her better. I disagreed and asked what fault, what blemish, what fickleness, was I to find that would change my affection. I said, "You may be right, but I don't think so. You say that the affections of young girls are generally migrating. Is this your experience? I would like to be a young girl for about one month — say in June — just to learn what is meant by 'migrating affections'."

Lynette's head had firm control and never lost it. In some measure she was correct in saying that I was idealizing her and making her more nearly perfect than she would claim to be. She was Irish in her outlook and independence, which was part of the fascination for me. Her control of English I have always marveled at, even before she had finished high school. In a long correspondence I do not recall observing a single misspelled word, a weak and faulty sentence, or censurable word choice. She had read considerably in good literature and absorbed a clear, winsome style of writing, which for me was an expression of the fine, discriminating qualities of the young woman. Her reserve and diplomacy attracted and held me happily. "I read your letters with perfect delight; I reread them, and each time I find something new." For her June was "the month of song-birds and roses," and her home town was like the laws of the Medes and Persians — unchanging.

In June I sent her a topaz ring, attended the Wasington and Lee commencement, visited the Ruckmans at Long Glade for a few days, and then off to Pocahontas and Lynette for the summer. Glorious summer — more letters, several visits to her home, and her admission that she was getting into deep water, with my assurance that the swimming was fine and that she need not fear drowning. I continued to pour out my heart in ecstatic letters, commenting, "Mysterious power of love! elevating, purifying, ennobling, soothing, delicious!" Once on a weekend visit in Marlinton I carried my suit to the point of sounding her out on an engagement, virtually a sly proposal, for which she was not yet ready. Her reluctance chilled my ardor somewhat but not my ambition to win her, even though a scheme was afoot to mar the romance.

The End of My Bliss

This movement grew out of the beauty contest which Lynette had won earlier in the year. A few of the contestants and their mothers were disappointed and by sinister frowning and sour comments sought to get satisfaction by revenge tactics, trying to reach me through members of my family and otherwise. When they failed to invite Lynette to their parties, I also declined to attend at least twice. They gossiped about Lynette so that I would hear, but I paid no attention to their talk until she, herself, acted in a way to give a shadow of substance to the gossip that a certain ineligible man had been too active in the beauty contest. After enduring this jealous annoyance through September and October, I wrote to her at Marshall College, and asked for an explanation. After two weeks and my pressing for a reply, she wrote me in some detail and satisfied me entirely, though she was hurt to the point of being made ill and disconsolate. This episode put our friendship in danger of grave injury or wreck. I did my best to get it back on a firm, friendly basis of trust and confidence. At Christmas we exchanged presents, and the New Year began pleasantly. In February, however, her letters stopped coming. Silence! Continued silence! Then came my topaz ring and a short letter, saying the correspondence had become a source of pain and distress and she could not continue her part of it. That was that! Malicious gossip had done its wicked work! So goes the old world. One memorable year of heavenly bliss was ended.

My First Trip to New York

During the holidays of 1910-1911 my friend, L. C. Caldwell, and I made a trip by boat from Norfolk to New York City, returning by Washington and Staunton. On the Old Dominion Steamship Company's *Princess Anne* we got acquainted with the Atlantic Ocean in a night trip to Manhattan. "How insignicant," I wrote, "our ship of 400 feet in length on the mighty deep! How utterly insignificant did I feel out there on the sea when I thought of our earth with its people and its mysteries and of the innumerable stars, which declare the glory of God!" We encountered a number of U. S. Marines who had been to Europe and various Asiatic ports and who were sad specimens of men long separated from the refining influences of home society, coarse boozers, morally corrupt and vitiated. While walking in the fresh air to ward off seasickness and the ill effect of looking at Mrs. Eddy's *Science and Health,* I chanced upon an old Dutchman calmly smoking a cigar, who told me of his many experiences at sea and in particular of his first sea journey when he became so desperately sick that he wished the whole d____thing would sink to the bottom of the ocean!

Stopping at the Broadway Central Hotel, we spent three days in seeing the sights of the great city — Broadway, Fifth Avenue, Wall Street, the Statue of Liberty, Central Park, Grant's Tomb, Columbia University, the Palisades, the Bowery, the Eden Musee, Anne Russell in "The Impostor" at Garrick's Theater, and finally the Hippodrome, where we found standing room for an enormous production with hundreds of actors, horses, engines, water nymphs at Niagara Falls, and an earthquake in the Andes Mountains. Stupendous for a novice! Thus we were introduced to the cosmopolitan mistress of America. Later I spent three years there as a graduate student at Columbia, realizing the truth of an observation made by Prof. William P. Trent that in time everything comes to New York. In Washington we spent one day, seeing the principal public buildings, and thence to Staunton and back to our teaching in Richmond.

But in February, my disappointment in love chilled my mind and heart. With 47 letters and several visits to my adored one I had sought to win her and had failed, failed completely, for the time at least. I was saddened and downcast and somewhat discouraged. I turned to my work with new zeal, to my reading, to my future plans, and to my other friends. In that very month of February, I received a cordial invitation from my college English professor, Dr. William Spenser Currell, to teach two of his freshman English sections the following year for $350, which he assured me was the best pay he had ever offered a beginning college instructor, and which would finance me while I was doing the master's work. I accepted at once. In Richmond, among my friends and the fair ones of the city, I found diversion though I had no ambition to try to wean any one of them from the attractions and opportunities of Richmond. Once I thought I had found Lynette's double in nearly every particular, but her parents were bent on marrying off an older sister first, who was far less winsome. I proceeded so cautiously as to get nowhere and was not disappointed since I had attempted little.

A Summer Romance

For the summer vacation of 1911 I arranged to spend most of the time visiting and working a little with my Ruckman relatives at Long Glade. Uncle Glen was absent much of the time on business, leaving Aunt Lillian, a lovely lady from South Carolina, and their children with the servants and farm workers. The two oldest of the children were girls, fast becoming beautiful young women, always kind and lovely to me. During the summer the younger of them, Sara, already as tall as I and precociously mature, had become secretly interested in a neighboring youth who was urging her to run away with him and get married, as I learned from the girl in strict confidence. I prevailed upon her to attempt nothing of the kind and I strongly advised her to see the boy no more and to drop him entirely as a rash and dangerous fellow. She promised to heed my advice on the continuing condition that I would not tell her parents. I thought it safe to agree to her condition provided I kept close watch on her movements and could divert her thoughts in other directions, as I did in my frequent talks with her. It was clear that her heart was bubbling with emotion just as mine had been a year before and that her longing and affection must have an outlet somewhere. Her case interested me as an example of feminine psychology, in which my own schooling was incomplete. My concern for her safety and welfare helped to distract me from grieving over my own disappointment in love. My cousins were almost as close and dear to me as my own sisters; indeed, they sometimes referred to me as their older brother, their own having died when quite young.

I read much that summer in the newspapers and magazines and books as was my practice if time permitted. My cousin-in-love said frankly that she thought this reading was a tiresome way to pass the time, and it was for her since she had not yet become interested in the diversion of reading. So the summer days passed quietly and peacefully for me though my cousin-in-love was restless and enigmatic. One fine morning while I sat on the front porch immersed in the latest newspaper, something wholly unexpected happened. My young cousin had decided to play a prank on me. She would teach me a lesson in feminine initiative. So, as I was reading the latest news, she tiptoed up behind me, impulsively threw her arms around my neck, gave me a smacking kiss on the forehead, and then ran away, laughing at my surprise and interrupted reading. "Well, well, her lightning has missed the neighbor youth and struck me," I mused to myself.

That was the beginning of a cousinly romance that lasted all summer and healed the heart wounds I had suffered earlier in the year. My cousin had thus sought my attention and love and I returned her generous and heart-warming affection. We understood and trusted each other perfectly, and we loved each other dearly. The sweetest and dearest kisses I ever received she gave me generously and unblushingly. She taught me what a woman's love could be so that I could never forget the lesson. Yet, we were first cousins, and I doubted the wisdom of going through to marriage. This aspect of the romance we did not discuss. In a manner I had not intended I won the girl completely away from any runaway match and was cured of my own disappointment. At the end of summer we separated without any plan or commitment. Later we each married in safer blood limits, but my cousinly sweetheart and I have always loved and treasured each other without even a shadow of distrust or disagreement. When I last saw her, I kissed her goodbye with the observation that her kisses were as sweet then as 40 years ago. That was the perfect love on earth, unspoiled by marriage. I realized that Tennyson was right in thinking,

'Tis better to have loved and lost
Than never to have loved at all.

CHAPTER 9

Winning a Wife

R EFRESHED and consoled by this memorable summer on Long Glade, I returned in September, 1911, to Washington and Lee to work for the master's degree in English and to teach two classes in Freshman English, to be followed by a second year of combined teaching and study. My roommate was my cousin, Glen Campbell, a freshman premedical student. At Castle Hill, a handsome hotel erected west of Lexington in earlier boom times, we had a large comfortable room and got our meals, within easy walking distance of the college and the business section of town. My cousin later graduated in medicine and is now practicing in Staunton, a popular and successful physician, with an enviable family around him.

Fraternal Experiences

Though previously I had avoided fraternities for personal and financial reasons, in the course of this year I was persuaded to join a local college chapter of Alpha Chi Rho Fraternity. The next year I also joined the Masonic Order in Lexington, taking three degrees in Masonry. In the course of a few years I came to think that both took so much time and money that I became inactive and have so remained to the present. For me, both appear to be outgrown institutions, however much they may have accomplished for society in the past. More and more the Christian Church seems to be getting into the same category as it clings to ancient dogmas and allows other agencies like the hospital, the press, and public schools to take over many of its former functions.

For the session of 1912-13, however, I was elected leader of the AXR chapter, succeeding Philip Murray, and I lived in our fraternity headquarters at the handsome home of Mrs. Clara D. Estill, where I became well acquainted with fraternity problems and rivalries. In joining this group, I made some friends but lost others who went to other fraternities and became competitors. Though the rivalry for new members was keen, we succeeded in pledging 10 fine fellows, increasing our chapter roll to 19 members. In December the chapter officers began to receive censorious letters from the national officers for failing to make routine reports to them. When we investigated, we found that our corresponding secretary had been grossly neglectful for several months, allowing seven letters to accumulate unanswered. He was speedily supplanted by a dependable brother and required to pay the fines assessed against us.

With 12 to 14 members living in the house, we operated on a budget amounting to about $1400 for dues and room rents. In spite of careful collections and management, we had, at the end of the year, $73 still unpaid. I gave my personal note to Mrs. Estill to cover $60 due her on the house rent and reimbursed myself from later collections. But the next year the chapter was $200 in arrears by Christmas, and I was glad to be elsewhere and free from the annoyance of such pesky fraternity problems. Once during the year a noisy Big Ben alarm clock involved me in an early-morning argument with its irresponsible owner, who, presuming to curse me for criticizing him and his noisy clock, speedily found himself staggering to the bathroom with a bloody nose and face. My remedy was so effective as to reform the brother and to win general approval. Since I had once practiced the art of boxing, on this occasion I used my knowledge to good purpose.

In December, 1912, I heard President-elect Woodrow Wilson speak at a well-attended celebration in his honor at his birthplace in Staunton, Virginia. In March, James Somerville and I joined a crowd of students and witnessed his inauguration in Washington, D. C. During the five-hour parade of 50,000 including the West Point and the V.M.I. cadets, the Richmond Blues, the Carlisle Indians led by painted and feathered chieftains, the Tammany and Chicago Democratic Clubs, and students from Princeton and the University of Virginia, Pennsylvania Avenue was a surging mass of jovial humanity from the Capitol to the White House. People were everywhere! Both Taft and Wilson looked sober and serious, but Bryan as happy as a lark. He and Mrs. Bryan, riding in a little electric automobile, were third in the parade, and all the way down the avenue they were cheered almost as much as the new president. Bryan and Clark were on the same platform at the inauguration ceremony, but memories of the Baltimore convention probably prevented any mutual felicitation.

While doing the master's work, I wrote and published in the college magazine an essay entitled "A Comparison and a Contrast of Byron's Manfred and Marlowe's Dr. Faustus," which made me eligible for the Santini essayist's medal. Since I was competing with two or three Phi Beta Kappa members and the judges belonged to the same scholarship fraternity, which was installed after my graduation, I especially enjoyed winning the prize, a

$60 gold medal. Since the names of authors were withheld from the judges, their decision was wholly upon the merit of the essays. Fraternal influence had nothing to do with it.

A Comic Episode

The summer of 1913 I was acting librarian at the college, reading history and literature in spite of afflictive boils and a skin malady, finally identified and cured as the itch. Harry Tucker and Ben D. Smith were attending the summer law school and added much to my contentment. Smith and I, in late July, agreed to occupy and protect the home of a rich Yankee widow, informal, big and jolly, who had a Collie dog and a lazy-looking cat, and who would be on vacation till September. Besides the cat and dog, the widow had two gentlemen admirers, an old fellow and a youngster. Before she got away the comedy of her pets and lovers almost killed me with laughter. In getting ready, she washed her cat and dog clean and sweet. At 8 P.M. she told her young lover (a professor at V.M.I.) goodbye in the darkness of the back porch, and at 9 P.M. she sent the old fellow away with a merry heart. When she looked for her dog, he was gone, paying his lady friends a visit. Next, I wound and set her alarm clock to awaken her at 3 A.M., and she went to bed, still whistling for her dog. When the alarm sounded to get her off on a 3:40 A.M. train, she got up and joyfully found her dog at home. She ate a lunch and fed her pets, and waited for a taxi to take her and her pets to the station. When the car came, she started off with her cat in an open basket and leading her dog with a chain. Once in the car, the dog got loose and hopped out with the widow in hot pursuit, calling, whistling, pleading, for it was nearly train time. As she and the dog re-entered the car, the cat jumped out and bee-lined for the house, with the old lady, now hot and puffing, in pursuit. Next, she banged on the door to get inside, and when in my night clothes I opened it, she almost ran over me. Going to my room, I laughed and laughed at the lover-dog-cat comedy, the widow missing her train and having to wait till noon for another.

With two years of combined study and teaching completed at Washington and Lee, I next accepted an offer of $900 with board to teach English, French, and German in the Horner Military School of Oxford, North Carolina. In October, the pine barracks burned down with loss of many personal effects including about two-thirds of my precious books, but the work of the session was completed under handicaps. With an offer of 10 acres for a new site and $25,000 in cash from Charlotte, N. C., Col. Horner decided to remove the school there. For a second year I accepted his invitation to make me headmaster at $1200 and board, and taught one year in Charlotte before going to Columbia for graduate English after prospecting there during the summer sessions of 1914 and 1915.

Cautious Prospecting in Love

With this summary of my work from 1911 to 1915, I must return to the affairs of my heart. Feeling sure that somewhere among the daughters of Eve, I could find and win one to share my adventures, I did not despair, however disconsolate I might be at times. Somewhat cautiously, I continued to prospect among the fair ones. Hereafter, I wished my head and heart to co-operate in a common purpose. In the year of my setback I met a fine, eligible Virginia lady (not my cousin) and developed a pleasant friendship with her, helpful, I think, to both of us, with visiting and corresponding. At Easter of 1912 I met another good prospect, then a student at Mary Baldwin Seminary, from far-away Missouri. She and my Ruckman relatives visited Washington and Lee while I was there. This lady and I exchanged cards and later letters, just friendly letters, after she returned to her home.

During the same period I sought to renew my friendship with Lynette after a year of severed relations. In August, 1911, I called to see her at her home without an immediate restoration of our friendship. But in March of 1912 we began to correspond casually at my request since I wished to prove to her that I harbored no ill will and wished to let bygones be bygones. As the months passed, our regard for each other grew. We liked each other's letters and we exchanged gifts. While I was doing the master's work and teaching my first year at Horner's, she was a student and literary leader at the Lewisburg Female Seminary. In 1912-1913 she and my sister Margie were there together and I visited them. Of course, the frank ardor of my earlier letters to her was missing. We were friends and correspondents, and we both were still prospecting. I declared to her that I was entirely resigned to being a bachelor for five years or until I had completed my graduate studies. Once when she complained that no one loved her any more, I replied playfully, assuring her that she knew better.

Dilemma Resolved in 1914

By the end of 1913 I began to realize that my interest was divided between my former sweetheart, Lynette, and my new

Misouri friend, Virginia Lee. For somewhat different reasons, I liked, admired, and even loved both young women at the same time just as a mother loves all her children at the same time. Both had shown considerable interest in me. The year 1914 was to be my crucial, wife-prospecting year. I had cultivated the friendship of Virginia Lee, because it looked as if Lynette and I would not reach an accord. The developments in 1914 surprised me as much as anyone else. I could not foresee nor predict the outcome. I was in a dilemma set for me by uncontrollable forces, and I was eager to find a happy solution. Though I was then engaged to neither lady, I would welcome either of them in a closer friendship.

The first climax of the action came in February and the second in September of 1914. During the holidays I visited Lynette and to my surprise and joy I learned that she loved me in spite of all her efforts to the contrary. I rejoiced at this turn of events, at this capitulation of her heart fortress after a four-year siege, though I was more wary and deliberate than formerly. But her heart-warming letters soon aroused my dormant love for her to such ecstasy that I felt like a new man, enriched and empowered by her love gained after a long pursuit. At the same time she wrote me that she had an offer of marriage from another source. In spite of my great interest in her I replied that I would not stand in the way of her accepting the offer if she wished to do so and congratulated her upon it. In response she assured me of her whole-hearted love for me, based upon her high regard for me and the knowledge that she had caused me to suffer much for her. Reassured by her professions and inspired by my own long-standing love for her, in February I proposed to her a second time in spite of my interest in my Missouri friend. Feeling sure that Lynette and I would succeed this time, I wrote Virginia Lee and told her the story of my love for Lynette, my winning her love, and my wish to remain loyal to her, and that unless I did so, I could not respect myself. Like a good sport, Virginia Lee commended my action and congratulated me upon the belated success.

I was soon much annoyed by Lynette's allowing some minor school activity to interfere with her answering my letters or her laconic, cavalier replies, which drew my fire without any rupture of our love for each other. Though I wrote her several letters requesting and urging an engagement to be effective on March 4, she observed that "a girl is always free to change her mind," which caused me to pause and ask if men were permitted to have the same weakness. Though assuring me of her whole-hearted love for me and her great happiness, she appeared reluctant to become engaged to me, saying that she was following the line of least resistance and could see no reason for an engagement. To be brief, I refused to proceed further on this basis, called off my proposal for March 4, and let the business drift to a more opportune occasion if it should ever arise. I continued to write to her, sent her a graduation present, and visited her once in June before going to Columbia.

On June 12, I sent her a long letter, frank and realistic, trying to analyze our difficulties and urging that our love for each other should prevent us from quarreling any more. "For the past two or three months," I wrote, "I have been trying diligently to find out why it is that we have had so many difficulties. I have never had violent disagreements with other girls; nothing of the kind. But we act exactly like two charges of positive electricity; when we get near each other, we are forced apart. Now, why is it? Here is my explanation: We have both always had our own way pretty much, and when two strong wills conflict, there's a contest. Then, too, we both have a sufficiency of temper, and that hasn't improved matters at all. Now I like temper; it is a good thing, but it must be controlled. I believe I have mine under fairly good control. The Horner boys frequently expressed surprise at my patience in dealing with them, though I know I am far from being perfect. Now you know more about yourself than I do. I have known you, however, to explode a time or two. You'll, perhaps, do so when you read this, but I am allowing plenty of time for you to cool off again before I see you. Now I had rather be in purgatory than with you when you are displeased or angry. There is a little food for thought, perhaps a task to perform."

In late April, Virginia Lee attended a D.A.R. convention as a page in Washington, and instead of going on to New York, as she had planned, she agreed to meet me at the Ruckman home in Staunton before returning to Missouri. From this time onward our correspondence and interest in each other were intensified, and in late summer I planned to visit her in Missouri and my Herold relatives in Kansas and Oklahoma. I attended the 1914 summer school at Columbia, sightseeing and studying diligently, and by letters keeping in touch with my reluctant Lynette McKeever and my prospective sweetheart, Virginia Lee Smith. My trip to the West was delayed from August to early September by a severe illness from typhoid fever of my brother Henry, who was confined for several weeks in a Staunton hospital; his recovery in doubt till late August. But I was able to spend the first week of September in Marshall, Missouri, where on September 7, I became happily engaged to Virginia Lee Smith, pledging our troth with my Santini medal and entering upon an ecstatic adventure duly celebrated in our letters. The following June I visited her for two weeks or more when she was very ill from an infection in her arm from a hypodermic injection.

On September 11, 1914, from Anthony, Kansas, I had written her in this vein: "To the Queen of my Heart, I have so much to write you that I scarcely know where to begin, and while traveling and visiting, my time is so much occupied that I seldom have an opportunity for anything but a card. Do not think me neglectful.————

"My own true sweetheart, let me tell you that Monday, September 7, 1914, Labor Day, is a red letter day in my life. Oh, the glory and the bliss that came to me on that day! I agree with you that our love for each other is the purest and truest that God gives his creatures. To me, you are an answered prayer, a treasure that money cannot buy. My whole heart is yours, and yours, mine. How good and how beautiful the thought of it. I am now in the Garden of Eden and life has taken on a thousand new charms." For 18 months the sailing was smooth, for she was my Loved One and Bride-elect and I was her Loved One and Husband-elect.

Then, from February to May, 1916, the seas got rough, misunderstandings arose, sharp words passed, and prospects grew dark. I was far away, and my would-be rivals were close at hand. By late June, 1916, our engagement was broken, giving both of us an opportunity to reconsider our treatment of each other. Learning of this sad state of affairs, one of my cousins acted as mediator between the two unhappy lovers, whose friendship and high regard for each other continued. Within a few months my cousin, Annah Ruckman, effected what she humorously called a Second Missouri Compromise, which the lovers fully ratified in September on my third visit to Missouri to attend to Cupid's business. After that passage the sailing was smooth and uneventful, and the Compromisers were married on June 21, 1917, in the bride's home in Marshall, Missouri. The newlyweds left at once for a bridal tour to the East, returning to Cincinnati in time for the beginning of my English work in the University of Cincinnati. Selah!

CHAPTER 10

Graduate-Degree Hurdles

WHEN I decided in 1910 to devote my life to teaching in high school or college, it was clear that in addition to my bachelor's degree I would need a master's in any case and a doctor's degree for efficient college instruction. A master's would suffice for high-school employment, but a doctor's was almost a *sine qua non,* or indispensable, for college work if one were to achieve satisfactory promotions and security within reasonable limits. I had won the bachelor's degree at Washington and Lee with such a rating as would enable me there to get a master's degree in one year of resident study. This vocational plan seemed to be sensible, because my four years of teaching had shown that I liked it and could hope to succeed in it if I were well qualified and persevering.

The requirements for the bachelor's and master's degrees at my *alma mater,* though unusual, were wise and far-seeing, because they fostered a comprehensive view of the domain of learning and well-rounded scholarship. In the academic college the subjects of study were arranged in three groups: In Group I were the foreign languages; in Group II, literature, history, philosophy, and economics; and in Group III, the sciences. To receive a bachelor's degree, one must have a total of 60 points with at least 15 from each group and with freshman English and mathematics required of all students.

Candidate for Master's Degree

For the master's degree, one must have 81 points with a minimum of 20 from each group, five A-or B-grade departmental certificates with at least one from each group, and a graduating thesis. Since I had earned extra points for the bachelor's degree, I needed only 13 more to meet all requirements. In the session for 1911-1912, then, I registered for two courses in German, two in English (drama and history of the English language), biology, and oral debates. These courses and my bachelor's credits would entitle me to certificates in Greek, German, English, philosophy, and biology. These subjects with Latin and mathematics I would be qualified to teach in high school. With this battery of teaching subjects, I could readily obtain high-school positions. The next year (1912-1913) I continued the study-teaching combination and registered for one English course in epic and lyric poetry and second-year French, while I supported myself and helped with the schooling of my oldest sister, Margie, by instructing three Freshman English sections.

My master's work in English with much required reading and many written papers was comprehensive and exacting. In the drama course, for example, which was equivalent to six credit hours, the topics covered were the history of the drama, its basic principles, Shakespeare's predecessors, Shakespeare himself, the later English drama, Ibsen, and other modern playwrights. In the course of a year Dr. Currell required about 40 short papers and essays and three long examinations based upon specific topics, done in lieu of the regular examinations, and counting one-half of a term's work. For example, mine on "Hamlet," requiring much intensive reading and study, grew into a 12,000-word document. Two other term examinations in drama were nearly as formidable.

From this course in drama originated my master's thesis on "Four Typical Tragedies," namely, Sophocles' "Antigone," Shakespeare's "Macbeth," Racine's "Athaliah," and Ibsen's Ghosts." The Creek play carried my study back to the 5th century B. C., Shakespeare and Racine represented the 17th century, and Ibsen the 19th. Without further instruction I was able to teach Shakespeare and modern drama with pleasure to myself and satisfaction to my many students through the years. Since I have long admired Sophocles, the grand, puritanic pagan, I quote one of my thesis paragraphs in praise of him:

"In other respects, the drama 'Antigone' is a marvel of perfection. It gives one an impression of completeness, unity, and beauty seldom experienced. Every word and phrase is alive with meaning and truth; the characters spring into being, life-sized, fresh from the hand of the artist; and the action moves forward to an inevitable climax. There is nothing left out and nothing extraneous put in. One reads and rereads with delight, because 'Antigone' is a play of inexhaustible thought and suggestion. The author is calm and serene like a god; his matchless expression and accurate psychology show forth the master dramatist."

My study in epic and lyric poetry under Dr. Currell, already classed as one of my three best courses, began with Dante and Milton and ended with Keats and Tennyson. The subject of the final examination was Tennyson's *In Memoriam*. My two courses in the drama and poetry I rate as high as any of my graduate work at Columbia for the doctoral degree. In fact, in each of these courses I did much more writing than in any at Columbia; in each of them I produced about 50,000 written words in essays, critiques, reports, and examinations. At Columbia, in a single year's course, two term papers of 8,000 to 12,000 words each would suffice. Dr. Currell's assignments were both extensive and intensive. At Columbia they were extensive, calling usually for a vast deal of reading with term examinations on the lectures and the required reading. Both methods were thorough and comprehensive and exacting. But I rate Dr. William Spenser Currell of Washington and Lee University as one of the most thorough and inspiring teachers I ever had. He cultivated in me a taste for literature that has remained my consolation and guide through a long life.

Teaching Interlude

My two years at Horner's Military School (1913-1915) were an interlude between my graduate study at Washington and Lee and at Columbia University. Though long located at Oxford, North Carolina, Horner's School after a disastrous fire was removed to Charlotte in 1914. My sojourn in the state introduced me to the cotton-producing South. While in Richmond, I had observed much growing of tobacco and the process of marketing it, but in North Carolina I saw great fields of cotton in cultivation or on the way to the ubiquitous cotton gins for seeding and baling. The snow-white fields of ripe cotton and the stooping pickers pulling long sacks behind them were a new spectacle.

Oxford was a pleasant old county seat, surrounded by sandy fields of cotton with Negroes and mules to cultivate and gather the crops. Its people were likeable, easy-going, conservative, and satisfied to live there in comfort. In contrast, Charlotte was a modern city, proud of its history, churches, schools, colleges, and its many profitable cotton factories. Every year its patriotic citizens celebrated the anniversary of the Mecklenburg Declaration of Independence, which had preceded Jefferson's version by one year. But, leaving behind its pristine political leadership, Charlotte had become a prosperous, industrial center with typical growing pains and ambitions.

At Oxford, in a single year, we encountered three serious impediments to our schoolwork. The first was a conflagration in late October that destroyed the three-story pine barracks, without casualties or injuries but with the loss of many personal effects, including two-thirds of my books, which in part I replaced with a set of the *Encyclopedia Brittannica*. Though the fire almost forced the closing of the school, I helped Colonel Horner to work out a plan for housing the boys and teachers and finishing the year. The second misfortune, coming in January on the heels of the first, was the threat of an outbreak of smallpox. One case of this dreaded disease was detected in a cottage with five or six boys, who were forthwith quarantined while the rest of us were vaccinated. Fortunately no other cases developed and in about three weeks the quarantine was lifted and the school work was normalized once more. The last but least serious affliction at the school was several cases of mumps, which laid me up with swollen cheeks for several days.

After the fire Colonel Horner received offers to move the school elsewhere. The best, a guarantee of a 10-acre site and $25,000 in cash from Charlotte, was accepted. With this gift and nearly $20,000 in recovered insurance, a fireproof barracks and dining hall were erected during the following summer in time for the school to reopen there in September. Pleased with my work for the last difficult year, Col. Horner offered to make me headmaster at $1,500 a year, an increase of $300, which I accepted even though I was then losing interest in military schools.

This incident shows my influence with the cadets. Once in Charlotte, several influential boys, becoming incensed at some of the colonel's criticisms and penalties, set about organizing squads of boys just before a vacation to smash a lot of the furniture by throwing it from the interior galleries to the cement area below. When student officers told me what was brewing, I called all the boys together, surveyed their grievances and plan to retaliate, advised, and shamed them into abandoning the plot.

Col. J. C. Horner was a fine, handsome gentleman well past middle life and a good churchman, but he belonged with the old regime of teachers. He was a stern disciplinarian and a firm believer in the schoolmaster's rod. If a boy failed to learn his Latin, the colonel would resort to it. I heard that in his earlier career this method of instruction was a feared reality among the cadets. However, owing to changing practices in teaching and parental protests, his observance of his rule had become symbolical. With a bundle of small switches on display to impress the boys, he would, after school hours in his office, require an offender to report there, and at a word of command to stand up and hold out his bare, open hand to receive a number of innocent strokes, which symbolized a humiliating punishment! During the smallpox scare the Colonel often had occasion to drive his buggy on a wide road past the quarantined cottage. However brave and honorable he might be in normal relations, he had so much respect for the fighting qualities of smallpox germs that, in passing the infected cottage, he always hugged the far side of the highway, looking straight ahead, much to the amusement of the boys and the teachers.

Col. Horner and his staff got on very well at Oxford, where the school met its obligations promptly; but in Charlotte the paying practice was so different that only twice did the teachers receive their full salaries on time. Usually we received half or less, scarcely enough for current expenses, and sometimes we borrowed from each other. At the same time, we observed that the Colonel had funds for various projects that could have waited. Paying his teachers was obviously not a first order of business. By April my personal protests had reached such a pitch that he threatened to dismiss me. Having a written contract for the year, I replied that if he did so, I would sue for my salary. Then, he decided to let well enough alone. Unfortunately, he had a reputation for getting into lawsuits with his patrons, which hurt the school. When May came, four of us teachers counseled together and decided to engage an attorney to make collections for about two months in arrears. When our grievances became known, a few Charlotte business men helped to negotiate a loan for $1,000, which was prorated among all the teachers, who then agreed to accept notes for the remainder due them. Those who joined me in the forceful measure were Capt. C. J. Ellison, a graduate of Washington and Lee; Major W. A. Burress, a graduate of Virginia Military Institute and our commandant, who later became a major general in the Army of the United States; and Capt. James S. Moffatt, my loyal friend from South Carolina, who took a doctoral degree at the University of North Carolina and became a professor of college English.

Doctoral Studies at Columbia

After examining the opportunities for graduate study at Harvard, Yale, Princeton, Chicago, and Columbia, I tentatively chose the last and matriculated there as a candidate for the degree of doctor of philosophy in the Faculty of Philosophy on July 6, 1914. That was easy enough, but the real hurdles were ahead of me. That summer I registered for two exploratory courses — one in English Usage under Dr. George P. Krapp and two half courses in the History of Education under Dr. Paul Monroe and Prof. E. N. Henderson in Teachers College. I was then trying to choose between education and English for doctoral work. With sight-seeing around New York City and up the Hudson to West Point, and two full courses to be completed in six weeks, I had a busy and inspiring introduction to my work and to the city.

When I returned for the summer school of 1915, I was accompanied by two of my sisters, Margie and Elizabeth, who wished to take college courses for teachers and who roomed in Furnald Hall while I returned to the Alpha Chi Rho house near Riverside Drive. I registered for the Teaching of College Composition under Dr. Charles Sears Baldwin and for American Literature under Dr. John Erskine, who was offering a short course in Poe, Hawthorne, Emerson, and Whitman. Both Baldwin and Erskine were enviable scholars, authors, and lecturers. Prof. Baldwin presented and reviewed with us the methods of teaching college composition in some ten leading institutions, placing plans and themes in our hands for examination, comparison, and evaluation. Erskine was a handsome man of rich and appealing personality, and with sure grasp of the material he fired my ambition to learn more of these four leading American authors.

By the end of this 1915 summer school I had decided to major in British and American Literature of the 19th century, supplemented by such earlier courses as might be needed. I decided to concentrate on the rich period since 1800, which reflects the political, scientific, and social ideas of the modern world. From this period in American Literature would come the subject of my doctoral thesis, and I would have an opportunity to compare British and American authors of the same century. I have had no reason to question the wisdom of this choice.

When my sisters returned home to begin their school teaching, I remained in New York for the fall session. To secure recreation and diversion, my friend Benjamin F. Luker and I planned a walking tour up the Hudson. He and I graduated from college together and were graduate students at Columbia, he in French and I in English. We rode on the subway to its terminus, where we pressed our feet and legs into service. Passing leisurely by the exclusive estates with barred gates and fierce-looking dogs on guard, we spent a bed-buggy night in a little hotel in Irvington, examined the places of interest in Tarrytown, enjoyed the countryside and river views, spent a second night at Ossining, near Sing Sing penitentiary, and thence to Newburgh above West Point. By that time, since we were thoroughly tired and running short of funds, we decided to take a train and return to New York by the shortest and easiest route.

Refreshed and ready for work, through the Columbia Employment Office we were engaged to officiate at a national tennis tournament on Long Island for a week. After that novel experience I read entrance English examinations for Cooper Union for several days, aided by another fellow who had the cheek to ask me to join him in padding our time sheets. I said no emphatically and threatened to report him if he dared to pad his own report. That settled the business and he submitted an honest claim. With some tutoring at $2 an hour and helping with the Columbia registration, by the Christmas vacation I had earned $105. In addition, on the basis of my master's work and summer-school courses, I won a Columbia scholarship worth $150. These credits, my savings at Horner's, and a later bank loan for $275 provided about $900 to pay for a full year of graduate study at Columbia and for other cultural advantages in New York City, especially those offered by the opera and theaters.

In October I heard former President Theodore Roosevelt speak on Americanism in Carnegie Hall at a celebration of the 423rd anniversary of Columbus's discovery of America. At Columbia University, I attended six lectures by another former president, William Howard Taft, on the powers, duties, and responsibility of our president under the Constitution. Then professor of law at Yale, Taft was a big, jovial, good-natured man of dignified bearing. When he laughed, his entire fat body rippled with infectious mirth. He told many good anecdotes of presidential experiences in the White House to illuminate weighty discourses, in which he favored a single term for the president, the admission of cabinet members to Congress without the privilege of voting, and Wilson's revival of the early presidential practice of addressing Congress with important messages. Another notable I saw and heard was Dr. Lyman Abbott, a clergyman turned editor of *The Outlook,* in a local Y.M.C.A. address. Though he was then an old man of 80 years, with bald head, thin face, and long white beard, looking like a poet or Hebrew prophet, he was mentally keen and alert. He spoke on "The Battle of Life," characterizing life as a battle for birth, for food and shelter, and for development. He observed that even peace is the fruit of battle.

Plays and Opera

At the end of 1915 I enjoyed several theatrical events. Besides Cervantes' "Don Quixote" on a movie screen, I saw two plays of fairyland with children in leading roles, Maeterlinck's "The Blue Bird" and Barrie's "Peter Pan," starring Maude Adams as Peter; the first pensive and profound, the second playful and diverting. On December 23, at the Metropolitan Opera House, the three-act opera, "Samson et Dalila," with the Italian tenor, Enrico Caruso, and Margarete Metzenauer of Germany in the leading parts, introduced me to the music and pageantry of opera. About 3,000 spectators with attentive ears and watchful eyes were thrilled by great singers, expert chorus, superb orchestra, beautiful scenes, and rich costumes — a combination of drama, music, and spectacle to delight the eye and charm the ear. At other times, I enjoyed Gounod's "Faust," Wagner's "Tannhauser," and Mozart's "The Magic Flute" and "Don Giovanni."

The 300th anniversary of Shakespeare's death was observed in this commercial and theatrical metropolis by the staging of several of his dramas. In April, 1916, I attended a spectacular performance of the historical "Henry VIII" by Sir Herbert Tree's English Company at the New Amsterdam Theater. I also saw and enjoyed "Romeo and Juliet" and "The Merry Wives of Windsor," in which Falstaff's misadventures with the merry wives elicited roars of cheering and laughter. The climax of the celebration was Sir J. Forbes-Robertson's presentation of "Hamlet," his farewell to New York, which about a dozen of us students attended together. A packed theater of attentive spectators heard the midnight hour, saw the ghost stalk before astonished guards, pale Hamlet dressed in black and pouring forth his pent up indignation and bitterness, Polonius in his dotage, the murder king and the faithless queen, poor Ophelia, and all the others — a masterpiece of the author, depicting the facts of life and sometimes lit up by flashes of wit under somber clouds. "Hamlet" and "The Merchant of Venice" — my favorite Shakespeare plays. My personal tribute was a sonnet on "William Himself," ending with this heroic couplet:

> Ever-living poet, imperious name,
> Imagination glowing, and passion aflame!

At the AXR house on West 115th Street, where I occupied a single room overlooking Riverside Drive and the Hudson River, we had occasional festivities. At Hallowe'en, for example, about 50 guests were present to get acquainted, be amused, or horrified in the Chamber of Horrors, where I played the ghost. Twice I was host to our graduate English group of about 12 men, who met weekly for reciprocal aid in our studies and for diversion. When John O. Beaty passed his preliminary examination, he celebrated by feasting the members and taking them to see D. W. Griffith's "The Birth of a Nation," a movie that was breaking all local performance records. Among our members were Roy Dibble (deceased), Walter Graham, Emory Neff, G. W. Mead, Mark Van Doren, J. W. Krutch, and Oral S. Coad, all of whom received doctoral degrees and made notable scholastic and authorial records.

In late September, after consultations with my professors, I registered for four graduate courses in English at Columbia, namely: For the History of the English Language under the linguistic authority, Dr. George P. Krapp; for Moliere in Comparative Literature under the well-known Brander Matthews; for the English Romantic Movement under Dr. A. H. Thorndike, chairman of the English Department; and for a Seminar in American Literature concerned with theses under Prof. William P. Trent. These four courses were real hurdles, for which my work under Dr. Currell was excellent preparation.

Invaluable and illuminating, though somewhat tedious, was the history of the English language from Anglo-Saxon through the Middle English of Chaucer's time to Elizabethan and Modern English. On these changes Dr. Krapp lectured and traced both sounds and words from period to period, placing examples on the blackboard for the class to copy. The seven parts of speech were thus traced historically so as to throw new light on many a verbal or grammatical problem. Since Dr. Krapp, though a fair and lovable man, had the reputation of being severe in quizzing doctoral candidates, most of his students sought to absorb as much of his meticulous learning as possible in preparation for their preliminary "Day of Judgment." Since from boyhood upward I had enjoyed finding explanations for twin words like *two* and *twain* or for the mystery why *manufacture*, literally meaning to make by hand, should acquire the meaning to make by machines, I was predisposed to like the course and did like it pretty well, though I later concluded that the graduate schools were unduly stressing linguistics to the neglect of other subjects such as our native literature.

In "Moliére" Brander Matthews, a fun-loving old scholar and author of many books, had a select, masculine class, for women were somehow excluded. He gossiped rather than lectured, and his gossip was both interesting and worthwhile. Jokingly he advised us to buy his book on Moliére at once and read it after he had quit talking. Always in a good humor and smoking a cigarette, he would talk charmingly of the great French dramatist and his times. Since he expected his class to read the plays in French, I complied in part in order to get ready for a test of my ability to read French. A picturesque and memorable teacher, Matthews sought to stimulate his students by discovering both diversion and substance in great literature.

The first half of Dr. Thorndike's course in the Romantic Movement included Wordsworth, Coleridge, Scott, Lamb, Jane Austen; a few minor authors like Southey, Monk Lewis, and Godwin; the drama, the critics, and for continental background some attention to the German Schiller, Goethe, and Kotzebue. With many thousands of pages to read, the course was one of my best and most inclusive. While reading Wordsworth's early and best poetry, I conjectured that he had a secret lover somewhere as scholars proved a few years later in the French Annette Vallon and her daughter. With the assigned fiction I followed Bacon's advice to sample it and pass on. For my term paper I wrote on William Godwin's political writings, which were almost as disturbing then as Karl Marx's in recent times. Since we had covered a vast field, most of us mistakenly dreaded the final, two-hour examination, which was surprisingly easy and fair. The course had dealt with the political, social, educational, scientific, and religious thinking of the period as modified by the American and French Revolutions.

Prof. Trent's Seminar in American Literature covered research methods and acceptable topics for doctoral theses in our literature. Being greatly interested in the Valley of Virginia, I asked whether Columbia would accept a historical novel on this subject instead of a formal dissertation. That very year Columbia did accept William Dyer Moore's original blank verse drama in lieu of a master's thesis. But for a doctoral historical novel, the answer was "No," which was doubtless wise for me and the department. A study of J. W. Riley's humor and realism was also ruled out. After considerable, inconclusive searching among possible topics, Dr. Carl Van Doren, then assisting Prof. Trent, suggested James Kirke Paulding, an early American author, as not only suitable but needing research.

After a tentative examination of some of his fiction and political writings, I accepted him as my doctoral topic. I then prepared a partial bibliography of books by and about Paulding and submitted it to Prof. Trent for suggestions. During the remainder of the year I began my research and note-taking, but a vast amount in Paulding's life, his books, and his magazine contributions engaged my spare time from teaching for several years. Part of two summer vacations I spent in the New York libraries finding, reading, summarizing, and listing his essays, tales, and verse contributed to 10 or 12 periodicals extending from *The Analectic Magazine* of 1813 to *The Literary World* of 1853. My original plan had been to write one chapter on his fiction, but I gathered so much matter on his tales that I decided to write one chapter on his 70 tales and another on his five novels.

In the second semester of 1915-1916, I registered for five courses, but later dropped one to lighten my load. They were the second half of Dr. Thorndike's Romantic Movement (1798-1832); the Anglo-Saxon Beowulf under Prof. W. W. Lawrence; the Seminar in American Literature under Trent and Van Doren, and a course in Comparative Literature under Prof. Jefferson B. Fletcher, translator of Dante. Though these courses provided an abundance of work, I also finished reviewing my Latin, French, and German. Latin and French professors examined me in my ability to translate passages which I was allowed first to look over without access to a dictionary. These two I passed, and much to my surprise for German, Dr. Thorndike later questioned me about the extent of my study of it and then exempted me from the test. Of course, at the time feeling against Germany was at a high pitch, which may have occasioned this short cut. Besides, my study of German had been much more thorough than my study of French.

During the year I probably overworked, even after dropping a course in Chaucer. From time to time I was annoyed by indigestion until, under medical guidance, I reduced my meat diet in favor of more fruits and vegetables. Once I was confined to my room for three or four days with sharp pains in my back and muscles, which I feared might be incipient pneumonia but which my physician named muscular rheumatism. His treatment and more regular exercise gave me relief, and I was able to complete my courses successfully.

I found Anglo-Saxon Beowulf as difficult as any Greek course at Washington and Lee, where I began the study of Anglo-Saxon in 1911-1912. After an interval of four years I had to review its grammar and vocabulary thoroughly and prepare every assignment carefully. I studied diligently and checkmarked every word looked up in translating. Then, just before the final examination, I reviewed every one of these words, making mental notes on a few skull-crackers. In the examination, when I looked at the passages for sight translation, I was gratified to find that I knew the meaning of almost every word. Since Prof. Lawrence was a fine scholar and specialist from Harvard, I was proud of the A-grade I received for this tough course in our grandfather language.

Dr. Thorndike steered us though Keats, Shelley, Byron, and their contemporaries in the second part of Romanticism, preparing us for Carlyle, Tennyson, and Browning of the Victorian Age. Prof. Fletcher covered a large field of the Renaissance in Italy, Spain, and France. Already I had studied Dante, a leader in the Italian Renaissance, but in Spain I knew little beyond Cervantes' "Don Quixote." In English translations I read considerably in the Spanish dramatists, Lope de Vega and Calderón. In

France we surveyed and read the prose masterpieces of Rabelais and Montaigne. This course provided an excellent introduction to three foreign phases of the Renaissance, although of necessity it could not concentrate on any one for most effective study. The Seminar in American Literature with lectures and student reports continued through the year.

During the First World War I taught three years at the University of Cincinnati except while I was in the military service in 1918. In September, 1919, I returned to Columbia to continue my studies and my research on Paulding. I registered for courses in Prof. D. S. Fansler's Chaucer, in Dr. Thorndike's Victorian Literature, in Prof. Trent's 18th Century, and in Dr. Carl Van Doren's American Novel. In the second term, besides teaching a section of freshman English, I continued Victorian Literature and the American Novel, on which Van Doren was then preparing articles for the *Cambridge History of American Literature*. Later he expanded them into the first history of the American Novel, for which he deserves the highest praise.

Erskine and Van Doren

At Columbia University I studied under and learned to admire both John Erskine and Carl Van Doren, then in their 30's. They were ambitious, gifted, and vigorous. I could scarcely determine which was the superior. Van Doren had a memory resembling Macaulay's and impressive power of accomplishment. As Professor Trent's assistant in a seminar in American Literature, he was ever ready to clear up disputed points, and as a lecturer on American Fiction, he seemed to have read and remembered all of it with fitting critical evaluations. Both men were popular and highly regarded by their students and fellow professors. My hunch, however, that Erskine was probably the more original and versatile was confirmed, I think, by later developments. Erskine's originality was evident in his stimulating essay, "The Moral Obligation to be Intelligent," in his witty and popular novels beginning with *The Private Life of Helen of Troy*, and in his musical and educational leadership. Both scholars wrote excellent autobiographies, which reveal the richness and breadth of their learning and associations. Carl Van Doren in his outlook and practical success reminded me somewhat of Benjamin Franklin, whose biography he wrote; John Erskine had much of Scott's charm and narrative skill and Matthew Arnold's love of Greek and French culture.

Two High Hurdles

Besides the required graduate courses of instruction, the two most formidable hurdles in the race for a doctor's degree were a preliminary, oral examination and a doctoral thesis. The oral examination was conducted by a committee of scholars who would seek to find out whether a candidate knew anything and was capable of mature thinking. Since about half of the candidates who took this Columbia test were said to fail, I wished to be well prepared before submitting myself to a high-mortality examination. So, I first completed the residence requirements and supplemented them by my own studies.

During my first year of residence I had obtained from the English group a prized copy of preliminary tests as remembered and recorded by 10 or 12 candidates over the period from 1907 to 1916, which filled 22 typed pages and furnished valuable clues to the methods and matters of the doctoral inquisition. The graduate English group used to review and discuss these questions and the correct answers, which I found helped in studying special problems. In this document Prof. Krapp was dubbed *inquisitor saevus* and *bete-noire* — the source of his undeserved reputation for inquisitorial savagery, as two students had reported.

While I was teaching at Bucknell University in Pennsylvania, I arranged a date, May 21, 1921, and came to Columbia for this dreaded examination. In preparation for it I had tried to review the whole domain of British and American Literature, especially the major authors and main literary movements, and I was careful to be in good mental and physical condition, eating very lightly on the appointed date. A repeated warning by successful and unsuccessful candidates was: "Do not try to bluff! Do not pretend to know what you do not know! If you do not know the answer, say so." To my great surprise in my test, I admitted lack of knowledge only about a few minor matters. To my very great surprise I enjoyed the two-hour quizzing adventure!

In American Literature Prof. Trent questioned me on Poe, Hawthorne, and Lowell, about whom I had read widely and had been lecturing to my students. So, I turned on my Poe and Hawthorne lecture records loaded with effective discourse. After a few minutes of this barrage Prof. Trent requested less detail, and I began to take short cuts to my destination. Later, while Dr. Thorndike was sampling my knowledge of the Victorian period, he asked about Matthew Arnold. I answered his question, and then volunteered the opinion that Arnold reminded me of

Sophocles and might be compared with the famous Greek dramatist. That was too much for Prof. Trent, who was sitting cross-
legged. With a quick movement, he uncrossed his legs and
stamped the floor, exclaiming, "How's that now? Arnold resembles Sophocles? Is in a class with Sophocles? Explain yourself!"

By this sudden crossfire I was startled and hedged a little,
saying, "Of course, Sophocles was a dramatist and Arnold an
essayist, but I think they had a few similar traits." I explained
briefly, searching for more ammunition, which one of the examiners, apparently sharing my view, helped me to find by asking several leading questions. With one professor agreeing and
one disagreeing with me, it looked like a drawn battle, and when
quiet was restored, they passed on to other topics. At the end of
the test I withdrew and waited in the hall for a report. In about
five minutes, Dr. Thorndike appeared and smilingly announced
that I had passed the preliminary. I thanked him and the others
and returned to Bucknell, feeling like Bunyan's Pilgrim with a
heavy load removed from my back.

When I had completed my thesis on James Kirke Paulding,
Versatile American, I submitted three typed copies of it to a
second committee of eight examiners. I was next invited back
to Columbia to defend it and my conclusions on May 8, 1925.
Since I knew far more about this limited field than any of the
committee members, I was cheerful about the outcome. Besides,
I had carefully guarded against factual errors and unsupported
conclusions in my study, the first part of which Dr. Carl Van
Doren had already examined, recommending more condensed
treatment. One examiner, however, I thought, was fussy about
minor matters and critical of my compact treatment, which meant
that he and Van Doren held conflicting views. Again, a pacific
examiner diverted us to another topic. In conclusion, the committee accepted my thesis subject to editorial changes and polishing under supervision. Once I flatly refused to make a requested
change in a factual statement and appealed the case to Dr. Thorndike, who sustained my position on the disputed passage.

After making a few additions, polishing the text, and having
the thesis retyped, I looked in vain for a commercial publisher.
Then, the Columbia University Press agreed to issue my study
and published it late in 1926. Since I had then surmounted all
of the doctoral hurdles, the degree of Doctor of Philosophy was
conferred upon me *in absentia* in December of the same year.
The previous summer I had traveled in eight European coun-

tries. The achievement of these difficult goals in 1926 makes the year memorable in my story.

CHAPTER 11

Instructor and Personnel Adjutant

IF life is a battle for birth, for food and shelter, and for development, as Lyman Abbott stated in his old age, then apprenticeships in the vocations are a part of the battle for the means of living and for growth. My first two, full-time, college positions I regard as parts of my apprenticeship in college teaching, in which I learned a great deal about my work and even more about college routine and pitfalls. So complex is the art of college diplomacy that few ever master it. A teacher successful in one set of circumstances may trip up in a different set manipulated by designing persons. Frequently, college deans, presidents, and boards of trustees are baffling to comprehend and perfidious to deal with. The percentage of crooks in college faculties is probably as high as in any other occupation. With greater intelligence they are more skillful in concealing their crookedness! High public professions may conceal much iniquity!

Negotiating for a Position

During my first year of doctoral studies I registered with the Columbia Employment Office to learn of college positions for the following year. One of my first contacts was with the University of Cincinnati, an excellent municipal institution supported by taxation and endowments. When its president, Charles W. Dabney, visited New York, looking for instructors, I had a conference with him regarding an English instructorship. Though the prospects were fair, the initial salary was then only $1200 a year, which was $300 less than I had last received in high school. Dr. Dabney insisted that he could not pay more without discriminating among beginning instructors and assured me, if I were engaged and my work proved successful, increases would come in due course. He suggested that I apply to Dean Frank W. Chandler, head of the English Department, sending him my record and personal references. Since later developments seemed to indicate that the president and dean did not agree on what was wanted nor on the extent of each other's authority, I quote my letter to Dr. Chandler. For a full month he acted as if he thought or felt that the president had infringed upon his own prerogative to recommend, and it seemed to me that I was caught between two sparring administrative offiicals. On March 19, 1916, I wrote this letter:

My dear Dean Chandler:

I am a graduate student in English at Columbia University, and yesterday afternoon I had a consultation with Pres. Charles W. Dabney concerning a position under you at the University of Cincinnati. It seems that Dr. Dabney was pleased with my record and recommendations, and at the end of the consultation, he offered me the position subject only to your approval and notified the Columbia English Department to this effect.

Altho my last salary was $1500 a year, Dr. Dabney, in order to prevent any friction or discord, preferred that I should be willing to begin with $1200 a year and look forward to a substantial increase at no distant date, provided, of course, my work is successful. I accepted Dr. Dabney's preference on this point, because I want a position in the Ohio Valley and because I am confident that my work will be successful.

I enclose some of my testimonials for your examination. Should you wish to communicate with any of the Columbia professors, I suggest the name of Prof. G. P. Krapp under whom I have done much of my work. I shall complete the required study in residence for the Ph. D. degree by June.

Trusting that I may hear from you as soon as you see Dr. Dabney, I beg leave to remain,

Very sincerely,
A. L. Herold.

On March 31, Dean Chandler replied to my letter, expressing regret for the delay in answering as due to pressure of many matters and his inability to confer with President Dabney. He also explained in some detail his wish to improve the quality of Freshman English, which was falling short of his expectations; and he indicated that most of my work would be in composition and perhaps one course in secondary English for teachers or prospective teachers. He wished to learn my preferences and whether I would be willing to take the composition; what I had published, when my doctoral thesis would be completed, and the like.

On April 5, in a two-page letter, I responded affirmatively to his requests. Then, on April 17, Dean Chandler wrote again that the resignation of a staff member had necessitated a delay and that he would let me know "at the earliest possible moment." After waiting another 10 days, I was so baffled and irked by the repeated delays that I sent him a letter withdrawing my application. At least, I could act and clear the atmosphere. Within two or three days I received from the dean the following special delivery letter, dated May 2:

> My dear Mr. Herold:
>
> I am returning the testimonials for which you asked in your letter just received. When your missive came, I had already sent in a recommendation to the President for your appointment as instructor in English, a recommendation which would have been favorably acted upon by our Board at its meeting this afternoon. I fear that you think I have been over-cautious and unduly slow in arranging matters, but I am sure that if you knew all the elements that entered into the case you would understand that I have acted as promptly as was possible. For one thing, the vacancy caused by the withdrawal of Miss McVea to accept the Presidency of Sweet Briar College was a contingency wholly unexpected. On the other hand, I cannot blame you for feeling a bit nettled by my delay, and I apologize for any distress that unwittingly I may have caused you.
>
> The instructorship will involve, I now find, two sections in Freshman Composition and Literature, a certain amount of conference work with Engineering students, a course in American Literature, and any other advanced course that you may care to give. For next season, I probably should not need to call upon you for the course in Methods and Materials in Secondary English, unless you desired it.
>
> I assure you that I shall be glad to do everything in my power to make you happy here. I think you would like the city and the university. If you still are willing to accept the instructorship at twelve hundred dollars, you have only to write me to that effect. I await your reply, and subscribe myself.
>
> Very cordially yours,
> Frank W. Chandler

At the time I was eager to obtain dependable work promptly, because I was then hoping to be married late that summer. Without this factor I think I should have either declined to negotiate

further or accepted the position provided the pay were increased
to $1500. Later I wished that I had made this demand. Instead,
I suppressed my spleen and accepted the position, which required
a lot of hard work at small pay, even though I received three
annual increases of $200, $100, and $100; that is, to $1600 for a
fourth year if I had not returned to Columbia for further study
and research on Paulding.

My Teaching Load

As to the labor, late in October the Dean's office requested me
to report on my total registration and my conference hours each
week. Here is the gist of my report, with a voluntary notation on
my weekly student manuscripts to grade:

I.   Classes

	No. of Students	Weekly Class-hrs.	Weekly hrs. Conferences
Two sections of Freshman English for Engineers	60	2	6
Two sections of Freshman English in Liberal Arts College	63	6	11
One class in American Literature for Juniors and Seniors	75	2	0

II. Manuscript received weekly: 654 pages in Freshman English
     and 150 pages in American Literature, totaling 804 pages.
III. Undetermined: Time required to correct and grade these
     MSS and time to prepare materials for the class meetings.

With 123 students in Freshman English and 75 in American
Literature, it is obvious to any experienced college teacher that
I had an excessively heavy load, even though I received student
aid for 10 to 12 hours weekly. Under administrative pressure to
improve the quality of Freshman English to meet public expecta-
tons, I worked 50 to 60 hours a week and I read so many manuscripts that by April I had to consult an oculist and get my
first spectacles. Though I was carrying almost a double load, and
for small pay, I stayed on the job for three years.

University Leaders

The University of Cincinnati, which then comprised seven
colleges including a Graduate School, had two administrators
of national standing. The first was President Dabney, genial
son of a famous theologian, former assistant secretary of agricul-

ture in President Cleveland's cabinet, and a skillful college president, co-ordinating diverse interests with tactful efficiency. Both in his office and his home he was genial, considerate, and dedicated to worthy purposes. In character and reputation he was what a college president should be but often is not. I never once heard him accused of trickery, deceit, or unfair dealing. He was truly a Virginia gentleman. The second outstanding administrator was Herman Schneider, dean of the Engineering College and originator of its famous co-operative system for combining instruction and work in a related job, with five full years required then to earn a degree. His system was copied elsewhere in colleges and high schools. While I was there, he was invited and handsomely paid to install the co-op system in the high schools of New York City. He was an original thinker and spoke and wrote with authority and persuasiveness. Later he became president of the University of Cincinnati. He, too, was a real man and worthy to fill exalted positions. I liked and admired both men and enjoyed being with and under them.

Among the best scholars there I would name Dr. L. T. More, professor of physics and dean of the Graduate School; Dr. Frederick C. Hicks, dean of the Commerce College; Dr. Max Poll of the German department; Dr. Frank W. Chandler, dean of Liberal Arts and head of the English Department, and Dr. Henry R. Shipherd of the English department. Dean Chandler, who had just published his *Aspects of Modern Drama,* was a brilliant scholar and effective teacher, with a flair for the dramatic and a touch of haughty conceit, which an object of his jibes might call intellectual snobbery. For example, upon one occasion, President Dabney addressed my large class in American Literature and other visitors on the genius of Edgar Allan Poe. Though literary criticism was not the speaker's specialty or forte, Dean Chandler spoke scornfully of the address, which most of us thought both instructive and appropriate. He was a demon for work and a man of high character and superior social qualities. His office was the liveliest on the campus and his home was unsurpassed for charm and courtesy. Dr. Shipherd, a Harvard graduate, was invited to Cincinnati for the express purpose of improving Freshman English, in which he had my loyal support. For three years there he and I shared an office and were congenially associated in our work. He was a ripe, experienced scholar, prized and praised by his students and friends.

A Bachelor's Life

Though only a bachelor, I was frequently entertained by

members of the faculty and administration. President and Mrs. Dabney were especially concerned for my welfare and happiness. He and I were Virginians and had studied at different colleges and different times under the same Greek teacher — Professor Addison Hogue. Within a day or two after my arrival Dr. Dabney invited me and his secretary to his home for lunch with Mrs. Dabney. When I called later, he enjoyed showing me his library and books written by his father. In late October Mrs. Dabney invited me to join herself and her friends on the stage of the Academy of Music to hear President Wilson speak in behalf of his campaign for a second term, which he won by a close vote of 277 electoral votes to 254 for Judge Charles E. Hughes on the vote-getting slogan, "He kept us out of war."

In all of Cincinnati I could scarcely have found a quieter room for study than in the comfortable Roanoke apartment of two retired, white-haired, Presbyterian ladies, the Misses Gaithers, who watched over me with motherly care. They were old-fashioned maids as trim and neat and busy as you please. Some minister had happily named them the Mary and Martha of his congregation. On Sunday at 10:25 A.M. they would be dressed and ready to take a streetcar to their downtown church, and usually they attended the evening services. Miss Carrie was the more conscientious churchgoer. Her soul's salvation apparently depended on her faithful attendance. Rain or shine, she went! In the evening her sister, Sara, would just as lief stay at home to read and rest, and once as they passed my door, she remarked to me, "Carrie is a great church girl. She *will* go and so I go along with her."

Besides musical and theatrical events of high quality, I recall, with pleasure, a series of popular lectures given by Prof. William Lyon Phelps from Yale. The topics of his three delightful lectures were "A Literary Pilgrimage to England," "The Present Condition of the Drama," and "The Modern Novel." The college auditorium was filled for every lecture, twice I was crowded onto the stage, and for the last one even standing room was at a premium. His lectures enlarged my own reading lists, and I became interested in authors heretofore lightly regarded. Later he would make newspaper headlines by inviting the heavyweight boxing champion, Gene Tunney, to Yale to speak to his students on Shakespeare. That was enough to bring the house down though Tunney was a real student of the dramatic bard. And what better way to dispel the athletic delusion that literature is fit only for "sissies—"?

During the winter our diplomatic relations with Germany

were strained to the breaking point; by March our entrance into the World War seemed imminent; and, in early April of 1917, President Wilson addressed Congress and asked for a declaration of war, which was promptly passed. The whole nation was stirred with preparations for fighting. Thousands of young men enlisted or went to training camps for officers. At the University of Cincinnati military drill supplanted athletic sports. I joined a home-guard company and drilled two hours a week. Though I was past the draft age, my sense of duty and loyalty to my country called for some form of participation.

During the spring of 1916, after a happy engagement of 18 months, my Missouri fiancee and I had agreed to disagree to such an extent that our prospective marriage in August was called off, and our amatory relations, like the nation's diplomatic ties with Germany, were strained for several months. Her friend and my cousin, Annah Ruckman, serving as mediator, succeeded in effecting what she called a Second Missouri Compromise, which the lovelorn accepted in September. In consequence of this rupture, however, my first year in Cincinnati was spent in single blessedness or cussedness, as one may prefer to call it, which my small salary made desirable. I could secure a single room for $16 a month and two meals in the Roanoke cafe for $20 a month, getting lunch at the university cafeteria. From my savings I began slowly to pay off about $500 of borrowed money. My life insurance was then costing $52 a year and monthly payments on my *Encyclopedia Britannica* $60 a year, making a fixed annual charge of $112, which was quite a drag upon my exchequer and cured me of installment buying except as a last resort. I was also advancing small sums to my sister, Lula, who had just begun her nurse-training at the Cincinnati General Hospital.

Marriage and Living Costs

After our marriage on June 21, 1917, Mrs. Herold and I honeymooned to Cincinnati and the two Virginias until September when we rented and furnished a Roanoke apartment to begin housekeeping and to wrestle with steadily increasing wartime costs of living. We enjoyed the many social and musical advantages of the city and heartily welcomed a $200 increase in my salary. At the same time we practiced strict economy, to which Mrs. Herold was not accustomed, but which, before our marriage, she knew would be necessary. In January, 1918, in a family account book I began to record every item of expense. My record for that month was:

Apartment rent, recently increased	$41.00
Electric lights	2.17
Groceries and meals	30.45
Travel expenses	20.35
Telephone and charity	8.77
Postage and newspapers	3.37
Amusements	2.39
Total January Expenses	$108.50
January Salary	166.66
January Salary minus Expenses	58.16

The next June by moving from the Roanoke apartment to a small four-room, second-floor apartment in a private home at $25 a month, without inconvenience or discomfort, we reduced our rent $16 monthly, which was an important offset to the increasing cost of groceries and other items. By these persistent economies for three years and after our marriage by occasional aid to Mrs. Herold from her mother, I succeeded not only in paying my school debts and buying some furniture but also in saving about $300 by September, 1919. With this sum and about $700 of lately collected income from an inheritance, I was able to return to Columbia for one more year of study and research — a strategic move that enabled me within two years to double my salary and to attain a modest standard of comfortable living from my college teaching.

Military Training

"By nature I'm a peaceful man," I wrote to a friend in May, 1917. "I love the ways of peace and quiet study. Thus I have lived so far. But, when Uncle Sam is needing men to help clean out a big, powerful den of intrenched outlaws, robbers, and barbarians, such as the Germans are proving themselves to be — at least the German military authorities — then I see the unwisdom of trying to be peaceful, and am willing to shoulder a gun and to do my share in making the ocean a safe place to voyage and the land a safe place to live."

However, at the age of 32, with the approval of President Dabney and other friends who agreed with me in thinking the war would soon end, I carried out our delayed marriage plans in June, 1917, and taught war-reduced classes the following session and summer to the end of July. But on August 5, 1918, with a few other members of the faculty I accepted President Dabney's appointment under authority of the Adjutant General to the Students' Army Training Corps Camp of 3,500 men to be held at Fort Sheridan, Illinois, from August 10 to September 16, and commanded by Major Edward W. McCaskey, U. S. A. (retired).

I enrolled as a private and was placed in Corporal Street's Squad 7 of Lieut. Mason's Company 18 for intensive military training. We put on uniforms, shouldered rifles, marched, and countermarched; we peeled potatoes, dug trenches, and studied U. S. Army Regulations; we learned to use a bayonet (horrible to remember!) and to throw hand grenades; we practiced on the rifle range at which I had won a medal in Cincinnati. When a boy, I had learned to care for and shoot guns — rifle, Winchester, and shotgun. I shared a tent with five other college instructors, among whom were the author, Dr. W. W. Sweet of Depauw University, and Dr. C. O. Gardner and Dr. E. S. Smith, both with myself from the University of Cincinnati.

Personnel Adjutant

Incredible as this may be, at the end of this five-week, training period on September 16, a lot of us to my surprise were commissioned Second Lieutenants in the U. S. Army, however little qualified we were when compared with a man who had spent four years at West Point. Of course, we were college graduates though our knowledge of military science was excessively meager. Many of my Horner cadets knew more about drilling men than I knew. No man can do a four-year task in five weeks. Fortunately, I was immediately placed in a seven-day School for Personnel Adjutants at Fort Sheridan, attended by 300 Second Lieutenants and supervised by Mr. J. J. Coss, a leader in the Army's classification of personnel. This school, too, was attempting the wellnigh impossible with no actual practice in doing the job. It is no wonder that military men have protested so violently against the unwisdom of trying to build an efficient army over a weekend or even in a month or two months. It can not be done.

In an effort to relieve captains and adjutants of some of their duties, the War Department in General Order No. 60 of June, 1918, created a system of personnel adjutants to handle records of induction, vocational classification, allotments, insurance, pay rolls, rosters, assignments, transfers, promotions, and related matters. The British Army had at first floundered badly in failing to place the right man in the right job — a problem of vocational classification. It is almost impossible in one week to master all the military forms and complex procedures pertaining to an army personnel office. A little experience in handling them would be a great boon. Even our instructors would get tangled up in trying to explain them!

Influenza Epidemic

While I was in this School for Personnel Adjutants, influenza was sweeping the country; the Fort Sheridan Hospital was crowded with ill men. I contracted an apparent cold, which got worse. To keep warm at night, I slept between blankets and two mattresses. Being assigned as personnel adjutant to the University of Cincinnati, I returned there on September 25 and reported for duty to the commanding officer, Major Raymond L. Percy, so ill that I could scarcely stand at attention and requested his permission to sit down. Immediately he instructed Captain Harper of the medical staff to examine me. Finding my temperature to be 104 degrees, he sent me straight home to my bed, where in the course of a three-week illness I learned that the Spanish influenza was more treacherous and dangerous than the military enemy. For many days I could sleep only after the relaxation induced by hot baths. My nervous system was so affected that my recovery was slow and for nearly two years I felt somewhat subnormal. In the training camps soldiers died by the hundreds and thousands from influenza or pneumonia complications. Camp Cincinnati was quarantined from October 5 to October 28, and 24 men died in service there between October 1 and December 20, 1918.

The Students' Army Training Corps (S.A.T.C.) at the University of Cincinnati was formally instituted on October 1; on the next day the induction of collegiate students began and was completed when the quarantine was lifted. The maximum strength of the unit was 1600 men, or including two city detachments, nearly 2300 men. The camp adjutant functioned for me during my illness and at my request for some time after my return in bad health. I rejoiced at the Armistice on November 11, at the demobilization of S.A.T.C. on December 20, and at my own honorable discharge with 18 other officers at Cincinnati on December 24, 1918 — three most genuine and welcome Christmas presents.

In January, 1919, I returned to my teaching at the University, feeling somewhat like an automobile with a flat tire and a defective spark plug but functioning under these handicaps. During the summer I wrote a careful 16-page account of the S.A.T.C. at the University of Cincinnati, which President Dabney incorporated and published in his annual report to the Board of Trustees.

Reasons for Leaving Cincinnati

At no time was I entirely satisfied with my position at the

University of Cincinnati. Besides the hard work, long hours, and low pay, already mentioned, I had other causes of dissatisfaction. I was aware that at $3 a credit hour I was earning $2400 a year or at $4 a credit hour, $3200, and that for the same amount of work the "big boys" were well paid. Though my personal associations were quite pleasant and though my opportunity to gain experience was valuable, fully two-thirds of my work was in composition, divided between liberal arts and engineering. The method of teaching English to the engineers I regarded as needlessly laborious for the instructor and difficult for the students, who without adequate preparation were required to write long technical reports on inspection trips to factories and water plants. With only one hour of class instruction a week, English instructors were expected to accomplish wonders with the students and their reports, assigned by engineering instructors.

The part I enjoyed most was the course in American Literature in spite of the inadequacy of the textbooks and the scarcity of library books for collateral reading in a large class. As the best available texts, we used Carpenter's *American Prose* and Page's *Chief American Poets*.

But after two years my salary was barely equal to my last in high school. As an appendage in two colleges, I regarded my prospects as dim. Besides, I needed change and rest from hard work and the ill effects of influenza. Carefully weighing all the factors involved in my situation, I decided in August to seek a release and to return to Columbia for one year of study and research. This procedure enabled me to get more attractive work at nearly twice my Cincinnati salary.

CHAPTER 12

The Bucknell Gauntlet

BY THE spring of 1920, I was gratified to learn that college salaries had improved markedly. To fill vacancies and to prevent transfers to other kinds of work, college officials had to increase the pay. When I left Cincinnati, I received a tempting offer from an insurance company, which I declined in order to cultivate my love of study and teaching.

Late in April I had a conference at Columbia University with the president of Colorado College regarding an English professorship at $2400 a year with annual increases up to $3000 or better, which I tentatively accepted though the location was inconvenient to New York for further research on Paulding. About the same time President Emory W. Hunt of Bucknell University became interested in my record, and after further negotiations and my visit to Bucknell at Lewisburg, Pennsylvania, he duplicated the first part of my Colorado offer, knowing that I wished to be nearer Columbia. The result was that late in May I secured a release from the Colorado position and accepted his offer to become Professor of English Literature in Bucknell University, a Baptist institution, long presided over by the able Dr. John H. Harris. The salary, though comparatively low, gave me a measure of comfort that I had not enjoyed before. I regret to add, however, that though the Bucknell prospects appeared to be good, they proved to be deceptive, because within a year I was confronted with a camouflaged gauntlet lined by alumni employees with jealously guarded interests in the college. To some of the faculty I was just about as welcome as General Lee with his invading army, though my stay was more prolonged than the famous invader's.

The natural beauty of the region, in contrast, was a ceaseless joy. Bucknell is located on a low hill among fine oak trees overlooking the comfortable and hospitable town of Lewisburg on the Susquehanna River in central Pennsylvania. The valley there widens into rich farm and grazing lands with wooded hills and mountains in the distance. Along the river are fine sugarloaf hills and attractive roads in all directions, especially to Eagle's Mere, a small lake on top of a flat mountain. Among our best friends there were Rev. Frank B. Everitt, pastor of the Presbyterian Church, and Mrs. Jane Cameron Harrison, of the Scottish Camerons and niece of Senator Cameron, a remarkable woman who could make and save money and spend it, too.

I found the English setup at Bucknell defective. One professor of rhetoric taught all the composition, another all the literature, and both were overworked. Just imagine one instructor trying to teach 250 students in composition, meeting them twice a week in seven sections. Near the end of my first year I advised with the dean and president on the need for a reorganization and was granted authority to carry out my proposals. The next September Freshman English became a six-hour course, meeting three times a week, in ten sections taught by an enlarged staff. We revised the grading system to prevent the unfit from getting credit and outlawed plagiarism. My inherited monopoly in literature I discarded, took charge of one freshman section, and distributed the composition and literature courses more equitably among the instructors, one of whom later showed his appreciation by spreading false reports about me. Reshaping the literary offering, I added two or three new courses. At the end of the year I was rewarded with, not an expected $200, but a $400 increase in salary.

In my efforts to gather an adequate English staff I prepared a table showing the ratio of English instructors to students in a dozen representative institutions, where the average was one English instructor for every 120 students. At Bucknell the ratio was one instructor for every 212 students. My own registration averaged 180. Since these figures demonstrated our need of additional instructors, we soon secured two more, who enabled us to do a much better job than under the old setup.

Student Magazine Revived

At the same time I sponsored a student movement to revive the college literary magazine, *The Bucknell Mirror,* which was then almost forgotten. Securing a competent editorial board and planning five issues of a 32-page magazine supported by subscriptions and a little advertising, we produced the first number in October, 1921. Seeking variety, originality, and literary worth, the editors brought credit to the college and the English Department. Besides essays, stories, and dialect humor, the first number carried two pages of charming "Susquehanna Lyrics" by Roy W. Sauers. Of particular interest were a free-verse tribute to "The Chair Factory" and an editorial in a later issue on "the Radiophone," or radio, which in 1922 was a brand-new invention.

Bucknell's Honor System

A distressing problem at the college was the prevalence of plagiarism and official indifference about it. Some students were being shamelessly carried along by their fellows. Others, however, were keenly alive to the evils of the common practice and eager to help correct them. *The Mirror* published an article by Miss Phoebe B. Davis on "The Honor System," from which I quote an excerpt:

"Anticipating going to college, many were the air castles I built. To me, college was the El Dorado, where one found the best types of students and the loftiest principles of life. These four years were to shape one's career so perfectly and faultlessly that the intellectual and moral training gained would enable one to enter life fearlessly. Of course, such air castles were beyond realization, but yet, I still feel that my airy visions had some grounds for further realization than the average college gives today.

"The final blow, which caused the entire collapse of my castles of ideals, was the total absence of an honor system of any kind at the college I had selected. Coming from a high school, where cheating or cribbing was considered a capital offense, the blow was unusually severe. Since my first term as a Freshman, I have seen practically no evidence of honor in regard to school work. I was gradually coming to the conclusion that Bucknell's idea of a college was an intensive and extensive training in getting away with everything one could. On the foundations upon which my air castles had fallen, I was forced to build actualities at which I shuddered to look."

Then she went on to point out what the faculty and students might do towards establishing such a moral atmosphere at the college "that a person would rather be tarred and feathered than be found cheating or cribbing." Another student wrote in December, 1922: "To the new student the most noticeable and deplorable condition is the faulty honor system. Selfish motives seem to govern our actions entirely. Many freshmen come from high schools where the honor system is in successful operation and they are amazed and disappointed at our laxity in such matters. Nevertheless, the atmosphere is such that in a short time they fall victims to the same habits."

These extracts revealed that cheating was the Bucknell dragon or octopus. Against it I was eager to enlist massed faculty action, but it became necessary to proceed by departments. So, the English Department entered the lists, and, to put teeth in the rule against cheating, it vainly sought an agreement with the administration to punish second offenses with dismissal. Yet, the administration ran an advertisement in *The Mirror* professing that Bucknell "aims to develop men and women who will apply true Christian ideals to every department of human endeavor."

The Bucknell Faculty

However much constructive work I might do, in my second year I began to realize that the college faculty was badly ingrown with its own graduates, who viewed outsiders as foreigners. The dean, two of my English associates, and most of the faculty were Bucknell alumni, who felt that they had vested interests to protect and who, if so minded, in various subtle ways could obstruct, delay, or block one's plans. Not all by any means, but a few would stoop so low. Some were real scholars and gentlemen. Even so, I began to doubt the wisdom of my coming to Bucknell and decided to seek a transfer elsewhere. After an experience of two years I wrote to the Columbia Employment Office, explained the situation, and expressed my wish to look elsewhere for a position.

Meanwhile, I had inherited from my grandfather, David V. Ruckman, a one-sixth interest in about 800 acres of improved and timbered land in Pocahontas County, West Virginia, which was in dispute or litigation for two years and, along with an attorney's aid, required my making two trips there to protect my interests. But in due course, the Herold heirs succeeded in dividing and selling the property advantageously in three tracts for a total of $32,265. With my share I had bought a small house on a good lot in Lewisburg and transformed it into a seven-room residence, which I later sold to advantage when I removed to Oklahoma.

End of My Apprenticeship

In our faculty meetings I did not hesitate at all times to protect the best interests of the English Department. One December, I recall, the students petitioned the faculty to extend the holidays by one week. Even though President Hunt showed an inclination to grant the request, possibly to reduce expenses, I opposed the petition vigorously, was supported by others, and the petition was rejected. On other occasions I faced similar problems and responded in the same way, perhaps to the annoyance and displeasure of the president. At any rate in my third year, when I was quietly seeking a transfer, he began to show his disfavor by word and act. When I asked for an explanation, he was evasive and sent me to the dean, who made two assertions that I could readily explain. In the end, I drew up a report and submitted it in mimeographed form with my resignation to the president and the board of trustees in June, 1923. My apprenticeship was over. I had been duly initiated into the mysteries of college politics. I ran the college gauntlet, and, like Moses Moore, striking right and left vigorously, I defended myself and survived to run again another day.

Trip to Chicago and Niagara Falls

In that same month of June as a reward for my foresight and Columbia's timely assistance, I accepted the headship of the English department in the University of Tulsa, the oil capital of Oklahoma. To conclude the negotiations, President James M. Gordon had invited me to meet him in Chicago on June 30, where we had a pleasant visit together and made plans for the following fall. My initial salary of $2,800 was steadily increased to $3,800 including summer school. In Tulsa I spent some of the happiest years of my life before ill health and Old Man Depression interfered in the 1930's.

From Chicago I returned to Pennsylvania by Buffalo and Niagara Falls, where I spent a day sight-seeing. Owing to the large quantities of water diverted to electric plants and owing, also, I suppose, to my exaggerated expectations, the falls were somewhat disappointing. Though the name *Niagara* is said to mean *thunderer,* the giant, when I was there, was not giving an impressive exhibition of his powers. The seven-mile gorge below the falls holds great geological interest, because it is both the scene and the monument of one of the earth's mightiest conflicts between stratified rock and running water. For thousands of years the waters of Niagara River have been pounding the rock to sand and dust and cutting the gorge, and ultimately Lake Erie may cease to be a lake and become a river valley.

My Tribute to Miss Davis

I wish to conclude this chapter with a tribute I wrote for *The Bucknell Mirror* of May, 1923, in Memory of Miss Phoebe Beatrice Davis, one of my lovely and most brilliant students at Bucknell:

"Among the rewards of a life devoted to teaching, none is sweeter than the discovery and observation of a pure and rarely gifted spirit. From day to day the instructor may observe it, developing, growing, unfolding like a flower to the beauty and mystery of life, and sending out in all directions delicate thought tentacles to support itself in its youthful and triumphant march onward and upward. In comparison with this discovery, the conquest of the North Pole and the finding of King Tut's tomb are indeed insignificant events.

"Such a reward was mine in meeting Miss Phoebe Beatrice Davis in a class studying Wordsworth's poetry in the autumn of 1920. I recall with pleasure how she penetrated the intricacies of the poet's philosophy of life and joyfully studied his wondrous lakes, his countryside, and homely sincere people. As appreciative and attentive as Dorothy Wordsworth herself, she found inspiration in "Tintern Abbey" and "Character of the Happy Warrior." Gentle, tactful, unpretentious, clear-eyed, and competent, she soon became the unquestioned leader of the class. Later, her merits and reliability induced me to engage her as an assistant in English; the following year when, with my aid and encouragement, *The Bucknell Mirror* was revived, she was elected as an associate editor.

"True seer that she was, she early became, according to an intimate friend, a dreamer of dreams. Even in the graded schools she had one goal, one fond hope, namely, to attend Bucknell. This dream she realized. Another ambition, also aroused early in her high school course, was to become a teacher of English. With what diligence and skill she worked in this field, her record in college is an eloquent witness. This ambition, unfortunately, she did not realize. Returning home in December, 1921, for the Christmas vacation, a leading member of the Senior Class, she was seized by a lingering illness and died October 3, 1922. During her college career, however, as her knowledge grew, all her minor ambitions focused upon one great aim — service to her friends, to her college, and to her people. This aim, rooted in and directed by love, enabled her to serve well her Alma Mater through its various organizations, and, as all her friends and associates will agree, she neglected no opportunity for service, and in every good cause she fought a good fight.

"Because of the purity, nobility, and uniqueness of her character, one may well apply to her a stanza from one of Wordsworth's most beautiful poems:

> 'A violet by a mossy stone
> Half-hidden from the eye!
> Fair as a star, when only one
> Is shining in the sky.'

I CHOSE TEACHING
Part IV. Adventures in Oklahoma and Europe

CHAPTER 13
The Oklahoma Frontier

WHEN in June, 1923, I became head of the English Department in the University of Tulsa, in the new city of Tulsa, a magic metropolis in the oil fields of Oklahoma, I had unusual opportunities to observe many fascinating aspects of the Southwest and to reshape the college English courses. Such freedom to experiment and to organize among liberal citizens in a region responsive to new ideas, I had not enjoyed elsewhere.

In 1900 Tulsa was a small, frontier, Indian town. Under the stimulus of the black gold of petroleum and other natural resources it had grown into a city of over 100,000 people, who prized comfortable homes, fresh water, and efficient schools for their children. Splendid modern hotels, banks, office buildings, and handsome churches adorned its central district. Westward beyond the Arkansas River loomed a huge oil refinery; northward to Kansas lay the rich oil and grazing lands of the Osage Indians; and to the south and east the rolling prairie, converted into cultivated farms and pasture lands. In 1923 the University of Tulsa, with four brick or stucco buildings and about 260 students, was on the eastern border of the city. Within ten years I saw it expand eastward and southward, leaving the college near its geographical center. An engineering feat costing $7,500,000 had just brought clear fresh water by gravity 60 miles from the foothills of the Ozarks to city faucets. Tulsa was a center of wealth, of energy, and of romance. Writing to an eastern friend, I said: "Your son's interest in the Southwest is well founded. There are perhaps ten chances here to one in many sections of

139

the East. The natural resources are abundant; the lands are rich and productive of cotton, corn, wheat, fruits, and so on; the climate is delightful; and the people are energetic and farsighted."

Tulsans were remarkably young and progressive. They had come from all sections of the country. They came from the North, the East, the South, and the West, especially from Pennsylvania, Illinois, Missouri, Arkansas and Texas, attracted by the lure of oil, lead, zinc, and a fertile region. One seldom saw old people, for they had stayed behind. Youthful vim was building the city and the University. Though they were predominantly white Americans, there were many Indians, who mingled and intermarried freely with the whites. Many a paleskin won an Osage woman for his wife. At the University some of the best students were of Indian blood. I recall one young woman gifted in music and another with literary talent who won a prize in poetry. On this Oklahoma frontier I was astonished to hear time and again the brilliant and liberal Methodist preacher and scholar, Dr. John A. Rice. From his pulpit he loved to blast superstitious religionists and beliefs. There I became acquainted with Dr. P. P. Claxton, former Commissioner of Education, who for several years, at a handsome salary, was Superintendent of the Tulsa Public Schools.

The administrative and teaching staff of the University, then numbering 25 but soon doubled, was a congenial and worthy group. Though at first not too well equipped with the higher degrees, they had both ability and character. President Gordon was a well-trained, experienced, likable schoolman, who at the end of my first year resigned and was succeeded by Dean Franklin G. Dill as acting president for the next three years. Dr. Dill, holding a German doctorate and well fitted for his work, cultivated friendly relations on the campus and in the city. My four years under these two competent and trustworthy administrators were among my happiest years of college teaching. I trusted them and they trusted me as my department grew and prospered. Dr. C. H. Kimbrough as registrar and professor of history was a nearly perfect example of a southern gentleman of the old school from Tennessee. Among others high in my estimation were Dr. William E. Howard in mathematics, Harvey D. Chase in biology, Senn Waddell in physics, Frances Reubelt in Latin and French, Margaret Wyndham in speech, Albert Lukken and the Ringos in music.

Revising the English Courses

My plans for the English department, based upon my teaching experience and a survey of many college catalogs, began to function in my second year. During my first I could only carry out the administrative and catalog commitments. Two English instructors, Miss Mary Allen and myself, taught 150 freshmen in four sections, 68 sophomores, and 40 juniors and seniors so far as they needed English. Among the freshmen were about 15 of unusual promise, including George Milburn, who later won distinction by his fiction. My first task was to strengthen Freshman English by reducing the size of the sections to 25 or 30 students and by improving the quality of instruction.

When I arrived at the college, the Sophomore English requirement was a six-hour survey of British Literature, the traditional setup that ignored our own literature. For two years at Bucknell I had tried using Greenlaw and Hanford's *The Great Tradition,* in which British and American authors were scrambled together. Since this method tended to confuse the two literatures, I then decided in Tulsa to offer a separate four-hour survey of British Literature and a four-hour survey of American Literature, to require all majors and minors in English to take both courses, and to allow other students the privilege of choosing six of the eight hours for degree requirements. Telescoping and abbreviating the old British Survey, we were able to give our students a comprehensive view of the British and American literary fields. That was my first satisfactory solution of the Sophomore English requirement. Twenty-five years later at Arkansas College, I decided to offer six hours of American Literature to sophomores, to move the six-hour British Survey to the junior level because of its remoteness and difficulty, and to require both surveys of students majoring or minoring in English. I prefer and recommend this second solution.

During my first year, to encourage original composition and to foster literary taste, I sponsored an English Club with 25 student members. In the second semester this Club and the Music Department held a song contest, which yielded an Alma Mater song by Carl Patterson and two pep songs for the Peptiac Club, of which I was faculty adviser. The English Club, later called Chi Nu Epsilon, stimulated interest in English studies, and in 1929 started an annual literary publication, named the *Miscellany,* of which I have six treasured numbers. So zealous were the students to produce it every year that they succeeded even in the worst years of the depression. As to the quality of the verse produced, I quote the first poem of the initial number, written by Mary Cornelia Hartshorne of Indian extraction and expressing both Christian and Indian traits in free verse.

Thanksgiving Hymn

Father, the people stand and look upward and thank you,
Thank you for the harvest, for tender globes of ripe fruitage;
For the sheltered days, Lord, and plenty;
For the beauty of autumn.

But for these things, also, I thank you,
Lord of Creation,
For these wonderful things:
For long, cold winds striding ruthless from hill to hill-top,
Stripping the trees, blighting the vineyards;
For cloud-splitting lightning that shudders across the heavens,
And the rumble and crash of thunder;
For flooding rain, stinging sleet, hail destructive.
For these things, that my soul may be whetted against them,
I thank you.

I shall go forth in the storms;
I shall go forth courageous.
I shall shout and sing in the hollow throat of the wind;
I shall answer the thunder.

And what though the winds lash me,
The sleet cut, or hail-stones batter?
Out of it all shall my soul come radiant,
Polished and gleaming,
Polished and tempered:
A strong, keen blade for the reaping of harvest.

Lord of my body and soul, for all these I thank you!

For several years I taught an introductory course in journalism, and served as chairman of the Faculty Publication Committee, which supervised the annual and the student newspaper. I soon learned that the best way to supervise was to get competent editors and managers who would need little or no censoring. Believing in joint student and faculty control, in 1924 I worked out a plan and secured its adoption, under which three faculty members appointed by the president and three responsible students chosen by the three upper classes formed a board of control with authority to choose editors and managers, to regulate their work and compensation, and, if necessary, to replace them. Four votes were required to act, but after getting full information and discussing it, the board often reached unanimous decisions. Once, when a manager mishandled the funds, this board ousted him in short order and chose his successor. This plan was such a gratifying success that I was proud of it. Sometimes student board members were more critical and outspoken than faculty members. For juniors and seniors I introduced a course in the epics of Dante and Milton and another in poetics with verse writing. I limited Shakespeare to one semester and added a semester's course in Modern Drama. Holding the British Novel to three hours, I introduced a course in Recent Literature and later in American Fiction. Along with the standard British courses, we later offered specialized work in Emerson and Whitman, and Poe and Hawthorne. Besides the introductory journalism, I started a course in Business English for commercial students. The department required English majors and candidates for the master's degree to do a course in the History of the English Language with considerable attention to Chaucer. After a few years I initiated a junior English test to maintain worthy standards. In order to carry on this program of experimentation and readjustment in the English department, twice I refused invitations to other colleges at better pay.

Debate with Oxford

Though Prof. Margaret Wyndham taught public speaking and coached plays in a separate department, for two years I scheduled and trained the debating teams for men and women. Not till my second year were we able to make an enviable record. In January, 1925, with Supt. Claxton presiding, we won front-page news stories by an international debate between our three-man team and a similar British team from Oxford University led by Malcolm McDonald, son of ex-premier Ramsay McDonald. On the Tulsa team were Forrest Fields, Alexander D. Moody, and Andrew Coleman, who like the Biblical David battled with the Goliath of English colleges and won an audience decision. The topic of debate was "That in a democracy ministers should be directly responsible to a popularly elected assembly." The visitors defended the parliamentary system of government, and the Americans championed the presidential system of the United States. To cover expenses, we charged an admission of 50 cents for adults and 25 cents for students. To my great surprise this debate attracted 2,000 from Tulsa and nearby towns. Their support enabled us to pay the English team a $250 guarantee and other expenses, with a $200 surplus. This was my most famous student debate, and it required much research and instruction in the science of democratic government.

Parental Protest Answered

In the following March I had an occasion to use my knowledge of exposition and argument in replying to the most formidable parental protest I ever received, written by a distinguished leader of the Tulsa bar. His letter and mine, both self-explanatory, I should like to reproduce in full, but limited space forbids. My full reply ended the tension and parental doubts as to my teaching and grading methods, and both the parent and his daughter became my good friends.

After two years of strenuous teaching, along with the completion of my doctoral thesis and a defense of it before a Columbia committee of English scholars on May 8, 1925, I felt the need of rest and relaxation among the mountains. So, in August of that year, with Mrs. Herold visiting in Pennsylvania, I traveled alone by train to Colorado Springs for my first view of the Rocky Mountains. On August 24, I ascended to the top of Pike's Peak by the Auto Highway, an exciting trip up and down, with the grandest of views from the cool, rocky summit 14,000 feet above sea level, but matched by forty other Colorado peaks nearly as high. Annually a million people or more visit this vast, cool, scenic wonderland, where Americans may enjoy the grand and varied beauties of nature. Unsurpassed are the natural wonders of Colorado and California. On this trip I bought an instructive, geological book, Dr. George I. Finlay's *Colorado Springs, A Guide Book,* with 42 plates and a map, which explained the geology of this region.

Accreditation

One of the major hurdles confronting the University was accreditation by the North Central Association of Schools and Colleges. In 1923-1924 the board of Presbyterian preachers, lawyers, and oil men by raising about $750,000 increased the endowment to nearly one million dollars. As a member of the library committee I helped to get more books and a professional librarian. Once, I personally secured a gift of several hundred dollars for increasing the book supplies of the English Department. At the same time I was putting the English staff and courses in shape to meet the required standards. In 1926 I received my own doctoral degree, and, as we shall see, I was careful to engage properly qualified instructors. By 1930 the registration of English students in the rapidly growing college required five full-time English instructors and one or more part-time. This combined drive by the board for funds and by the faculty for scholarship led to the accrediting of the University in 1928-29 at the top of a list of 45 applications, according to the reports. Accreditation gave the college appropriate official standing and terminated apologies on this score.

My Investments

After renting a furnished house for one year, I paid $4,800 in cash for a new five-room bungalow situated within easy walking distance of my work, and I moved our furniture and books to it from Pennsylvania. The next year for about $600 I bought my first automobile, a 1924 model-T Ford sedan, which, though a little topheavy on sharp curves, served me well for eight years, taking me there and bringing me back, as advertised. After watching and studying the growth of the city for four years and hearing many alluring tales of increases in land values, I became desirous of trying my luck. I foresaw correctly that Tulsa would not expand much either northward or westward but southward and especially eastward. Then, I looked for acreage in the path of the most likely development, found a ten-acre tract suitably placed on a thoroughfare east of the college, and studied its possibilities. Though $1,000 an acre was the price asked for it, I rated it at $700 an acre, which I offered to pay. Had I been wise enough to foresee the future, I would have stuck to that price or not bought. However, a salesman looking for commissions weakened my powers of resistance by specious claims, and I took an option at the price asked. Later I closed out by paying $1,800 in cash and signing notes secured by tough-hided mortgages for the remaining $8,200 payable with interest over a three-year period. From my salary and the sale of lots I was confident that I could pay this obligation within the allotted time.

But I could not foresee the approaching ten-year DEPRESSION! When that struck like a tornado in late 1929, I still owed $2,100 on the lots, not to mention money borrowed on my home and life insurance. After an early sale of two lots on a prospective business corner for $1,550, I could sell no more lots for twelve long years. Frequently the mortgages made me feel like a man on a scaffold with a hangman's rope around his neck! They specified that if either interest or principal should be unpaid when due, then the entire amount obligated would become due and payable at once by foreclosure. In spite of the depression and the perfidy of a new administration, I succeeded in keeping continuous employment and in meeting my financial obligations in the midst of widespread unemployment and financial disaster. But not until 1942 could I clear the mortgage on my home.

By 1940 I was able to sell my remaining business corner to an oil company for $3,500 in cash, which made $5,000 for my two business corners. Then, 18 of my residential lots were marketed for $600 each, less a builder's commission. Finally, in 1945, I sold the 18 remaining lots to an insurance company for $7,600 in cash. My conjecture that the ten acres would eventually sell for about $25,000 was well founded, though the ten-year depression upset my golden expectations. Interest charges, taxes, surveying, grading, cutting streets, sewer and water lines, commissions, and one legal scrap that cost $1,000 to settle, reduced my profits to about four per cent on the investment. In other words, United States bonds would have yielded nearly as much income without any financial worry or responsibility. Though I completed the deal, no salesman could induce me to repeat it. Seeking business experience, I got it to satiety. Let me add, however, that the 36 residential lots in Herold Addition and the two business corners in Franklin Addition to the city of Tulsa with all their improvements are now probably worth $300,000.

In October, 1930, as the owner of this real estate, I joined three of my Tulsa neighbors and other affected citizens in opposing an all-inclusive zoning plan then pending before the City Commission. We circulated several thousand handbills calling a mass meeting of eastside citizens on October 14 in the University auditorium. At this clamorous meeting the proposed zoning ordinance was discussed pro and con. I came to it armed with a two-page resolution blasting the proposal as arbitrary, retroactive, confiscatory in its wholesale changes of classification, promotive of congested districts, and unknown to the people of the city since only 25 copies of the ordinance were available for the information of 142,000 citizens, which resolution the mass meeting adopted. As secretary of this group, I later appeared before the Zoning Commission to present it and to hear many other individual protests including one by a young woman who in choice English flayed alive the promoters of the Bartholomew Zoning Plan. The Commission was so blasted with withering protests that the plan collapsed completely.

Secretary of Education League

In 1926 Dr. W. B. Bizzell from Texas became president of the University of Oklahoma, Charles A. Lindberg the next year flew the Atlantic Ocean to Paris and fame, and the Tennesee Evolution Case was discussed far and wide by scientific scholars and mediaeval theologians. When an Anti-Evolution Bill to restrict the teaching of science in the public schools was proposed in the Oklahoma Legislature, a group of Tulsa citizens, including Dr. P. P. Claxton, Dr. John A. Rice, three science teachers and myself from the University of Tulsa, and fifteen others from the city, met on February 13, 1927, in Dr. Rice's church to oppose the bill. This group chose officers and an executive committee to direct the fight, and subscribed $80 for expenses.

The next day attorney N. J. Gubser submitted to the committee a resolution listing five specific violations of constitutional guarantees in the bill and stating other reasons for opposing it. The Executive Committee authorized Dr. Claxton to rewrite one section of the resolution, made minor adjustments in its phraseology, and then approved its publication and distribution to members of the Legislature. The committee also engaged Judge M. M. Eakes to visit Oklahoma City and to lobby for the group against the proposed law.

It was my duty as secretary of the group to print and mail copies of the resolution to members of the Legislature. I was also authorized, upon my suggestion, to secure 200 copies of a pamphlet opposing "Anti-Evolution Laws" published by American Civil Liberties Union in New York. These I telegraphed for and with a letter of transmittal mailed a copy to each member of the Legislature. Combined with much statewide opposition, our efforts helped to defeat the bill and to free the state from the menace of similar reactionary legislation.

Funds for New Buildings

Recognizing the need of new buildings for the library, the fine arts, and the sciences, and an opportune time to raise the funds, I drew up a resolution setting forth reasons for them and suggesting that a campaign for funds be started to appeal to different classes of people and to construct them within three years. In February, 1927, the faculty approved the proposal, which was published, and within six months three large gifts were pledged amounting to about $700,000 for the three buildings thus requested of the board of trustees. By the end of 1929 their construction was so far advanced that I induced the faculty to authorize the art department to prepare appropriate Christmas booklets with sketches of the buildings, greetings, and inscriptions to be signed by the student officers and the members of the faculty for presentation to each of the donors. Thus, we happily concluded a successful campaign for the three buildings just as the cyclonic depression began to strike. I was also privileged to choose inscriptions for the library from Thomas Carlyle and Emily Dickinson. Emily's, placed in the reading room, is

"There is no frigate like a book."

The donors of the library were Mr. and Mrs. Robert M. Mc-Farlin; of the fine arts, Mr. and Mrs. Harry C. Tyrrell; and of the science or petroleum building, Mr. Waite Phillips. These buildings were formally dedicated on June 1, 1930.

Loss of Boyhood Friends

At the same time remorseless Death was operating on the Virginia frontier. In 1927 two of my boyhood friends and cousins passed away. First, Cousin Brown Moore, an old man in feeble health, passed to his final rest in the Moore cemetery near our ancestral Moses Moore. Less than a month later, his son, Roy Paris Moore, my boyhood friend and playmate, also died, aged 44, and was buried at Glade Spring in the Valley of Virginia. For twenty years or more Roy had worked as surveyor or manager for pulp and lumber companies in West Virginia and North Carolina. In an automobile accident in 1925, he had received severe head injuries, which forced him to retire to a farm. His wife wrote me that instead of improving, he grew worse and developed creeping paralysis, which caused his death within three weeks. My trusty and loyal boyhood friend was survived by his wife and an 11-year-old boy bearing his father's name. The next year Roy's sister Florence of my age, mother of six children, died of a lingering disease at Warm Springs, Virginia. In the same year my Cousin Letcher Herold, aged 69, died on the ancestral farm adjoining ours, survived by his wife and three children. Cousin Letcher was a good, modest, industrious farmer, who once wryly remarked to me that he would have to die to get his name in the newspaper! He was fond of hunting and fishing, and he married late, winning a local teacher from his older brother Millard, a gifted storyteller, who soon joined his brother in death.

When I was a boy on Knapp's Creek, Cousin Millard would often stop with us on his way to or from his home to tell us all the news far and near, and well did he know how to create suspense and to keep one bursting with curiosity to know what happened to that farmer or his wife or the dog or whatever it was. With a smile and genuine animation, addressing my father, he would begin, "Now, Wise, what d'you think I saw at Huntersville this mornin'? Mercy me! You could never guess, but 'pon my word the most outlandish thing down there in a power of people! Now just lissen." And off he would go with a yarn to fascinate a boy.

Once he told of a hunting experience, in which being placed at a stand to watch for deer passing through, he shot at one and knocked it down. Dropping his gun, he ran to the deer as it was getting on its feet. Cousin Millard always declared that he grabbed the deer by its horns as it began to drag him down a hill, kicking and horning so savagely as to tear off much of his clothing and finally getting away and leaving him scratched and bruised and nearly naked. When the automobile came, he sold his horse and buggy and bought a Ford runabout. Then he engaged my brother Henry to teach him to drive it. After a few days and much instruction about levers and gears, starting and stopping, Cousin Millard consented to get behind the steering wheel to try his luck. After much fumbling, he succeeded in getting the car started up the road, but when the car began to climb a bank, he reverted to horse-and-buggy technique and in his excitement cried out, "Whoa! Whoa! Stop! Stop!" as Henry, convulsed with laughter, took the wheel and stopped the car. Never again would Cousin Millard try to drive an automobile!

Cousin Newton Herold, a brother of Letcher and Millard, had like my Uncle Russell gone West as a young man in the early 1880's. He worked his way up on farms and became a succesful owner of grain and stock lands near Bates City, Missouri, where on my trips to Marshall I sometimes visited him, his wife, and two children, Raymond and Naomi. Like Cousin Millard, he had a lively sense of humor and enjoyed telling stories, and, like his father Andrew and grandfather Christopher, he lived to a ripe old age of nearly ninety.

CHAPTER 14

My Trip to Europe

JUST as I put love and marriage aside till I had received a college degree, so I postponed foreign travel till I had completed all requirements for a doctoral degree except the publication of my thesis. For many years I sought the time when my work and finances would permit me to travel beyond the United States. My first dream was of a world tour in 1926, but the cost of such a long trip restricted me to one summer vacation of foreign travel. So, I joined a special tour to Europe sponsored by the Students' Travel Club of New York City, which had worked out a popular system for seeing Europe with dependable service, intelligent sight-seeing, and congenial companionship. It provided all necessary traveling expenses to eight countries from New York for $695, except passport, visas, and personal items. Since my personal expenses were about $300, the total cost of my trip was $1,000.

On my way east from Oklahoma I visited relatives in the Virginias, and I came to New York in mid-June to arrange for the publication of my thesis by the press of Columbia University. The publisher agreed to have the galley proofs ready to correct by September 4, when I planned to return from abroad to New York. Then, for a fortnight Mrs. Herold joined me for a visit with our old friend, Mrs. Jane Cameron Harrison of Lewisburg, Pennsylvania, where my wife, like a daughter, had many long and refreshing sojourns with this Lady Cameron of Pennsylvania, and where she returned after seeing me off in New York on the steamship *Lapland* on July 7, 1926.

For nearly four days in cool weather and smooth sea, our pilot steered almost directly east from New York before turning southeast toward the Madeira Islands. Besides seeing two or three ships, about noon of our first day we ran into a school of several hundred dolphins, sometimes misnamed porpoises, each five or six feet long, with pointed noses, swimming along with our ship and nearly as fast, emerging at the trough of the waves, and enjoying themselves immensely. I wondered what they thought of us and whether they knew where they were going and had a pilot to guide them! On the second day we noticed the warmth of the Gulf Stream flowing toward England.

My Talk on Modern Italy

On Friday morning, July 9, Miss Jane B. Taylor, chaperone of our party and professor of speech at Vassar College, invited me to speak the next evening to its members on some topic related to our tour. Having lately read several articles on the new Italy led by Benito Mussolini and having some of this material with me, I agreed to talk on "Modern Italy."

On Saturday evening, student members of our party started the program with a clog dance and a piano selection. Then Miss Taylor introduced me to a group of 200, nearly twice the size of our party and filling the dining room. Owing to the noise of the ship's engines and propellers, I was fearful my auditors could not hear me and at my request they were told that if any could not hear, they should feel free to leave the hall. But the party listened attentively. Some stood throughout, and hardly anyone left. I spoke slowly and deliberately for 25 or 30 minutes to the group. Nearly all were strangers to me, and many well traveled. They were generous with compliments, and thereafter many of them sought my acquaintance, adding much to the pleasure of the trip. Surely, speaking thus in the middle of the Atlantic Ocean to the hum of machinery was a novel experience!

Among the college teachers on the tour was Prof. Edward B. Spencer from Grinnell College, Iowa, who lectured one evening on the Azores, Madeira, and Canary Islands — their volcanic origin, population, products, and government. One day I had a long, instructive talk with Prof. Nils Flaten, our conductor, on traveling in Europe. Though professor of languages at St. Olaf College, Minnesota, he was very modest and disinclined to address large groups. The stalwart son of Norwegian parents, he was a worthy son of Norway — large, plain, upright, and efficient, reminding me of Henrik Ibsen.

Scenes and People at Madeira

Our boat came to Funchal, Madeira, about four A.M. on July 15. We were due to go ashore at nine o'clock, but Madeira came to greet us soon after daylight. First I heard beside the ship a clamor of voices with broken English: "Small boy, give him ten cents," or "Small boy, give me twenty dollar." When I came on deck, I saw by the ship a dozen small boats, each with a grown man rowing and one or two small boys, brown, athletic, and stripped except for a breech cloth. Some early rising passengers were tossing coins into the sea for the boys to dive after.

Three or four motor boats took us ashore to a stone pier, where we came upon the quaintest of quaint towns. Under electric signs and near fine-looking hotels we saw ox teams sledding trunks to a boat, a two-seated canopied sled drawn by oxen, mules pulling loads on crude sleds and carts, and ragged people coming and going or eyeing us. An advance agent of our company, planning the day for us, had lined up 25 or 30 automobiles of French and Italian design for our convenience.

The rugged Madeira Islands, long ago settled by the Portuguese, had a population of 200,000, mostly very poor and illiterate, using primitive methods of travel and cultivation, but industrious and peaceable. As our train of autos wound through the city, tooting and honking like a four-ring circus, it attracted much attention. Men, women, and children came out to see us pass — the children throwing us flowers and begging for money

— begging all over town, running along and behind our cars — hungry and underfed, for the people looked thin and haggard. Once when our car stopped, a little wizen-faced girl of four or five years put out a begging hand so appealingly that two men in our party gave her a handful of coins. Children and cripples congregated at the churches. Hungry and poor: the islands over-populated and nowhere for the people to go. The hillsides terraced for grapes — Madeira wine — and every square inch cultivated. Wonderful flowers and grapes everywhere! Also, bananas, palm trees, and other tropical plants.

The Rock of Gibraltar

Late that afternoon our ship left on a 500-mile cruise northeast to Gilbraltar, which we were due to pass about midnight; but, when a few passengers petitioned the captain to see the famous rock by daylight, he graciously ordered the boat to slow down and announced that we would pass there early the next morning. In close-up pictures the Rock of Gibraltar always looks stupendous and impressive; but when viewed from a distant, passing ship, I found it somewhat disappointing and unimpressive. Our ship did not stop there, but passed through the Strait of Gibraltar to the Mediterranean Sea on its 400-mile jaunt to Algiers, French Morocco, where we went ashore to find a beautiful and prosperous-looking sea-front, and to get glimpses of the Mohammedan world. For lunch we were taken to a hotel several miles inland over hot and dusty roads, and then, back to our ship for an uneventful 600-mile cruise over a smooth sea between the islands of Sicily and Sardinia to Naples, Italy.

After unsatisfactory trips to Pompeii, Capri, and the Blue Grottoes, I protested the poor management to our conductor, who was not personally responsible for the plans but who secured satisfactory adjustments thereafter from the company. One obstacle to good connections was inefficient telephone service. The next morning I visited the Naples Museum, where I could study a model of Pompeii and observe many fascinating relics — petrified bodies, statuary, mosaics, and utensils, excavated from the ancient Roman city buried under 15 to 20 feet of volcanic ash from Vesuvius, which is still a live volcano!

Three Days in Rome

From Naples we traveled by train to Rome, lodging in the Hotel Esperia for a three-day visit in the Eternal City, which fulfilled my expectations. In the Capuchin Church, where several rooms were adorned with the skeletons and bones of ancient monks, we felt so creepy and nauseous that a welcome change of scene was the Vatican with its ancient manuscripts, mediaeval relics, and imperial display of gold, statuary, and paintings. But the queen of museums was the Borghese with a fine mingling of choice paintings and statues. At St. Peter's Cathedral, impressive, beautiful, and costly, I was amused at a regulation which denied admission to bare-armed women. A few members of our party had not been forewarned.

On our free day there I bought reprints of pictures, views of Rome, and began a collection of madonnas, which are primarily a glorification of motherhood. In the afternoon by taxi I visited the English cemetery, where the remains of the poets, John Keats and Percy B. Shelley, are buried appropriately near Roman antiques.

Florence and Venice

At Florence, an inland city of the fine arts in central Italy, we visited the Duomo, Dante house, Savonarola spot, the Old Palace, and art galleries. My group stayed at the Hotel Porta Rossa, a former palace converted into a comfortable hotel with excellent service. The Brownings once lived in this city, rating it restful, artistic, and inspiring. I was disappointed to find so few relics of Dante, Italy's greatest poet. Seeking a small marble bust of him, I found none to my liking till I reached Venice. There I bought my favorite literary idol. In the English cemetery of Florence, I visited the tombs of Mrs. Browning, A. H. Clough, W. S. Landor, and Theodore Parker, an American.

In Venice the chief attractions were five-domed St. Mark's Cathedral, the Doges Palace, and the marine streets. In gondolas we passed under the Bridge of Sighs and the picturesque Rialto, where Shylock, in Shakespeare's "The Merchant of Venice," shocked the Christian world by lending money at interest! In the Italian cities, as in Madeira, were evidences of overpopulation, not so marked but distinctly observable in the wages paid for work and in the physical appearance of many children and workers. I wondered how all the people there could get enough to eat and something to wear.

Stresa to Nice

Passing through the rich valley of the Po River, we visited the resort city of Stresa on Lake Maggiore with its beautiful little islands made more beautiful by art. Spending one night in

Milan and viewing the handsome cathedral there, we passed through Genoa to the French frontier, where our passports and baggage were examined. Arriving in Nice, beautifully situated on the Mediterranean Sea and adorned with palm trees, our entire party of more than 100 stopped at the Regina Hotel.

Switzerland

Traveling up the valley of the Rhone, we lunched at Lyon, an ancient and attractive city; and in the afternoon we arrived for the night in Geneva, capital of the oldest modern republic and at that time seat, of the League of Nations. Surely, belligerent nations could hardly find a more suitable place to cool off and settle their heated controversies, because this handsome city, astride the Rhone at the west end of Lake Geneva in view of Mont Blanc in the icy Alps, is a famous center of culture, art, and light industries like watchmaking, prosperous, healthful, and beautiful. Though one could well spend a week there, we had time to visit only the Palace of Peace, the Woodrow Wilson Quai, and a few other points of historical or artistic interest. Harmonizing French, German, and Italian elements in its domain and befriending all peoples, Switzerland is one of the most civilized nations in the world.

Passing through several towns and 50 miles of fine wheat fields on the north side of Lake Geneva, we lunched at Montreux and visited the Castle of Chillon, widely publicized by Byron's narrative poem, "The Prisoner of Chillon." With much rain on fertile limestone soil, the entire region of cultivated farms and piny forests on the lower mountains was beautifully green and fresh as if newly created. By an ingenious, corkscrew, electric railway, we were uplifted from the lake and carried eastward through a truly fascinating and picturesque region of neat farms, clear lakes, deep gorges, and vacation resorts among the foothills of the majestic Alps to Interlaken for one day of sightseeing, and two August nights so cold that I gladly slept between feather beds in the giant icebox which is Switzerland! Seeing this wonderful region of cultivated or grazing lands, blue lakes, and green or white mountains — the Jungfrau in the eternal white of snow and ice — all so cool, fresh, varied, and beautiful, I declared that surely the Garden of Eden was here — here the Creator finished his work and rested on the seventh day! In Interlaken my conjecture was partly confirmed when I observed a garden and hotel named Eden!

Four Days at Paris

On Sunday, August 8, my birthday, we rested in Lucerne. The next morning, taking a fast train for Paris, we passed through fine wheat fields via Belfort and arrived at our destination at nine in the evening for a four-day visit in gay Paree, then sobered by fresh memories of the First World War. Our first trip included the Eiffel Tower, highest in the world, Napoleon's Tomb, and the Arch de Triomph, where the grave of France's Unknown Soldier is honored by a memorial flame. In the evening we enjoyed "Carmen" in the Opera Comique. The next day ten of us visited the Louvre, seeing the more important sculpture and painting, especially Leonardo da Vinci's "Mona Lisa", Rembrandt's "Bathsheba," and Greek and Roman sculpture including "The Venus of Milo" and "The Victory of Samothrace". One evening in the National Opera House we attended an excellent presentation of "Thais".

On our third day we toured the Battlefields about Rheims and Soissons, both mutilated by artillery bombardments. We entered the beautifully kept American cemetery at Chateau Thierry. We passed countless numbers of black German crosses and hundreds of English and Italian crosses at the graves. At one place the French, English, German, Italian, and American dead were buried in adjoining plots -- united in death! But how sad to see the visible signs of the numberless youthful dead!

On our last day we motored to the Versailles Palace, erected at great cost to please a vain old autocrat and preserved as a beautiful pile by the French government. Beautiful, worth seeing? Yes, but already too much has been written about it and I pass on. Back in Paris, I suffered my only mishap on the entire trip. By taxi I went shopping to a big store, bought a 600-franc gift to take home, got in a taxi to look for another shop, and in my searching and weariness left my gift on the seat of the taxi, which disappeared with my present. But I refused to talk or worry about the loss of the $17 spent for the gift. For diversion that evening I enjoyed seeing an excellent dwarf comedian at the Palace Theater.

Down the Rhine River

The next day, through Metz and Forbach, we traveled to Wiesbaden in Germany, a popular health resort, where we had a restful night. On the morrow we enjoyed a refreshing eight-hour boat trip down the Rhine River to Cologne. With an illustrated guide to the river, I was able to identify most of the famous castles and towns along the high river banks — castles in use and in ruins, and such famous towns as Mainz, Bingen, Koblenz, Remagen, and Bonn. Between the towns and cities were highly cultivated farms and terraced hillsides for vineyards.

A Look at Holland

Entering Holland at Venlo, we spent August 16 and 17 among the thrifty and well-fed Dutch. On our way to Amsterdam we passed through fine meadows and pastures where thousands of cattle and milk cows were grazing. Though I saw a few of the ancient windmills, I learned that steam and gasoline pumps were replacing them. At the much-publicized Isle of Marken we observed the simple homes and the quaint costumes of the fisher folk. Our car passed through an area five to ten feet below the level of the ocean, which strong dykes hold back and to which water from the land returns in elevated canals. About 10,000 acres were annually reclaimed from the sea, and a plan was afoot to drain all of the Zuyder Zee, a tremendous undertaking.

Amsterdam, nicknamed the Venice of the North, I enjoyed very much. At the American Hotel we had comfortable rooms and exquisite meals, the best of the tour. In covered buses on a rainy morning we toured the city, seeing one of many diamond cutting factories operating there, the Royal Palace, the Rijks-Museum with Rembrandt, Van Dyck, and Jan Steen masterpieces to charm the eye and mind, and a model residential district of the successful Dutch. I liked Holland and Amsterdam, and enjoyed my trip there, which included the Hague. The city of Amsterdam is well built, much of it on piles, with marine streets and bridges like Venice; it is clean, handsome, and prosperous. The people are industrious, alert, and intelligent. They patronize well-stocked bookstores and art shops. There was not so much fuss over cathedrals and religion as in Italy and France. How fitting that these liberal, industrious, economical, sea-going Dutch should establish the colony and city of New Amsterdam that became the great metropolis of New York!

After two satisfying days in Holland among the Dutch seafighters, who do much of their farming below the level of the ocean, we took a night boat for England over smooth waters that induced a quiet stomach and sound sleep. On the train to London we had a memorable British breakfast of porridge, hot coffee, bacon and eggs, and toasted bread. In London our entire party lodged at three small hotels on opposite street corners near the Victoria and Albert Museum. I was at the Leicester Court Hotel, formerly a palatial residence but converted in lean years into a private hotel with home-like accommodations. There I was filled with the peace and comfort I used to feel when a boy visiting my grandparents. I was the wanderer returned to the fireside at home.

London and Will Rogers

Ten of us spent our first afternoon in the manuscript and statuary departments of the British Museum. We viewed the precious manuscript of Anglo-Saxon *Beowulf*, dating from the eleventh century A. D., other old books, and many manuscripts by leading British authors. Among the classical statuary we gazed upon the famous Rosetta Stone, which enabled linguists to read Egyptian hieroglyphics, the Elgin marbles that stirred Keats' imagination, and many other relics. Later, I called at the Museum to check its Paulding possessions, and I found most of his books catalogued. About the same time, a few of us attended an English production of Ibsen's "Pillars of Society", the pillars being truth and justice, one of Ibsen's best plays.

On the second day our half of the party visited Piccadilly, St. Paul's Cathedral, London Bridge, and the Tower of London, which is an ancient prison where the royal jewels are now securely and happily incarcerated. We passed Dickens' Old Curiosity Shop, Johnson's Coffee House, Trafalgar Square, and the Parliament buildings on our way to Westminster Abbey, where a guide told us about the distinguished and the obscure entombed there, a few in upright positions, so precious is the free space. Is it any wonder that Shakespeare and Carlyle preferred to rest elsewhere on their backs! Just another mark of the greatness of these two authors! But the Abbey was not so large and impressive as the one that Irving's essay had conjured up in my imagination. In London, monuments to Americans are excessively scarce. In the Abbey are memorial tablets to Longfellow, Lowell, and W. H. Page. Near the Abbey is a handsome monument to Abraham Lincoln, and in the grounds of the National Gallery is a statue of George Washington, dwarfed by its surroundings.

We also visited Tate's Gallery of modern paintings including masterpieces of J. W. Turner, celebrated by John Ruskin in *Modern Painters*. Alone I looked up Thomas Carlyle's residence in Cheyne Row, which is now a Carlyle museum with many choice relics of Thomas and his wife, Jane Welsh, including Tommy's sound-proof study on the third floor. In the Victoria and Albert Museum I observed with special care the meteorites and the relics of prehistoric man, arranged in chronological order.

Though I liked the National Gallery's 1100 paintings, I preferred the adjoining National Portrait Gallery, where among 1200 portraits one could find many fine specimens of British manhood. Especially attractive was the collection of English authors, many of whose faces I had not seen before or whose poses were unfamiliar. Outstanding were those of Browning, Wordsworth, Carlyle, and Arnold; also, minor writers, like Gray, Walpole, William Godwin. and Froude. For this fine gallery I could spare only one short hour.

On Thursday evening, August 19, Miss Jane Taylor, our chaperone, and her sister, Dr. Macmillan, and I attended Cochran's Revue at the London Pavilion, which was a silly, dancing, singing, costume show with many fantastic and outlandish outfits intended to display the feminine form. Fortunately I was on this occasion saved from utter boredom by the American Will Rogers, who was the principal attraction and whom I saw and heard for the first time in the city of London.

This wit and entertainer came on the stage near the end of the show. He was greeted warmly, but in telling his first yarns, he seemed uncertain of himself and somewhat halting (perhaps that was part of his technique). But when he was encored time and again, his confidence improved, and his jokes on London and Americans were wildly received. He was easily "the hit" of the evening. He began by telling us who he was, likened himself to Bernard Shaw as always finding fault, and to James Barrie as an entertainer of children and adults with infantile minds. He said that Britain and the United States would always be friendly, because they can look at each other and laugh; that if he had been consulted, the problem of the war debt would have been settled long ago, because he would not have lent any money in the first place. He suggested that traffic problems be solved by letting people travel east on Tuesdays, Thursdays, and Saturdays, and west on the remaining days of the week. And so on for 30 or 40 minutes, a stimulating and original feast of witty remarks, couched in somewhat slangy, disconnected English by a sharp observer of current events. Though he shrewdly flattered the British at the expense of the Americans, everyone enjoyed the fun and wit of the American cowboy from Claremore, Oklahoma.

One late afternoon in central London I saw thousands of shop and office workers going home. I observed them sharply, and decided that most of them were smaller than the average American, shorter and less vigorous. Centuries of the limitations of city life could account for the difference, if it exists. These thousands also were wearing wool hats or caps in August, ready for rain at any time, because in England it can rain a good shower most unceremoniously — fickle, fickle weather! In close and rapid succession, sunshine, clouds, and rain.

In St. George's Chapel at Windsor Castle I was fascinated by a unique and memorable piece of impressive statuary named the Princess Charlotte Cenotaph. The central figure is the prostrate form of the Princess, completely veiled and surrounded by a group of four mourning figures, kneeling at an altar and completely veiled so skillfully that they look lifelike. Above the deceased Princess and the mourners is an ascending human form accompanied by two angels, one carrying an infant. Behind the ascending group two flowing marble curtains open at the center, as if to a tomb. This original and magical white marble monument is eloquent of grief and hope and the mystery of life and death.

Oxford, Stratford, and Windermere

Since Oxford was not on our regular tour, forty of us petitioned the London office to take us there by a special car on our way to Birmingham. For an additional fee of five dollars we were able to visit the famous Oxford University consisting of twenty-six separate colleges with beautiful campuses scattered throughout the city. With a guide we walked through the labyrinthine grounds. Though the central library and the dormitories were closed, we viewed dining halls and chapels adorned with paintings and stained glass windows. One fine example was a most beautiful stained glass window of symbolical figures, namely, Christ adored by the three graces and the four virtues, so light and graceful that they seemed to be floating up to heaven!

From Birmingham, an industrial city, our party motored to Stratford to visit Shakespeare's birthplace, the home of Ann Hathaway, and the poet's tomb in Stratford Church. The visit caused Ann to grow in my estimation. I had always thought of her cottage as a hovel and herself as socially below William; but judging by the handsome Hathaway home, the grounds, the furniture, and other household effects, I concluded that her family had plenty of starch and feathers. Then, too, in choosing William and securely attaching him to her chariot, she proved to the world that she was a good judge of men. Along the paths leading to her thatch-covered home, lovely flowers smiled at us as I suppose they smiled and Ann smiled at William Shakespeare more than three centuries ago.

From Stratford we drove through an attractive farm region to Rugby, where we boarded a train for Windermere in the celebrated Lake Region of England. The next day by buses we visited Wordsworth's Rydal Mount and Grasmere, crossed the divide to Keswick, once the home of Coleridge and Southey, and in the afternoon, returned to Windermere for the night. Beyond any question this home and haunt of William Wordsworth and the inspiration of his best nature poetry is a beautiful region with an enchanting mingling of fresh lakes, bare hills, and green countryside. However, the bare-topped hills disappointed me who am accustomed to Virginian hills and mountains wooded to the the very tops. Many sections of the United States would have inspired Wordsworth as they did Bryant, Longfellow, Whittier, and Whitman.

Edinburgh to Glasgow

The next afternoon we went by train across Cumberland and Scotland to Edinburgh. The following day we visited the principal tourist attractions: Edinburg Castle with drill grounds and St. Margaret's Chapel (built about 1100 A. D.), art galleries, parks, churches, college, and shops. Undoubtedly Edinburgh is a beautiful city. Princess Street facing the Castle and the principal park, I should rate the most beautiful I ever saw. Looking west, one sees handsome business buildings on the north side, and on the south side the long park with flower beds in the foreground, the Scott Monument looking like a cathedral steeple; then statues, fountains, trees, the two impressive art galleries, and to the far left, Edinburgh Castle looking down upon the bewitching scene. Yes, the Scotch love the beautiful as well as the true and the good. I am proud that some of their fine blood got into my veins!

From Edinburgh we motored through purpled heather hills to the Trossachs, which are charmingly depicted in Scott's poetic story, "The Lady of the Lake". On the way there our bus driver, a real Scotchman, stopped so often for alcoholic refreshments that he developed a mania to pass all other buses, sometimes rounding sharp curves on what seemed like fewer than four wheels! Once again I lodged a stiff protest with our conductor and a request to eliminate the chariot races. On our free afternoon a few of us made a special automobile trip to Abbotsford, the baronial home of Sir Walter Scott, weaver of popular verse and wizard of romantic novels. His fine library and study are preserved as he left them, and on the grounds we saw some of his young descendants.

On Saturday, August 28, we traveled by train down the coast to Glasgow, Scotland's chief commercial and shipping center, where we boarded the *Cameronia* for our return trip to New York. Passing north of Ireland into the Atlantic Ocean, we soon encountered rough seas on the edge of a storm area, so a petty officer told me, belittling the disturbance. However, becoming quite seasick, I was confined to my cabin for two or three days. I lost weight, and did not fully recover till our boat neared its destination. So my return was a complete reversal of my pleasant outward journey. My journal I was unable to finish till months later. But, arriving in New York on Saturday, September 5, I picked up the proof sheets of my thesis and boarded a train for Tulsa, Oklahoma, arriving there just in time for the college registration. Soon afterwards, the manager of radio station KVOO Tulsa invited me to give a radio lecture on my trip, called "America and Europe Compared", which is reproduced in the next chapter.

CHAPTER 15

America and Europe Compared

Radio Lecture as given on KVOO, Tulsa, Oklahoma,
Thursday, November 4, 1926.

Ladies and Gentlemen:

DURING the past summer I spent two months in six European countries, and from Tulsa to Tulsa, Oklahoma, traveled about 14,000 miles. Crossing the Atlantic Ocean by way of the Madeira Islands, Gibraltar, and Algiers in North Africa, our party landed at Naples, Italy, and moved northward through Italy to France, Switzerland, Germany, Holland, and then to England. At the end of August, we left Glasgow, Scotland, for New York City. An interesting feature of the trip is that I saw wheat harvests all summer — Oklahoma's in June, Pennsylvania's and Italy's in July, the French and English in August, and the Scotch at the end of August.

So many Americans go abroad nowadays that there is no longer any particular distinction in making such a trip. Last season more than 500,000 visited Europe. In fact, they are getting the reputation of being the greatest travelers in the world, and elsewhere, if an incident I heard can be accepted. As the story runs, several of them were one day visiting the volcano

Vesuvius, and were looking down at the boiling lava in the crater. When one of the Americans remarked to his companions that the fiery scene reminded him very much of the infernal regions, an English lady, overhearing the comparison, exclaimed to her companion, "My, how these Americans do travel!"

One of the principal pleasures in traveling is the joy of coming home, and I have been interested in comparing our country with some of the European countries so as to make clear certain differences in appearance, resources, and living conditions. Though my conclusions are based upon somewhat limited observation and are therefore subject to restriction or modification, still I believe they are fairly trustworthy, because I submitted them to persons who know Europe more intimately and who are in substantial agreement with me.

In making a comparison of Europe and America, one should, of course, bear in mind that the European nations are old nations with an old civilization deeply rooted in the past. Modern Italy, for example, stands on the impressive ruins of the Roman Empire, and even in England one finds many remnants of the Roman civilization. One should remember also that Europe is densely populated. For example, in Italy and Germany for every square mile of land there are more than three hundred people; in Great Britain there are about four hundred and sixty people for every square mile. But in the United States there are only forty persons for every square mile. In other words, the European nations are about ten times more densely populated than the United States.

With these facts in mind, I wish now briefly to point out three aspects or ways in which Europe seems to surpass the United States; two in which they are about equal; and five or six in which the United States surpasses Europe.

So far as I could observe, Europe is superior to America in magnificent and beautiful cathedrals, patiently and lovingly erected by a devout people in the course of centuries. In the medieval period city competed with city in trying to surpass each other in the building of cathedrals, and their efforts were blessed by the popes. The most famous are the splendid St. Peter's in Rome, St. Paul's in London, Notre Dame in Paris, those at Rheims, Cologne and Milan, and hundreds elsewhere smaller and less well known. Most impressive of all is that at Cologne, a huge and towering pile of stone supported on the inside by one hundred lofty stone pillars each ten or twelve feet in diameter. But for all their costly magnificence, they are not nearly so serviceable or well fitted for instructional purposes as many American

churches of which we hear very little. For example, the First
Presbyterian Church here in Tulsa is for all practical religious
purposes superior to the towering Cologne cathedral. The renowned St. Peter's in Rome for all its beauty and Roman-like
magnificence was so enormously costly as to help bring on the
ecclesiastical abuses that precipitated the Protestant Reformation.

Europe is superior also in art galleries. For centuries the
great painters and sculptors of Europe, encouraged by an appreciative public and in many cases indeed supported by wealthy
patrons, or the church, or the government, have vied with one
another in creating objects of renowned and treasured beauty.
The finest collections are in Rome, Florence, Paris, Amsterdam,
and London. But American dollars have enticed many specimens
to American museums and art galleries, native artists prosper,
and so in Washington, New York, Chicago, and elsewhere, many
Americans can satisfy their love of art works without making a
trip to Europe.

In the third place, Europe easily surpasses the United States
in historic and legendary associations. For many centuries the
facts and fables and remains of history have been slowly accumulated. How rich are Rome, Florence, Paris, London, and Stratford-
on-Avon with the records of great events and great person-
ages of the ancient world! How the banks of the Rhine, the
Tiber, and the Thames bristle with crumbling or renovated
castles each the center of historical or romantic legends! Fortunately, the U. S. has some associations and attractions of this kind,
but Europe is superior.

In two aspects, namely, in natural beauty and in attractive
cities, it seems to me that the United States and Europe are
about equal. No less an authority than Washington Irving, after
living for seventeen years in Europe and seeing it thoroughly,
declared that the mountains, rivers, lakes, and countryside in
America, though unheralded and unsung by travelers, are just
as lovely, just as beautiful, and just as worthy of admiration as
any similar scenes in Europe, with Switzerland perhaps excepted.
Surely the lakes of New York, the Appalachian valleys and
wooded hills, the prairies, the Great Lakes, Yellowstone, and the
Far West are worthy of our pride and praise. Even in Oklahoma,
I have seen landscapes to delight the heart of a Wordsworth or a
Scott.

And American cities, though new and somewhat uniform,
compare favorably with those of Europe. All things considered,
Washington is as beautiful as Rome or Paris, and a much more
desirable place to live in. New York and Chicago are as impres-

sive as London, or more so, and certainly much easier to get around in. Why, in London, even the taxicab drivers get lost, so crooked and irregular are the London streets! And for physical attractiveness Tulsa may be classed with Florence, and for energy is her superior.

I wish now to consider some ways in which the United States surpasses Europe, keeping in mind that my ideas are somewhat tentative and subject to amendment, if need be. I am not at all dogmatic, and rather expect that some people will disagree with me.

But in reference to the first point, namely, American superiority in natural resources of almost all kinds, I am confirmed in my opinion. Our country, being virtually self-sustaining, enjoys a tremendous advantage over most foreign nations. I mean that the United States has great supplies of coal, iron, copper, lead, petroleum, cotton, timber, wheat, corn, meat, and dairy products. In contrast, Italy has little or no coal, or iron, no petroleum, and little timber. Were there no petroleum in the United States, Tulsa would still be a small town, and the streets of our cities would not have the traffic problems created by the 18,000,000 motor cars owned by Americans. The wealth of the United States is astounding, and confers upon the people of the country both an opportunity and a responsibility. Consider these figures taken from a series of articles written by Isaac F. Marcosson and published last summer in the Saturday Evening Post, namely,

That the United States with six per cent of the world's population and about six per cent of the land surface of the earth possesses one-half of the world's gold supply. With great natural resources developed by an energetic people, by commerce, and by the trade currents set in motion in our favor by the Great War, the United States has become enormously wealthy. Please consider also that annually our country produces:

38 per cent of the world's coal output,
40 per cent of the world's lead out put,
46 per cent of the world's pig iron,
52 per cent of the world's lumber,
25 per cent of the world's wheat,
30 per cent of the world's other cereals,
55 per cent of the world's cotton,
58 per cent of the world's paper,
38 per cent of the world's installed water power,
58 per cent of the world's telephones and telegraphs,

33 per cent of the world's railroads,
70 per cent of the world's petroleum, and
83 per cent of the world's autos and motor trucks.

Without these great resources, we should have little to develop, and far less national wealth.

Again, the United States is on the whole better and more wisely governed. Our form of government, a federal union, has the deserved confidence of the American people, and thus far has proved itself to be sufficiently strong, flexible, and efficient. The great emergency of the World War was met with scarcely a slip in the machinery of government. Great powers, war powers, were conferred upon the President and executive boards without endangering the liberties of the people. Far-reaching reforms, like woman suffrage and prohibition, have been launched. Most significant it is that for a hundred years many nations have copied our form of government; most recent is Germany. We have profited from all the experiments in government that the old nations tried, and have set a new style in a new land free from age-old abuses and customs.

In the third place, our school system is superior in reaching all classes and maintaining a high average of intelligence. Americans may differ in politics, in religion, and in color, but in education they are a unit, they agree; they are wedded to the principle and practice of educating both the young and the mature when they want an education. While our system is far from perfection and tolerates abuses, still it has accomplished wonders. Our grade schools, our high schools, our colleges, our universities are the best in the world, and we are justly proud of them. Of course, Europe has excellent schools and colleges; but, if cathedrals and art galleries are the glory of Europe, then our colleges and universities, illuminating the mind of man, are the glory and pride of the United States. In this connection, it should be noted also that our books and magazines help greatly to build up the intelligence of our people. While the Europeans are great consumers of printed matter, especially the Germans, English, Swiss, and French, the Americans are even more eagerly prying into the mysteries of science, literature, philosophy, and religion.

Again, the United States excels in business organization and in inventiveness. American railroads, telephones, telegraphs, factories, and machines are probably the best in the world. Evidence of this appeared recently in the New York Times Book Review. In scores of books on the United States, German authors and observers have recognized the supremacy of the U. S. in business efficiency, and some of the them have strongly advised that German industry be Americanized. It is significant also that a settlement of the Franco-German reparation problem carries the name of an American, Vice-President Dawes, and that American engineers and experts of all kinds are much sought after in Europe.

The United States is superior in sobriety and energy. Say what you will, the American are more sober and more energetic than Europeans. They accomplish more in less time. They have more initiative; they like work. The settlement and development of the United States is one of the wonders of the modern world. Never before were wildernesses and prairies converted to the uses of man so quickly as here. Roosevelt called part of it "The Winning of the West." Substantial cities have sprung up in a few decades. Admiring our ways, millions of foreigners were attracted here before limits were placed upon immigration.

It is also recognized that in the comforts and conveniences of life, in all that pertains to the home, the shop, the office, the factory, the farm, the Americans are most fortunate. It is our good fortune to live in an earthly paradise, with a beneficent sun shining down upon a fair and prosperous land, filled with the good things of life, a land literally flowing with milk and honey. All classes of Americans live comfortably and enjoy unusual opportunities for self-cultivation and self-development. American living conditions are so attractive as to arouse the envy of the world.

In conclusion, my friends, let me say that, though we are richly blessed and share the favor of heaven, there are yet weak spots or indications of a falling away from our high estate. As in the story of a certain rich man in the Bible, our fields have produced abundantly, our barns are full and new ones are needed, and we are inclined to eat, drink, and be merry, forgetting perhaps at times that our souls must eventually render an account. I refer to such weak spots as corruption in public office on a large scale, involving cabinet members, and even whole states, such as Illinois and Pennsylvania. And we show little vision in our foreign policy, but conduct ourselves so as to offend rather than to befriend other peoples. Some of our public men lack courage and vision; they cannot see beyond the borders of our own land. As a people, we are wasteful and extravagant, enjoying the fat years and taking no thought for the lean years that may come our way. Generous and charitable though we are, we are also sometimes selfishly indifferent like the rich man in the parable.

For us a fitting prayer is Kipling's famous lines:

> If, drunk with sight of power, we loose
> Wild tongues that have not Thee in awe —
> Such boasting as the Gentiles use,
> Or lesser breeds without the Law —
> Lord God of hosts be with us yet,
> Lest we forget — lest we forget!
>
> For heathen heart that puts her trust
> In reeking tube and iron shard —
> All valiant dust that builds on dust,
> And guarding calls not Thee to guard.
> For frantic boast and foolish word,
> Thy Mercy on Thy People, Lord.

Printed December, 1926.

After this introductory report, I spoke at the same station on "Italy and Mussolini," "Switzerland and the League of Nations," and in response to requests from my radio listeners on "See America First."

CHAPTER 16

Progress in Adversity

IN THE summer of 1927 John D. Finlayson, Th. D., a native of Canada, succeeded Acting President Dill, with the title of chancellor and a salary double that paid his predecessors. He came to Tulsa after a short term as president of the University of Wichita. Youthful and ambitious, boastful and aggressive, he succeeded in selling himself to our Board of Trustees, and the following year with pretentious formality he was inaugurated. His first mistake was to get an unsatisfactory secretary. Though I sought to maintain friendly relations with the flashy newcomer, that was frequently quite difficult. For example, in March of his first year, in getting an additional English instructor, the chancellor carelessly engaged a young woman whose letters soon convinced me that she was not fitted to teach English either in high school or college. I showed him two of her letters with 24 elementary blunders clearly checked, hoping that he would take the initiative in dropping her, but he left that to me. So, I drafted the following letter to him:

April 24, 1928

Dear Dr. Finalyson:

I have carefully re-examined the two letters of March 23 and April 13, 1928, which I received from Miss V — L — and which I showed to you a few days ago. I regret to state that her two letters contain almost all the errors that a sub-freshman in English is likely to make — errors in sentence construction, choice of words, spelling, punctuation, tense of verb, capitalization, and omission of necessary words. Moreover, the construction and tone of the letters show an imperfect, halting, uncertain, and inadequate control of written English. Since her letters contain no fewer than twenty-four plain errors in technique, it is evident that she can not be depended upon to correct, revise, and proofread the manuscripts of students in English composition.

It appears, also, that the recommendations supplied by the University of Wisconsin were somewhat misleading, though most of the instructors can claim that they recommended Miss L — for a high-school position, not for college work. Surely, there is a wide gap between their statements and her actual performance in the letters. When our freshmen submit such horrible letters, we require that they be carefully revised and rewritten.

In her proposed coming to the department of English, I anticipate nothing but grief for Miss L —, for her students numbering perhaps more than one hundred, and for the University of Tulsa. I am certain that a readjustment is necessary in order to protect and conserve the best interest of all who are concerned. A course or two done in the Summer School at the University of Wisconsin will make very little change in the case, because the faults are deep-seated and exceedingly difficult to eradicate. It is my candid opinion that Miss L — needs to do much intensive work in composition and literature in order to qualify even as a fairly competent instructor of high-school English.

With all kindliness for her and with the best interests of our students clearly in mind, I must request and recommended that Miss L — be given the privilege of speedily resigning from her work in English, because to resign now will be much better for her than to be forced out in disgrace some time next year. I feel sure that she will recognize the wisdom of this course, and the proverbial stitch in time will save perhaps ninety and nine.

Very cordially yours,
Head of English Department

That forceful letter led to her resignation, and I was then privileged to negotiate for a competent instructor, though the mishap, I am sure, peeved the inexperienced administrator. A little later his unwise and haughty dealings with the students incited an outburst from them. A large group of 96 incensed students petitioned the Board, urging it to investigate the new administration, asserting that the University needed a man more in sympathy with its ideals and purpose and "one possessed with a more agreeable personality", and declaring that their only aim was "to regain the harmonious spirit among the students, faculty, and business men", which the present administration had lost in a single year. Though the Board did nothing, the students had evaluated the chancellor correctly. Two years later, after he had replaced several members of the faculty with his own adherents, he had the audacity to claim that these changes had markedly stimulated the older members of the faculty. "The English Department", he wrote to the Board, "reports 20 per cent better work than heretofore," although I had made no such report. Thus, he sought to conceal his own mistake in engaging an incompetent English instructor.

With such an administrator to deal, it was almost inevitable that our relations would go from bad to worse. Within two years I was heartily despising the man under whom I was unfortunately serving. In the end he undermined my prospects and hopes at the University of Tulsa.

Ill Health

In the fall of 1928 I became much concerned about my own health. I had a chill, followed by fever, with pains in my back and pelvic region. Dr. Malcolm McKellar diagnosed my malady as a pelvic infection originating with the prostate gland, aggravated by septic tonsils and infected teeth. After the extraction of my tonsils in December, 1928, my recovery was slow and incomplete. Though I was carrying a heavy load of work, especially in 1931-32 when one instructor was away on leave of absence, I was physically weak and underweight by several pounds. In the course of four years I visited this physician seventeen times for treatment and advice, but I continued my work, conserving my strength in every way possible. Later I became convinced that carbon-monoxide poisoning from a defective gas stove in my basement college office affected my physical and mental health to such an extent that my teaching became laborious and even a little walking was mysteriously tiring. Since doctors knew little or nothing of this modern hazard from the widespread use of gas and gasoline, I made a careful study of it and wrote an article, called "Gas and Gasoline Hazards", which was published in *The Texas Outlook* for January, 1938, and to which I will refer again later in this narrative. Yet, neither the new dean nor the chancellor showed any real interest in my health problem except to use it adversely against me, as we shall see.

Occasionally I had charge of our chapel program. I find that on November 12, 1928, I offered the following prayer at our Armistice Service, which clearly reflects my study of Dante and my hatred of war:

"Our Heavenly Father, Creator and Preserver, who set the stars in heaven, who established the earth, and who, in love and wisdom, made man and gave him power and dominion over himself and the earth, we come to Thee on this Armistice Day to hallow Thy name and to pray that Thy kingdom of peace and good will may be fully established in our minds and hearts and in the minds and hearts of Thy people in all nations.

"Deliver us, O God, from pride, from envy, from anger, from sloth, and avarice, which are the causes of strife and discord: but fill our hearts with humility, fraternal love, good will, zeal, and liberality, which promote peace and harmony. Purge us, we pray, of that spirit which led Cain to slay his brother Abel, and fill us with the spirit of Christ, who taught us to love our fellowmen and do good unto them.

"Today, in distress and sorrow, we would remember the battle fields of the world reddened by human blood, but especially do we remember the millions of homes desolated by the Great World War, the millions of young men mutilated, sacrificed, and buried on the plains of Europe, the millions of fathers and mothers left desolate, the sisters, wives, and sweethearts inexpressibly saddened by the infamy and brutishness of war. Remembering these, may we all highly resolve to nurse the war spirit no more, but to think of peace and justice and to seek after them zealously for ourselves and all men everywhere. May this era of peace and social justice begin in our own daily practice, extend to all the world, and last forever.

"We thank Thee, O God, that the great Christian nations have pledged themselves to abandon war as a national policy and have solemnly agreed to settle their controversies in future, not by the sword, but by arbitration and the dictates of right reason and Thy will. Bless this striving after peace and good will, and dedicate our minds, hearts, and lives to Thy service, and to justice, righteousness, and peace. Amen."

The Miscellany

As already indicated, in May, 1929, my literary students began the publication of a small, annual magazine of student verse and prose, called the *Miscellany*. Almost any type of worthy, original material was acceptable, though restricted in length: short stories to 1,500 words; essays, feature articles, and speeches to 800; editorials and book reviews to 500; descriptions and letters to 200 or 300 words; and poems to 60 lines. As instructor of poetics, I was specially interested in the verse and suggested that the poem winning first place should begin each number. Here is the list of authors and poems in the lead over a six-year period:

1929: Mary Cornelia Hartshorne's *Thanksgiving Hymn*.
1930: Doris L. Allen's *Heart Songs*.
1931: Doris Lorraine Allen's *I Am in Love with Fleeting Things*.
1932: Rosemary Hoffman's *Youth's Cry*.
1933: Rosemary Hoffman's *Metamorphosis*.
1934: Marguerite Griffith's *I Would be Remembered*.

Though all of these were girls with two names repeated, the boys also won places in the verse contributions. Reid Swindler, a gifted music student, though blind from childhood, wrote good verse, graduated with high honors, and thrilled his hearers with organ selections. Kermit C. Shelby, then an employee of an oil firm, who later placed his short stories in *The Saturday Evening Post*, wrote for the 1934 *Miscellany* a fine poem, "I Have Found Love", which I quote here:

I thought that love would never come to me —
That Fate had slated me to live alone
Leading a robot life, existing, breathing,
Performing endless duties. Yet never living really;
A moving something, not dead, but not alive:
A restless atom, drifting without meaning.

But now I know the joy of sharing love,
Of binding intimacy brought forth by sharing sorrow.

I am a sleeper, roused from lethargy,
To find new worlds, new ecstasy unending,
To know at last why people are created.
I am alive; I walk strange paths of bliss;
New beauties come my way.
I have found love.

Among the contributors, Mrs. Marie Mott, a gifted balladist, writing both prose and verse, later published her verses in periodicals and book form; Henry T. Chambers was also successful in reaching the newspapers and periodicals, earning enough to fire his ambition; Alvin DuVall became a journalist, and Edgar A. Albin, a professor of art at the University of Arkansas. Ben Henneke is now, I think, teaching speech at the University of Tulsa. The second *Miscellany*, edited by Dolores Mary Silsby and containing my picture, was graciously dedicated to me as "friend, advisor, and critic, who has at all times encouraged and aided the literary students at the University of Tulsa".

Cousin Mary's Poetry

About the same time I became acquainted with my mother's first cousin, Mrs. Mary Erwin Overholt, then living at Fayetteville, Arkansas. As already shown, she and my mother had grown up together at Mill Gap, Virginia, but were separated when Cousin Mary and her husband emigrated to Missouri and Arkansas. Though she was then in her seventies, she was very much alive and lived to be nearly 97. When I learned that she liked to write verses, I investigated and in her manuscripts I discovered many fine poems she had composed through the years. I was overjoyed to learn that she had this gift and I praised her work so convincingly that her children agreed to publish it privately under the title of *Year in, Year Out, at Echoes* (1934), the name of her lovely home on the border of town. This belated recognition of her talent so stimulated her gift that in the next two decades three more small volumes were published, making her the poetic genius of the family.

In *The Arkansas Gazette* for March 4, 1951, I briefly reviewed her four volumes of verse — nearly 500 pages with 400 titles, celebrating the mountains, rivers, trees, birds, flowers and people of Arkansas and treating all aspects of her active, cheerful life as mother, teacher, observer, thinker, and poet. I mentioned "Farewell to Red River" as one of her best poems, noted her vein of humor mixed with wisdom, and quoted the lovely lines —

The robin sings when it's raining,
The mockingbird sings in the sun,
But the whippoorwill sings in the moonlight
After the day is done.

Reviews and Articles

Besides writing occasional book reviews for *The Tulsa Tribune* and special articles for periodicals, I was invited in September, 1930, by Allen Johnson, editor of *Dictionary of American Biography*, to contribute a 1200-word article on James Kirke Paulding, which I prepared and submitted the following January. This *Dictionary* in 22 volumes was made possible by a large contribution from Adolph S. Ochs of the *New York Times* and engaged the services of over 2,000 specialists in American biography and history. My thesis on Paulding qualified me for the assignment, supplemented by my rating in *Who's Who in America*.

About the same time I began an intensive study of *shall* and *will* in modern usage, which became my topic at a meeting of Oklahoma teachers of English and grew into a careful article published in the College Edition of *The English Journal* (October, 1936). This investigation of a puzzling problem in usage was the most difficult I ever tackled and I reached firm conclusions that simplified my teaching of the words. My article and the contributions of other scholars have in 25 years so clarified and liberalized the meaning and usage of our future auxiliaries as to be recognized by most grammarians and lexicographers. The chief improvement is the recognition of *will* as an appropriate auxiliary for the simple future with all three persons. Since this usage was secure for the second and third persons, the battle ground was the first person. My conclusion was: for the informal or simple future, use *will* with all three persons; for the formal or emphatic future, use *shall* with all three persons. I should add that Leonard's *Current English Usage* (1932) encouraged my own heretical beliefs in English grammar.

Raising English Standards

When I came to Oklahoma, a movement was on foot to raise the English standards of accomplishment in the high schools and colleges. At a meeting of the Oklahoma Education Conference in February, 1924, I read a paper on "Definite Relations between High-School and College English". I asserted that, to begin wisely, we should discard three delusions regarding our work, namely, the practice of using literature to glorify war and the war spirit, the tendency to regard physical work as unworthy or unfitting any one for education, and the practice of permitting any "flapper" or athletic hero to attempt English instruction regardless of their qualifications. With these delusions cleared away, I said, we may hope to co-ordinate our efforts by preventing needless breaks or uneven standards between high-school and college English, by striving for a better understanding of each other's province and special problems, by treating composition as a thought process to transmute our experience and knowledge, by emphasizing the practical uses of composition as in letters, by stimulating interest in current events, by teaching American Literature as a main support of our democracy, and by avoiding fussy, mechanical, pedantic methods of instruction. "We must remember", I declared, "that all true literature is the spiritual inheritance of the race, profitable for self-development, for knowledge, for correction, and doctrine; it is a rich fountain of ideals, traditions, thoughts, and aspirations". In fact, this paper was a summary of my philosophy of English materials and methods.

In the following years the Oklahoma heads of college English departments met at least once annually to devise better plans for Freshman English. We agreed to give a uniform freshman test and to place very weak students in subfreshman sections till they were fitted to do the regular course. We also kept in touch with the leaders in high-school English and later arranged to let Prof. J. W. Shepherd of the education department of the University of Oklahoma serve as co-ordinator and gather English data from the schools. In this work I was closely associated with Professor T. H. Brewer and S. R. Hadsell of the University of Oklahoma, Dr. W. F. DeMoss of Oklahoma A. and M. College, and other heads of college English departments. They were real scholars and my good friends.

For the year 1933-34 I was honored with the presidency of the Oklahoma Council of Teachers of English. Among my fellow workers my efforts had been well received. Besides a good deal of additional correspondence, my principal tasks in this position were to preside at a meeting of our Executive Committee in March, 1933, and to plan for a luncheon and general session of our English teachers on February 9, 1934, both events being in Oklahoma City. For speakers I engaged Dr. W. S. Campbell (Stanley Vestal) to address the group on "Advising Young Writers" and President A. Linscheid of the State Teachers College at Ada, to speak on "English, the Master Subject". A committee reported on the revision of the high school English curriculum, and our delegates to a recent meeting of the National Council of

English Teachers told of their impressions and new methods. About 400 English teachers with their friends attended our general session, which came off smoothly and agreeably and ended my presidential duties except that of acquainting my successor with the details of this English organization.

From time to time I induced the college to engage lecturers and living poets to address our students. Among these I recall especially Rollo W. Brown, who spoke on the writer's art and opportunity, and two poets, Bliss Carman, who was a Canadian of considerable merit and distinction, and Edwin Markham, then a venerable personage, who in 1899 had achieved international fame with his call for social justice in "The Man with the Hoe," which was followed by "Lincoln, the Man of the People".

The University of Tulsa in 1928 relinquished control by the Presbyterian Church and became an independent, non-sectarian institution, governed by a self-perpetuating board of 36 trustees. This change tended to liberalize the college and encouraged non-Presbyterians to contribute more freely to its support. In the same year the School of Petroleum Engineering was started in an old frame house. The next year, while the three new buildings were under construction, the Board put on a campaign for $1,550-000 in additional funds for endowment and construction, which, colliding with the Depression, was only partly successful. Skelly stadium was started but not fully paid for. With the collapse of the New York stock market in the fall of 1929, many rich Tulsans either lost heavily or were impoverished. I heard that Mr. W. G. Skelly was saved from bankruptcy by his friend, Waite Phillips, who had lately sold his extensive oil holdings for cash, and weathered the financial crash successfully. After our student registrations and salaries had held up well for about two years of the Depression, they began to spiral downward sharply.

Employment Hazards

The session of 1931-32 was hazardous for me. Since one of my English Instructors was away on leave for graduate study, I tried to carry on without a substitute, anticipating a drop in registration, which failed to develop. Giving two freshman sections to a speech instructor, I discontinued one advanced course and added one to my already full load. Thus, with 18 teaching hours per week, my own registration ran up to 204 students. Being in subnormal health, I soon felt the weight of a crushing load, and, giving up all special activities and conserving my strength, I got through the first semester, though on a few occasions I let my classes out before the end of the class period.

The act of teaching was laborious and even my voice was somewhat undependable. In the second semester I lightened my load somewhat and finished the year, taking care to acquaint the dean with my health problem. That very year the chancellor announced that my absent instructor would not return though he had been definitely assured of continued employment. Stressing our need of him and our obligation to him, I succeeded in having his contract renewed, even though the finances of the college rather than of my department were getting in bad shape under the chancellor's rash leadership.

In the spring of 1932 the Finlayson administration decided to teach the faculty a thing or two by putting on a Teacher Rating Test with members of the senior class acting as judges. Dean L. S. McLeod either secured elsewhere or cooked up a two-page questionnaire monstrosity under twenty heads or teaching traits with a scoring apparatus of one to five, but only four scoring spaces. Using one of these scoring sheets for each of his instructors, the seniors were asked to reduce teaching skills to a mathematical formula or standard. If such a scheme were properly prepared and honestly administered, it might have some slight value for supervisors. When I heard of this maneuver, I reminded my students that I had lately been working under difficulties and I have reason to think that my students, well disposed toward me, made allowance for my ill health and overload of teaching, because in the fall of 1932 the editor of *The Collegian* circulated his own questionnaire, which rated me as one of the seven most popular instructors on the campus. (During World War I an Army Test had placed me in the upper half of the Engineering Faculty at Cincinnati).

Finally, however, in the fall of 1932 the dean reported the results of the spring test to the teachers individually with a letter of transmittal emanating the superior wisdom inculcated by an objective test of qualities not susceptible of mathematical evaluation. In general, instructors with small classes and reputations for easy grading led the procession, as one might have anticipated. Some of the best instructors in the college including this writer competed for the lowest ratings. On the report made to me I showed the dean two grave blunders in tabulating the totals — an obvious error of 27 percent affecting my report adversely. After a lapse of 22 years I have scrutinized the Rating Scale thoroughly and am morally certain that faulty placing of Arabic figures on the sheets almost certainly led to grave errors in tabulation. For example, what looks like a record of 2.4 and 3.6 is actually only 1.4 and 2.6. This misleading ambiguity was oc-

casioned by placing five numbers on a four-unit scale and ignoring the fact that units of measure on every measuring stick and
on every clock face are placed at the completion of the unit and
not at its beginning. On this rating scale 2 was placed where 1
should be and 3 was placed where 2 should be. To illustrate:

1	2	3	4	5	(wrong)
0	1	2	3	4	(right)

My protests then and later to the dean and chancellor that
something was radically wrong were unavailing. That same year
the chancellor had sought and received a special grant of authority from the Board to reorganize the staff for economy, as he
claimed. He had blanket authority to do pretty much anything
he wanted to do. Armed with this grant of power and the falsi-
fied ratings, in March of 1933 he belatedly notified me that the
"best interests" of the college and his economy measures required my resignation, but I did not complacently resign. The
chancellor was too late. Under the terms of my employment,
buttressed by previous board action, my position was secure for
the next term at least. Then I engaged an attorney to advise me
and protect my interests in court, if necessary. Together we
drafted a letter to "little baldy" threatening to sue unless my
rights were recognized. Within 24 hours the chancellor offered
me a settlement for the next year, which, when reduced to writing, I accepted. Thus I weathered one more year of the depression, though my salary in four years had declined fifty per cent.
My proposal that the work of my department be prorated, allowing each instructor three-fourths time, was rejected, though
similar practices were followed in other departments and elsewhere.

The following tabulation shows how my salary including
summerschool and extension payments varied over the ten-year
period of the great depression:

In Oklahoma		In Texas	
1929-30	$3724	1934-35	$1880
1930-31	3340	1935-36	2450
1931-32	3015	1936-37	2450
1932-33	2686	1937-38	2750
1933-34	1722	1938-39	3000
Down and out!		Up again!	

My most critical years by far were 1933-34 and 1934-35 when
my employment was insecure and positions were excessively

scarce. In Tulsa 4,500 heads of families were reported without work, and in August, 1934, Teachers College of Columbia University informed me that 40,000 teachers were on its unemployed rolls looking for positions. In that tempestuous period I left no employment stone unturned. Far and wide, through friend and stranger, I sought employment, running down every clue to a job. During that spring and summer I could get nothing at all, for a single opening might have 50 to 100 applicants. For the minor position I secured in Texas I was especially indebted to President W. B. Bizzell of the University of Oklahoma and my English friends there. In response to a request from President Sam H. Whitley of the East Texas State Teachers College for an English instructor, Dr. Bizzell, who had come from Texas, recommended me by telephone to fill a temporary vacancy. In Dr. Whitley I found a good friend for a depression period, who offered me employment for a second year and helped me get a more secure position at the State College for Women. In Texas economic conditions were much better than in most states, because the new East Texas oil fields were filling many an empty purse.

I was very fortunate to be continuously employed during the depression, for I could live and pay interest and something on the principal of my debts. I think that a single year of unemployment might have allowed mortgages to swallow my Tulsa lots and perhaps my home just as other countless thousands lost their homes, farms, or businesses, and were forced into charity lines.

After Dr. Finlayson's second move to turn me out in December, 1933, I conferred with two or three powerful board members, exposed his blundering administration of the college, and thus perhaps had some part in bringing about his resignation in March, 1934, to accept a position in a local insurance company, probably arranged to ease him out of the chancellorship. Had a friendly administrator succeeded him, I might have been reinstated; but, in resigning, he succeeded in steering one of his satellites into temporary leadership, who carried on for his master. Later, however, I decided that my transfer to Texas was fortunate, a blessing in disguise.

I CHOSE TEACHING
Part V. Adventures in Texas

CHAPTER 17
American Literature in Hard Times

IN SEPTEMBER, 1934, as already related, I accepted a substitute English position in the East Texas State Teachers College at Commerce, one of the seven teacher-training colleges in the vast state of Texas. In President Sam H. Whitley I found a competent and trustworthy leader of about 1,000 students taught by a faculty of 75. At the time the state department of education was requiring better preparation of its teachers so that summer and extension courses were in strong demand for the bachelor and master degrees. Once a week I met a Saturday extension group at Texarkana, making a round trip of 250 miles at state expense and teaching a class of teachers from 6 to 9 P. M. At the end of a year in Dr. Whitley's courteous organization I was unexpectedly elected for a second year with an increase in salary and appointment to a faculty committee to initiate the master's degree. Though I accepted this position, toward the end of August I resigned it in order to take an offer to become an associate professor of English at the Texas State College for Women at Denton.

During this year of substitute employment I had been constantly looking for an English department headship and I almost secured one in Kansas. But, observing a rapid growth and building program at the only Texas state college for women, I got in touch with President L. H. Hubbard, who invited me to visit the college in August. In a conference with him and Dr. L. M. Ellison of the English department, I learned that they were interested to employ a specialist in American Literature to teach and to develop it in the college. In this conference I observed that the President, who had taught English, was taking the lead to promote American Literature and that the department head was somewhat reluctant. Within a day or two I received a phone call offering me the position. To avoid any misunderstanding, I requested the president to reduce the offer to writing and to mail it to me. This letter was so important in my life and work for the next decade that I reproduce it in full:

August 25, 1935

Dr. Amos L. Herold,
East Texas State Teachers College,
Commerce, Texas

Dear Dr. Herold:

In accordance with the terms suggested in my conversation with you yesterday, I am offering you the position of Associate Professor of English in the Texas State College for Women, College of Industrial Arts, at a salary of $2200.00 for nine months. In addition to this regular session salary you are guaranteed six weeks of summer school teaching at a salary of $250.00. If the present plan of additional compensation for the direction of masters' theses is continued, as it doubtless will be, you will receive additional compensation for this in the summer if it is carried in addition to the teaching of two three-hour courses, the regular summer teaching load. (Fifteen hours is the regular teaching load in the regular session.)

Our object, in asking you to join our staff, is partly to assist in the development of graduate work in the field of American Literature. This field needs expansion, and we believe you can accomplish this.

In considering this offer, remember that both the salary and rank are subject to advancement. The former legislative salary for this position, before the depression reductions, was $2700.00 for nine months and every effort will be made to restore it.

Assuring you of our pleasure of having you with us,

I am,
Yours very truly,
L. H. Hubbard
President

The next day, after phoning Dr. Ellison to learn what my teaching schedule would be, I sent President Hubbard a telegram accepting his written offer, since in a conference President Whitley had so recommended and reported that the offer had better prospects than anything he could propose. Then I wrote

Dr. Whitley a somewhat regretful letter of resignation in which one paragraph was:

"I wish, therefore, to resign from the position to which through your kindness I was elected last June. In doing so, let me assure you of my appreciation of the many acts of kindness and assistance that I have received during the past year. Though I came here an utter stranger, I soon was made to feel at home, and I have really had a busy and pleasant sojourn upon the campus of E. T. S. T. C. There is a fine spirit of service and democracy here that ought to characterize all the American colleges, and the growth of this spirit, I am sure, is due in great part to the fine quality of the leadership in all the administrative offices from the president down. Last spring in answering a pesky questionnaire, I made the point that the administration here is one of the best and most economical that I have ever observed, and I have been about a number of colleges in the East and Middle West. But, in going to Denton, I am hopeful of finding the same fine spirit of service and democracy."

Promoting American Literature

The commission and opportunity to teach and expand American Literature were potent reasons for my accepting a position in the Texas State College for Women. For ten years in Oklahoma I had promoted the study of our native literature. In February, 1924, in a paper I read to a conference of high-school and college teachers of English in Oklahoma City, I stressed the importance of our own literature in acquainting our students with American traditions, intellectual progress, and democratic aims. "There is," I declared, "no better way to Americanize young Americans. In our older and recent authors there is a wealth of mental pabulum for our future citizens." I then set an example for the colleges, as previously reported, by reorganizing the English courses to include both British and American authors.

Dr. Ellison had already indicated that my program of teaching would be two freshman sections, two of sophomore English Literature, and American Literature for juniors, seniors, and graduates. For seven years that was my agreed and acceptable schedule. But when soon after my arrival at the college I proposed expanding the course in American Literature from three to six hours — a year's work, in order to announce this expansion in the forthcoming catalog to be used for two years, the head of the department objected and to my surprise and dismay proceeded to assert that American Literature was so inferior to

British that a single three-hour course should suffice. I set forth reasons for its worth and for its expansion. When two or three visits to his office failed to get a favorable response, I began to despair of being able to do the very thing that I had been commissioned to do. Though I supposed that Dr. Ellison was acquainted with the letter that the president wrote me, he was long unaware of the explicit commission, which years later he agreed necessitated my seeking expansion in keeping with my engagement. However, a few days later the department head requested me to rewrite the catalog announcement providing for six hours of American Literature — three to the Civil War and three since this War. So, reshaping the first term's work at once, I offered the new course the second semester to my appreciative students. By perseverance and persuasion I had secured a 50 per cent expansion, which for a while would meet the terms of my employment.

But after 55 students had registered for the second semester, Dr. Ellison notified me that my registration in American Literature should not exceed 40 to 50 students and he insisted on an immediate reduction and the turning away of other students. This decision to ration American Literature was a continuing annoyance for six years. My suggestion that a second section be formed was ignored till the session of 1941-42 when two sections, totaling 80 students, met the demand without excluding anyone. The rationing was objectionable and unsound, because many needed the course for teaching and others for purely cultural reasons. In spite of the rationing my class twice numbered 60. Term after term I turned away five to 20 applicants for the course. Once a persistent girl staged a sit-down strike. When I excluded her, she left but soon returned, sat down near me, and declared she was going to sit there till I signed her for the course! She amused me so much that I capitulated and registered her for American Literature regardless of the rationing! In the summer school with only half as many students in attendance there was no problem since only 20 to 40 wished to register for my course.

In spite of the stupid rationing and refusal to accommodate the students, I enjoyed teaching English 437 and 438 — American Literature. I had specialized in 19th century American and British Literature and written my thesis in the home field. I loved the subject and I enjoyed teaching it. Knowing both the history and the literature of the United States, I could co-ordinate them and present them clearly and effectively. My interested students worked like beavers, because I gave them plenty of work. Using Snyder's *American Literature* as an overall text and Thoreau's *Walden* in the first semester and Whitman's *Leaves of Grass* in a selected edition the second semester for class study and recitation, I required five book reports each semester, half written in class and half outside, which enabled me to check their work. The graduates did a term paper. In all each student read or studied 18 average volumes during the year. Once a crooked woman tried to bluff me into thinking she had read Irving's *Astoria*. When she failed to answer a few specific questions about it, she admitted her neglect and ignorance, but tried to bribe me to give her a grade anyway. I think she was the most crooked woman that ever entered my classes.

At registration time students regularly stood in line to enter my various classes, and, if turned away, they were all the more eager to come the next term. The rationing advertised my courses, and when the students joined them, I gave them good service. My method of instruction was informal. I talked without notes, for I was filled with my subject. Occasionally I took a seat and let prospective teachers report to the class on some phase of the work. To avoid monotony, I varied the procedures during class time, which for me and most of the students passed quickly. Besides tests and examinations, sometimes I would choose ten words from the class assignment to be spelled and defined or explained, which gave a good rating of the students and kept them on the job.

Experimental Course

In 1938-1939 I conducted an experimental sophomore course in which, while doing the regular British survey, the students were encouraged to compare certain British authors with Americans. For example, one or more would compare Dr. Johnson and Franklin; another, Swift and Thoreau, Tennyson and Whitman, or Carlyle and Emerson. The students examined the pair individually and reached independent, written conclusions. Virtually without exception, these students showed a decided preference for the American authors and gave convincing reasons for their opinions, a few of which I quoted in a magazine article originating with this class and my various teaching experiences. This paper, which was named "The English Major Reconsidered," was published in *College English* for December, 1942.

In this article I advocated at least three adjustments in our conception of the English major and the college English department: first, a redefinition of English Literature for America to mean and to include both British and American Literature; second, adequate acquaintance of American students with the American scene, point of view, traditions, and way of living; and third, a telescoping of ponderous or lengthy British courses and offering less linguistics to make room for native authors in the college curriculum. Among the objections to some British authors I listed obsoleteness of vocabulary and the fostering of political, religious, and social institutions different from our own. Then I quoted three of my students who gave their reasons briefly for preferring three American authors to three British. This article I closed with a call for a better job of teaching American Literature in high school and in college, insisting that every candidate for a master's or doctor's degree in English should have a respectable knowledge of his own literature.

In 1940 Dr. Ellison, following the lead of the University of Texas, surprised me by initiating a three-hour course in the American Novel, which he had heretofore barely touched upon in teaching the British Novel. This new course drew about 25 students, but did not reduce the strong demand for my six-hour course in American Literature. By 1941-42 about 12 per cent of 900 juniors and seniors in the college were studying American Literature, whereas all of some 600 sophomores were required to take six hours of a British Survey, divided into 20 sections. Under the restrictions and rationing of these hard times I estimated that only one girl in six at the college was able to study the literature of her own country, though three sections of American History were serving about 40 per cent of the graduates.

While the experimental class was in operation, I was also planning a volume of selected sophomore readings from British and American authors in the proportion of two parts to one, respectively. Eliminating obsolete and minor British writings and reducing the space for major authors, I planned a single, compact volume of 1200 double-column pages to be supplemented by as much collateral reading as instructors might wish. I made a tentative table of contents, combining without scrambling the two literatures into a single year's work for sophomores, and was proceeding to do the job when I learned that three Texans — David L. Clark, William B. Gates, and Ernest E. Leisy — were producing a two-volume sophomore text called *The Voices of England and America* (1939), combining the two on a 3-to-1 basis.

With this text in prospect, with war clouds in the world getting blacker and blacker, and with unexpected interference developing in my Denton position, I decided to put aside my project for more favorable circumstances. But in 1948 as head of the English department in Arkansas College, deciding that much of the British survey was either too difficult or unsuitable for sophomores, I won faculty approval to offer them a six-hour course in American Literature and at the same time I moved the old British survey to the junior year, requiring my English majors and minors to do both surveys — a plan that worked successfully and is probably destined to become the standard procedure. This solution I arrived at after 25 years of experimenting with the British survey. I had tried a scrambled course, using Greenlaw and Hanford's *The Great Tradition,* and I had tried two four-hour surveys of British and American Literature. *The Voices of England and America* I did not care to use. During this period I have been reassured by student demands for American Literature, by its rapid expansion in many leading colleges and universities, especially in the Middle and Southwest, and by the publication of more and better textbooks in American Literature. (See also Chapter 20).

Old and New Friends

In coming to Texas, I became associated again with two of my favorite fellow students at Columbia University — John O. Beaty, professor of English at Southern Methodist University in Dallas, and William Dyer Moore, professor of French and Spanish at the Texas State College for Women. Beaty on a three-year fellowship from the University of Virginia had entered Columbia two years ahead of me. Writing a thesis on the Virginia novelist, John E. Cooke, he graduated in 1922 and later wrote or edited a number of college textbooks, a novel of Anglo-Saxon times for young people, and an exposure of Communist intrigue in this country, entitled *Iron Curtain Over America.* W. D. Moore was a native Texan, a poet, scholar, and perfect gentleman, who began his teaching career in a San Antonio high school and ended it at the Women's College in Denton. Many times we visited in one another's homes and had a grand time talking over our schooldays in New York and the acts of women and men in a puzzling world. Beaty's poetic wife was from New York City; Moore's fine lady from Louisiana; and mine from Missouri's Little Dixie, a full-blood Southerner. Socially, however, past antipathies were forgotten.

One of my new friends in Denton was E. V. White, Dean of the Women's College. Though a native of Louisiana, he had grown up on a ranch in central Texas. After his military service in the Philippines, he graduated from the University of Texas and engaged in schoolwork. Dean White was a typical Texan, large, handsome, generous, dependable, witty, and popular. Besides textbooks in mathematics he published several small volumes of proverbs mingled with fascinating little stories and anecdotes, many characterizing likable negroes. In Austin I frequently saw him before his death in 1955 at the age of 75.

CHAPTER 18

Diversions and Casualties

THIS employment in North Texas within 250 miles of my property interests in Tulsa enabled me to attend to my business there and to become acquainted with the liberty-loving people of our largest state, which takes pride in being the only state that was once an independent nation with a lone-star flag. This position also freed me from administrative duties and allowed me much time for research and writing on four current problems, namely, the future tense in modern English, the place of American Literature in college, the hazards of carbon-monoxide poisoning from gas and gasoline, and democracy and freedom in the American colleges. Of these four topics two concerned literary questions, one dealt with a health or scientific subject and one with political and civil rights and freedoms. Each one grew into a published magazine article.

My associations in Texas were at first altogether pleasant and stimulating. The contacts so happily begun in Commerce continued on an enlarged scale in Denton, where two state colleges were located — the Women's College with about 2,000 students and 120 on the faculty, one-third men, and the North Texas State Teachers College with about 1,800 students and 100 on the faculty, well divided between men and women, and both colleges growing rapidly. Denton itself was an attractive town of eight or ten thousand people, an hour's drive north of Fort Worth and Dallas, two rival and ambitious cities. The climate was delightful with little or no winter and roses blooming the year round, and the surrounding area was productive farm land and pastures. After storing our furniture and books for two years in Tulsa, we rented a Denton bungalow and, moving them there, we settled down to quiet work and peaceful living. For exercise, in fair weather, I walked six to twelve miles weekly through the year.

One popular and attractive feature of the Women's College was the practice of bringing celebrities like Lowell Thomas, Will Durant, Thomas Mann, and Lily Pons to the campus for addresses or entertainment. For example, in the session of 1939-1940, Mrs. Franklin D. Roosevelt, well known in her own right as Eleanor, dedicated a Little Chapel in the woods, where the graduates often get married. A traveling company presented "Rip Van Winkle" and Cornelia Otis Skinner entertained with dramatic monologues. The violinist Fritz Kreisler and conductor Vladimir Golschmann with the St. Louis Symphony Orchestra led the musicians. Among the speakers that year were Professor William Lyon Phelps, the dramatist Channing Pollock, the naturalist William Beebe, the Irish poet Oliver Gogarty, and a few lesser figures. For all of these events students and teachers could get season tickets at comparatively small cost.

The Denton Forum

Soon after coming to Denton, I was invited to join a men's scholarly group of 32 members, mostly faculty from the two colleges, called the Forum, organized in 1931 and meeting eight times during the school year. Its informal programs consisted of three parts: dinner at one of the colleges, a careful paper not to exceed 40 minutes in reading, and a discussion of the paper by each member for not more than four minutes. Knowing many months in advance of his appearance on the program, each member had ample time to choose and prepare an original document. Here I was associated with the most active leaders in the town and the two colleges and had a chance to sharpen wits with them. The Cato of the group was Dr. W. H. Bruce, a retired old man, long president of the Teachers College. Two leading educators were Dr. G. A. Odom of Teachers College and Dr. R. J. Turrentine of the Women's College. From Denton were superintendents R. C. Patterson of the town schools and R. L. Proffer of the county schools and a business man, E. J. Headlee. Our historians were L. W. Newton and C. A. Bridges, who was our secretary. The chairman of each meeting was the member who had read the last paper. A program would last from 6 to 9 P. M. or longer.

All sorts of current topics and problems were discussed. About 1940 Dr. Bridges presented a searching analysis of the F. D. Roosevelt administration, so biting in its criticism that he would not risk its publication, fearing loss of his position and having a wife and children to support, as he told me privately. Other members treated various topics in education, science, and sociology. In the course of seven years I prepared and read two papers on "The Genius of Thomas Jefferson" and "Faculty Participation in College Government," which after revision and condensation was published in *The Texas Outlook* in 1943 as "Democratizing the Colleges." This article I rate one of my best contributions, which I read to the Forum while I was being secretly hazed and victimized for expanding American Literature and asserting my civic rights at the Women's College. Loving debate from my boyhood upward, I enjoyed this Forum, being seldom absent and only for a potent reason.

Playing with Verse

During these happy years I sometimes played with verse, as in Oklahoma, where I composed a fanciful ballad called "Neptune's Daughter," suggested by a vivacious girl named Neptune in her bathing suit and red cap. In the beauty-spawning land of Texas, associated as I was with some of the most beautiful and intelligent women in three colleges, it was inevitable that they would catch my fancy or fire my imagination. At the Women's College fresh beauty was everywhere, modest, discreet, and virtuous. Most memorable of the girls was a golden-haired blond with the fine intelligence and erect bearing of an Indian princess, for her mother was mostly of Indian origin and her father was a fair-skinned German. What a blend was that and what an exotic beauty resulted! Her mind was keen and penetrating, a match for her beauty! How could one fail to admire and praise her? But another who fired my imagination was a handsome teacher, able, courteous, discreet, alive with quiet beauty and a doctoral degree!

Texas Centennial

In 1936 in Dallas the people of Texas celebrated the centennial of its independence from Mexico by an exposition of the state's history and activities to promote its prosperity and culture. Long in preparation, expensive, and well advertised, the show attracted not only Texans but many thousands from other states. It was a great exposition, creditable to the state and the nation. As a member of the Texas College English Conference, I visited various parts of the state in attending our annual meetings to discuss ways and means of improving our instruction. While in Texas, I also made subsidized train trips to Cincinnati, Indianapolis, and New Orleans at the Christmas season to attend the annual sessions of the Modern Language Association of

America, where one could hear and meet language leaders from all parts of the United States. I think the most memorable talk I heard there was Howard Mumford Jones's brilliant advocacy of the study of American Literature at the Cincinnati meeting.

More Articles and Radio Talks

In Texas I continued my study of the future auxiliaries, *shall* and *will,* which I had started in Oklahoma. These words required the most intensive study of the literature about them and their changing usage. My original impulse for the study was unadulterated annoyance with the conflicting and stupid rules contained in the textbooks supposed to guide instructors and students. For many years I tried to practice and to teach conformity to the crisscrossing rules for the use of *shall* and *will.* Finally, I rebelled against them and tried to find better methods, and I succeeded to my own satisfaction and with the approval of many scholarly friends. After four years of careful research and observation of usage in speech and print and much writing and rewriting, I had a compact article ready for publication. My exposition, argument, and conclusions entitled "The Future Tense in Modern English" were published in the College Edition of *The English Journal* for October, 1936. Of all my research I regard this article as the most difficult and perhaps the most convincing in delicate questions of English usage.

In March, 1936, under college auspices, I gave a short radio talk over WFAA, Dallas, on O. Henry, or William Sydney Porter, who came from North Carolina to Texas for his health and lived for a few years on a ranch. While clerking in an Austin bank, he became involved in bank shortages, and after a stupid trial was sent to a federal prison, where he began to write and publish short stories. When released, he became our most prolific and most popular writer of short stories. In Austin I talked with men who had known him and who assured me that funds could have disappeared without Porter's knowledge owing to the loose system permitted at the time. I gathered a lot of data, which I boiled down to 850 words. I classed him with Mark Twain in his ability to capitalize his personal observations and experience in brilliant, humorous narratives, which won friends, income, and fame for O. Henry, but a shadowed life for William S. Porter. Though much of his work may be forgotten, I said, enough will be treasured to insure the author an enduring fame.

During my first year in Texas I read Admiral Richard E. Byrd's account of his solitary observation camp near the South Pole, of his illness, and near death from carbon monoxide gen-

erated by oil-burning stoves in narrow quarters with little ventilation. I observed a close parallel between his symptoms and
mine in Tulsa, Oklahoma, in somewhat similar circumstances. A
visiting lecturer on health discussed the carbon-monoxide menace
and referred me to the research pamphlets prepared by the Federal Bureau of Mines and issued by the U. S. Public Health
Service. At once I secured three of these pamphlets and began
an intensive study of gas and gasoline hazards from carbon-monoxide poisoning. I read all the available literature on this topic
and applied my knowledge of biology and hygiene and my own
experience with gas-burning stoves. A mine inspector and I
made a special trip to the University of Tulsa to test the stove
in the little basement office that I had occupied for several years,
and we found it discharging injurious quantities of carbon-monoxide, as I had correctly conjectured from my studies and symp-
tons. Though our report induced the college to replace the
faulty stove with one of safer construction, the college at no
time offered any replacement to me for the injuries I sustained
there.

Assembling and organizing my information on the carbon-
monoxide menace, I wrote a non-technical, 3800-word, expository
article entitled "Gas and Gasoline Hazards," which was published
in *The Texas Outlook* for January, 1938. I quoted Dr. Harvey
G. Beck, an authority, to the effect that carbon-monoxide as a
cause of accidental and suicidal deaths in the United States ranks
second to automobile accidents. I showed that the fearful affinity
of this gas for red corpuscles produced a slow devitalizing suf-
focation when the concentration in the blood reached 20 to 50
per cent. The brave scientist, J. S. Haldane, tested various concentrations upon himself and literally touched the garments of
death to acquire knowledge. I showed that low concentrations
in the blood may produce a tired feeling or headache, and, if long
continued, sleeplessness, weakness, mental dullness, anemia, nervous disorders, and even suicide. The chief remedy: knowledge
of the hazard and the sources of danger and proper stoves and
proper ventilation.

College Teachers in the Depression

For most Americans the Great Depression between the two
World Wars extended from 1929 to 1939, but for a host of college
instructors it lasted from 1930 to 1945 — a long period of 15 years
with many casualties. That is, the Second World War of 1939-
1945 by drawing most young men and many young women from
the colleges to the armed services or other wartime employment

left thousands of college teachers with no employment or reduced time and pay. Though I attended the New York Exposition of 1939 with visits to my eastern relatives, this war period was for me more disconcerting than the ten-year depression
as I knew it in Oklahoma and Texas, because in 1942-43 I had
no employment and I spent the year like a sabbatical at my own
expense, resting and studying at Teachers College of Columbia
University. While the war lasted, college teaching staffs were
being reduced and new positions were very scarce. In 1943-44 I
worked as civilian editor for the U. S. War Department at Camp
Lee, Virginia, and the next year I taught at the Wentworth
Military Academy, Lexington, Missouri — both temporary, emergency positions. Not till 1946 and the return of the veterans
to college were positions available in plenty. To get through this
insecure period I had to draw on my savings, which I replaced by
teaching till I was 68 and qualifying for social-security benefits
under standards liberalized for older persons.

The long depression with its hardships and losses and dis-
appointments probably shortened many useful lives. My father,
who remarried in 1910 and lived to 1932 and the ripe age of 75,
declared he had never known or observed such distress in the
Greenbrier Valley as in the years 1930-1932: bank failures, factories closed, work very scarce and little money circulating, farms
and stock selling at great losses, some people looking to the Red
Cross for their food, and even mortgages of little value since
properties would not sell to meet them. Before the federal government organized the Home Owners Loan Corporation to float
new loans under easy terms, farmers in the Middle West were
almost up in arms in opposing cold-blooded foreclosures by
powerful insurance companies. This Corporation gave me a loan
on my Tulsa home, which helped me to weather the depression.

In Febraury, 1936, two of my good friends at the University
of Tulsa, Professors Dill and Kimbrough, succumbed to maladies
aggravated by the depression and a pitiless chancellor, who held
over both men the menace of dismissal. Though Dr. F. G. Dill
at the age of 59 was in good financial condition, Dr. C. H. Kimbrough at 56 with five persons to support was forced to let a
mortgage take his beautiful Tulsa home. Especially Kimbrough
and in some measure Dill were victims of maladministration
and the depression. Both men had served the University of Tulsa
long and faithfully as professors and administrators. Though the
new President C. I. Pontius tried by kind treatment to rehabili-
tate both men, especially Kimbrough, it was too late!

In 1941 my Aunt Lucy Wade, aged 73, mother of nine children, living at the old Ruckman home at Mill Gap, Virginia, departed this life; and the next year my Uncle Glen Ruckman, aged 69, died from ill health precipitated partly by the hardships and financial losses of the depression. In the first part of 1929 he had bought cattle and sheep in large numbers to be shipped that fall and winter, but, when they were sold on a broken market, he sometimes lost $10,000 in a single week. In spite of tremendous losses he kept his contracts faithfully. Though always popular and generous, he was thereafter much handicapped and broken. When his only son died ten years later, the male line of my Grandfather Ruckman ended.

An Ideal Citizen

In November, 1943, my good friend, James H. Price, aged 61, former governor of Virginia, died suddenly from a cerebral hemorrhage in Richmond, with his burial in Staunton. On December 2, *The Times-Dispatch* published my tribute to him, entitled "The Ideal Citizen," with which I close this chapter:

"As a college mate and friend of James H. Price, I was pleased last week to observe the universal expression of sorrow and regret at his untimely and sudden death in Richmond. Though I have known members of the Price relationship in West Virginia since I was a boy, and though we had many friends in common there and in Staunton, I did not meet James H. Price till he came to Washington and Lee University to study law in the fall of 1907.

"All the Prices were fine, virtuous, public-spirited citizens, loyal to God and country and interested in state and community projects. The one I knew best was Dr. William T. Price, an honor graduate of Washington and Lee and a beloved Presbyterian minister, who achieved considerable distinction as an author and a clergyman. Some were editors, lawyers, and physicians; two or three wrote some verse.

"But, fine as they were, the jewel of the family, in my judgment, was James H. Price, whose life and work afford a splendid theme for those of us who admire genuine democratic society and institutions. In learning to love and in honoring such men as Price, the good people of Virginia confer distinction upon themselves, for as long as democracies can find and use such men for leaders, democracies will be safe. At college, he was a topnotch student of the law, universally liked and admired, and honored by his fellow-students with the presidency of his graduating class. His ambition led him to Richmond, where the fine qualities of his rich, serene, superbly integrated personality flowered in friendships and in public service and in devotion to the true, the beautiful and the good; for truly he was a treasury of the virtues and people he met instinctively recognized this fact and trusted him and honored him. In his life and character the Golden Rule was enshrined. While he bore himself with the simplicity and humility of a true Christian, he wore the robes of high office with ease, grace, and distinction. To meet him was a pleasure and an honor and to enjoy his friendship was a high distinction. His unique achievement in personal character and in public service was that of the ideal citizen."

Amos L. Herold

Petersburg

CHAPTER 19

Against Third-Term President

FROM my youth upward I have been a lover and advocate of the American charter of freedoms and rights as set forth in the Declaration of Independence and the first ten amendments to the Federal Constitution, called the Bill of Rights. I refer especially to the rights of "life, liberty, and the pursuit of happiness," the right of the people to choose the form of government, and to petition for redress of grievances; freedom of religion, of speech, and of the press; the right "to be secure in their persons, homes, papers, and effects against unreasonable searches and seizures," and freedom from "cruel and unusual punishments."

In comparatively few ancient and modern nations have the people been secure in the possession of these rights and freedoms. Dictators and the dictator spirit bred by the possession of great power have constantly tended to deprive the people of these inalienable rights. In the modern world, Hitler, Mussolini, and Stalin have exemplified the worst forms of rule by fear and coercion. Against autocracy Thomas Jefferson and his followers swore eternal hatred. Long have I shared their faith and their hatred of dictators. In the 1920's and 1930's the trend toward autocracy in the fascist and communist nations encouraged similar tendencies in the United States, and many thoughtful

Americans became much concerned about the preservation of their own freedom.

In the United States this tendency to a single absolute power showed itself in Franklin D. Roosevelt's ambition to monopolize the presidency and to make the Supreme Court and Congress his subservient satellites. In this Roosevelt's three administrations there was a tremendous sweep toward dictatorship. Nothing stirred my indignation quite so much as his overweening ambition for third and fourth terms contrary to the practice and advice of our ablest presidents, the imbecility of some of his partisans in rating him the indispensable man, and his frequent attempts to dictate to the people of several states who their congressmen and senators should be. I followed closely the various maneuvers and political tricks that preceded the claim that the third-term nomination was forced upon an unwilling man! So obvious was Roosevelt's pretence and deceit that I could not endure to look at his picture in the newspapers. With my bare hand I would cover his wily face while I read the news or I would fold the paper so as to hide it. Though I had supported and voted for him in 1932 and 1936, I opposed him tooth and nail in 1940 and 1944, and I lived to see the American people approve my views by adopting the 22nd Amendment to the Constitution limiting the presidential tenure to two terms. Thus, the Roosevelt presumption and vainglory were terminated by the supreme law of the land, and a grave weakness in the original Constitution was corrected.

I proudly record that from Denton, Texas, on July 17, 1940, I sent President Franklin D. Roosevelt at the White House this telegram: "Better follow the example of Washington, Jefferson, and Jackson, for third-term issue will either defeat you or lead eventually to dictatorship. (Signed) Democrat." Though his subordinates may have suppressed this message, I had then and I still have the satisfaction of having sent it.

During the campaign I looked up the various sharply-worded statements that Thomas Jefferson had made against aspirants for third terms, and, reducing them to a compact letter, I sent it to the *Dallas News* for publication over my name. This statement from the founder of the Democratic Party was a hard-hitting blow to Roosevelt supporters that they could neither dodge nor explain away. While professing to be followers of Jefferson, they were obviously rejecting an important part of his teaching.

When Wendell L. Willkie was nominated for the presidency by the Republicans, I studied his record and his speeches carefully before I decided to support him instead of the third-term candidate. While still undecided as to my course, I sent on August 11, 1940, the following letter to Willkie:

Dear Mr. Willkie:

I am a Southern democrat of independent leanings, who supported Roosevelt in 1932 and 1936, but who, much opposed to the third term and some of the New Deal doings, may go elsewhere this year. In the college atmosphere here I know of many others who share my views and who are looking forward to your coming acceptance speech with unusual interest. My prediction is that the extent to which democrats break away from their party candidates for the presidency will depend largely on that speech.

Should you in that speech show any inclination to Lindbergize with the dictators of the Old World, most dissatisfied democrats will swallow their third-term objections and support the democratic ticket. Should you show an ambition to an indiscriminate junking of the New Deal, they will do the same thing. Should it appear to them that Wall Street and utility companies can dominate your policies, they will do likewise. If, however, you satisfy them on those important issues, they will be disposed to turn to you.

You can win thousands of democratic votes and the good will of many democratic congressmen and senators by a strong declaration to devote yourself as president to national and international affairs, leaving the election of congressmen and senators to the people of the districts or states that they are to represent in accordance with the Federal Constitution. Roosevelt's interference and purges have been very displeasing to hosts of democrats. Such a declaration might win Delaware, Maryland, West Virginia, Missouri, Oklahoma, and other states, and make victory secure elsewhere.

My personal opinion is that we should view the Monroe Doctrine as our shield of protection against foreign aggression and the two-term policy as our shield of protection against dictatorship within the country, the two being complementary and equally important. Thus far, the two-term policy, accepted heretofore by both parties, has a perfect batting average, whereas the Monroe Doctrine during the Civil War was imperfectly enforced.

The best way to win democratic votes is not through regular republican spellbinders but through bolting democratic speakers like Al Smith, Wm. H. Murray of Oklahoma, Senators Burke and Reed, and others. It occurs to me, too, that a convention of bolting democrats at a central point like St. Louis in September would be a capital way to get publicity for the movement and give democrats a more plausible reason for leaving the party than if the movement is wholly under the wings of the republican organization.

Make no mistake that FDR is not already campaigning on his trip to Boston and in the September call to prayer. Why not join the call to prayers and make it unanimous?

Support Willkie

Though I had been an original supporter of F. D. Roosevelt in his first two campaigns for the presidency, his attack upon the Supreme Court in 1937, his later attempts at party purges, his financial irresponsibility and wastefulness as proved by his father's will, his manipulation of the Chicago Democratic Convention through his underlings for the third-term nomination, and his shameless willingness to junk the two-term policy long recognized by both major parties as an essential part of our political practice — all of these offenses in spite of his first-term accomplishments convinced me that the Democratic Party had left me and its moorings and induced me to join the opposition party. In the exciting campaign I wrote many letters to my friends and to quite a number of newspapers seeking to defeat Roosevelt.

In one letter to the newspapers I sought to show that if Thomas Jefferson were living in 1940, he would certainly oppose the third-term candidate, to which a reader replied in the *Tulsa World,* seeking to weaken my argument. By the middle of October I was able to combine my various lines of reasoning into a single compact statement, which I named "A Rational View of Presidential Tenure." I reviewed the development of the two-term practice, quoting Jefferson and Congressional resolutions in support of the custom. I summarized the president's tremendous powers to command, to appoint, to direct foreign affairs, to propose legislation, to veto, to use patronage as a weapon, and to name judges likely to be responsive to his will. I stressed the point that these powers are *cumulative.* "So, with Franklin D. Roosevelt," I wrote, "the conditions that Jefferson feared have arisen. Roosevelt is popular, shrewd, and ambitious. To many he appears the indispensable man. His appointees fill the land, secured his third nomination, and campaign for his election. About twelve million persons who have lately gotten on the federal payroll and their friends are naturally interested in his re-election. . . .In eight years the Roosevelt power has become so enormous over his party, over the legislative and judicial departments, and over federal beneficiaries that the only safe course for the people to follow is Jefferson's advice."

But his powerful political machine, supported directly and indirectly by federal funds and credits, and the baseless charge that Willkie's German origin could not be trusted led to Willkie's defeat. Though this reverse was a great disappointment, one of my friends, Andrew Ashburn, and I sent our candidate the following telegram from Denton, Texas, on November 8, 1940:

> Congratulations on your magnificent fight. We foresee victory for the crusade in forty-two and forty-four and a constitutional amendment against third terms. Do not accept New Deal appointment, but let it hang itself. From your mid-western farm, be sure to visit your Southern friends.

> (Signed) Amos L. Herold, Andrew Ashburn.

I can not better indicate my great concern for the future of our country at this time than by transcribing a copy of letters that on November 11, 1940, I sent to my Texas Congressman, Hon. Ed Gossett, and the two United States Senators from Texas. Here it is:

Letter to Texans in Congress

As one of your Texas supporters and as a loyal American greatly concerned on this Armistice Day with preserving our American democracy with all its rights and privilges, I write to you earnestly urging that, in these trying times when FDR says it is not safe for him to be away for more than half a day's travel, you and your fellow congressmen and senators observe the same precaution by staying on the job during these critical times to protect your own powers and our liberties.

In my judgment the election of FDR to a third term despite all his fair speeches about democracy puts the menace of dictatorship unmistakably on first base, to speak the language of baseball. In my judgment the House is on second base, the Senate on third, and the Supreme Court at home plate, with the people, I sincerely hope, holding a final veto in 1944, when the menace may be ended once and for all by an amendment to the Constitution.

I urge you not only to stay on the job and refuse to be mere errand boys for any one but that you scrutinize and circumscribe by time limits and otherwise whatever legislation you may find it expedient to pass. From time to time short recesses may be expedient, but it may be better to follow the practice of the British Parliament and remain in almost continuous session or be ready for quick assembly. Do not give any occasion for being short-circuited or detoured around by the Chief Executive, or rule by executive order with the attorney general determining the limits of executive power. Of course, co-operate and expect co-operation as the New York *Times* pointed out editorially last Friday or Saturday.

Remember that you and your fellows are not the servants of the Chief Executive, but you are the servants and elected representatives of the people of Texas and of the other states. If the limits of executive authority as set by the Constitution and the laws of Congress are not scrupulously observed, do not forget that the trump card of impeachment is yours if no other recourse is to be had. Just the determined threat of its use may suffice for any emergency.

And I am in deadly earnest, because I know that eternal vigilance is the price of liberty.

FDR called the recent campaign a "funny" campaign, which epithet reminded me of Nero's fiddling while Rome burned.

Very cordially yours,
Amos L. Herold

In February, 1941, I wrote Senator Burton K. Wheeler to congratulate him upon his brave stand in the Senate in behalf of freedom of speech in examining and criticising an aspect of our government and in defending the basic rights and privileges of the American democracy. At the same time, I warned against the suicidal practice of filibustering to kill proposed legislation as dictatorship by a minority. On May 5 of the same year I sent the following signed letter to the *Dallas News* on choosing a United States Senator:

Qualifications for Public Office

Texas voters will soon be called upon to choose a new senator to fill out the unexpired term of the late Senator Sheppard. Never was a graver responsibility placed upon the people of Texas than now to choose well and wisely, for these are times to try men's souls and to require vision and courage.

Woodrow Wilson, I have heard, used to ask three

questions about a candidate for an appointive office, namely: Is he honest? Is he loyal? Is he competent? Certainly, if a candidate is honest, loyal, and competent, he ought to be successful.

But, it seems to me that in the Congress of the United States at the present time other qualities are needed. Since we live at a time when the executive branches of government are encroaching upon the legislative and judicial, when the general movement is away from democratic processes and toward what Jefferson called monarchial government but which we call totalitarian, dictator, or one-man government, the people of Texas and the United States need in Washington representatives who are not only honest, loyal, and competent, but independent, courageous, and determined to maintain our form of democratic government in all its integrity, with the Congress and the Supreme Court receiving just as much respect and confidence as the Executive Branch.

Candidates who pledge themselves in advance to do no thinking, to be mere followers of somebody else, to be complacent yes-men; candidates who make rash and irresponsible promises and who indulge in unrealistic views of society, finance, economics, and international questions; candidates untried and inexperienced, or known to lack independence, tenacity of purpose, and courage arising from deep-set convictions about our government and a lively sense of loyalty and responsibility to the people who elect them — are they or any of them entitled to the suffrage of the people of Texas or any other state?

So, as never before, examine, scrutinize, question, test in every way possible the claims of the many candidates, and choose well and wisely.

Amos L. Herold

Then on August 20, 1942, I sent a second letter to this paper entitled "Commander-in-Chief," which I signed with a pseudonym, "C. L. Smith," as a precaution against possible reprisal in my employment, though careful readers probably recognized the camouflage.

Commander-in-Chief

In recent months there has been a good deal of confusion in the minds of some people regarding the meaning of Commander-in-Chief as we find the term in the Constitution of the United States. Many people need to read and reread the Federal Constitution if they wish to think clearly and do their part in preserving our democratic

form of government in a world threatened by dictatorship. And what we need to preserve is not merely the form,
but the democratic substance of our own government. It
is perfectly possible for dictatorship to overwhelm us under
the camouflage of constitutional forms. Do not forget that
Adolf Hitler came to power, dictator power, in Germany
in the trappings of democracy. The German Reichstag,
chosen by the German people, gave him dictatorial control
over Germany. The lesson for our own country should be
obvious and unmistakable.

Now the Constitution of the United States provides
that "The President shall be Commander-in-Chief of the
Army and Navy of the United States, and of the militia
of the several States when called into the actual service of
the United States." The President is not Commander-in-
Chief of the Senate of the United States nor of the House
of Representatives nor of the Federal Courts nor of the
people of the United States nor of the people of Texas
or any other state. The Constitution of the United States
regards the President, not as the master of the American
people or their representatives in Congress, or in the state
legislature, but as the executive servant of the American
people.

Although eighteen sections of the Federal Constitution
enumerate the powers of Congress and only three or four
are needed to enumerate the powers of the President,
nevertheless for a long time the powers of the Presidency
have more and more encroached upon the powers of Congress and the powers of the Judiciary. At the present time,
fully three-fourths of the Federal judges are appointees of
the present administration and naturally disposed to look
with favor and approval upon its policies and legislation.

If, in addition, the Congress of the United States be-
comes a spineless herd of yes-men, who regard the President
as their Commander-in-Chief contrary to the plain intent
of the Constitution, then the end of the American Democracy is near at hand. Consequently, any candidate for office,
whether it be for justice of the peace or the Senate of the
United States, who declares in advance he is going to
function as an imbecile, as a child, or as Charley McCarty,
ought to be denied public office, or who by his actions is
known so to function ought to be denied public office.

C. L. Smith

In the campaign of 1944 against the fourth-term candidate for
the presidency I was so intensely active in opposition that, after
technically qualifying the preceding year as a resident citizen

of Marshall, Missouri, I left my employment at Camp Lee, Virginia, and returned to Marshall, Missouri, in March for the purpose of entering a congressional primary in the Second District on the Republican ticket. Though my prospects of success against the regular candidate supported by the Republican organization were slight, I was so eager and determined to blast Franklin D. Roosevelt by mail, by the press, and by the radio that I campaigned vigorously in fifteen central Missouri counties including the towns of Booneville, Columbia, and Jefferson City, making four or five short radio talks and expending about $800 in a month's campaign. Though I entered the contest as a stranger and newcomer, I made a creditable showing by winning about 3,500 votes in the primary to about twice that number for my opponent, who was already serving in Congress. This candidacy also enabled me to try out my boyhood dream of entering politics like William J. Bryan and reforming the country!

Three years later widespread demands for a constitutional limitation on presidential terms induced Congress by more than a two-thirds favorable vote in the House and Senate to propose the Twenty-Second Amendment to the Federal Constitution and to submit it to the states for action in March, 1947. In that same month Maine led a procession of ratifying states from all sections of the nation. When Nevada on February 26, 1951, became the 36th state to ratify the Amendment, it immediately became effective. I hailed the revision as the realization of one of my dreams in which I had invested much effort and some money. A grave defect in the original Constitution was corrected by the nation with little regard to political associations, because Missouri, Mississippi, and Virginia joined Maine, Illinois, and California in approval. Though the incumbent president was not affected, President Harry S. Truman wisely chose not to run again. In condensed form the Amendment provided that no person shall be elected to the office of president more than twice and no one succeeding another elected person to the presidency and serving more than two years shall be elected more than once.

Amendment XXII was the last of seven fundamental changes in our Constitution which I witnessed between 1913 and 1951. The first, Article XVI, was the income-tax authorization, championed by Bryan and other liberals. Next, Article XVII provided for the election of United States Senators by the people, who in a number of cases had learned that state legislators had accepted bribes for their votes. The famed XVIIIth prohibiting the manufacture, transportation, and sale of intoxicating liquors, which was approved by all except two states and became effective in January, 1920, was repealed after a trial of 13 years by the adoption of Article XXI. In August, 1920, Amendment XIX enfranchised women. Article XX, effective in February, 1933, fixed the terms of Representatives and Senators to begin on January 3 and the terms of President and Vice-President to begin on January 20, which became the date for the inauguration instead of the original March 4. These basic changes were preceded by a vast deal of debate and public discussion. Article XVIII is notable as the first and only Amendment to be repealed.

CHAPTER 20

A College Monarchy

WITH this account of American political events from 1932 to 1951 and my reactions to them as a background of my life and work, I must now return to the last years of my employment at the Texas State College for Women. Though the faculty, the students, and the general arrangements about the college were good and commendable, I regret to record that my hopes and first impressions of the college administration proved to be mistaken and disappointing. While it was very attentive to the comfort and welfare of the students, there were times when the status of the faculty seemed to waver between that of college teachers and paid servants.

Within a year or two I realized that the smoothly performing administration was a polite, gloved, presidential monarchy. Every phase of the college was ruled by the president, who delegated little of importance to his subordinates and converted faculty meetings into an opportunity to announce decisions, already made usually, and to lecture the staff, mostly women, upon their duties and conduct. For minor slips, competent teachers might be dismissed to discipline those that remained.

In giving me a commission to develop American Literature, the president had assumed charge of the English Department, though at the time I supposed that he and the department head were agreed as to the terms of my employment. When the Federal Treasury Department invited the college employees to buy bonds or saving stamps, the administration virtually converted the request into an order for monthly purchases with occasional reports or punishment for anyone adjudged neglectful of this patriotic duty!

In the course of four years by administrative assumptions and manipulations, President Hubbard took over a charity fund, set assessments, made collections like a tax collector, and spent this fund of more than $3,000 as he saw fit, making no report to the faculty, who paid nearly all of it. For a few years I acquiesced and paid my share without question, but more and more I was boiling with indignation at a system that treated the teachers like children or imbeciles. After receiving in 1941 in cash or notes with interest about $12,000 for half of my Tulsa lots, which paid my debts and left a comfortable balance in the bank, I began to feel much more independent and determined to assert my rights as a teacher and a citizen. Already on the political front I had written in a way to displease the Roosevelt underlings and satellites, of whom Hubbard was a leader, playing ball with the politicians, whose interests were divided between the welfare of the country and the rewards of office. In the very year (1940) that Mrs. Roosevelt visited the campus I protested in *The Dallas News* against breaking the two-term tradition.

Later I learned on good authority that one member of the board wished to turn me out in 1941 without the customary notice in advance. Since I was due to receive such advance notice, it seems that President Hubbard quieted him with assurances that he would attend to the business in due course, that is, the following year, as discovered by a later investigation made at my request by the American Association of University Professors.

Taxing the Faculty

On September 15, 1941, President Hubbard came before the faculty and passed out an assessment sheet with blank checks to each member of the staff to fill out for his share, listing 13 agencies to benefit from the fund without indicating the amount to each and requesting or instructing the faculty to perform. In previous years there had been the formality of faculty approval, but not in 1941. Mr. Hubbard was handling this business! By a rare act of self-control, I kept quiet and filled out my check for $21.60 for the Faculty Activities Fund of T. S. C. W., which, paid and cancelled, I still have as a trophy of my adventures.

Inquiring as to a similar Civic Fund at the Teachers College, I learned that its system was very different from ours. Getting a copy of its assessment and administration, I enclosed it to the Committee supposed to be in charge of our fund, with the following letter of mild protest. It went straight to Hubbard, who was the committee.

T. S. C. W.,
Denton, Texas,
November 10, 1941.

To the Commitee in Charge of
The TSCW Charity Fund,
Denton, Texas.

Gentlemen:

A few days ago I was privileged to see and secure a copy of the Distribution of the NTSTC Civic for 1941-42. For the information of our committee, I enclose a copy of it, with the request that it be returned to me as soon as it has been looked over.

As this report to the NTSTC Faculty shows, the rate of assessment at our neighbor college is only one-half of one per cent, without discrimination as between nine-and twelve-month employees. With this relatively low assessment, all deserving obligations are taken care of, the total outlay being $2025. I understand, too, that the fund is handled by a faculty committee without bothering the administrative officials; that this committee prepares the budget for faculty comment and approval; and reports annually upon the allotments made from the fund. This procedure seems to be fair and truly democratic.

Last year NTSTC contributed $500 to the Denton Chamber of Commerce, whereas our committee threw down the bars and allotted $750, making a total of $1250 for the two colleges. Though I have heard one or two plausible explanations of this allotment, it has always been to me obscure and doubtful for this reason: that, though I once had fourteen years of experience teaching in municipally supported colleges, I was not once called upon to help defray the operating expenses of the local chamber. By no stretch of the imagination can the Denton chamber be classed as a needy, ragged object of charity. Since the two colleges expend large sums of money here annually and afford exceptional educational opportunities for all the young people in town at small cost, I personally should like to see the tables turned upon our commercial friends by asking them to create substantial loan funds for students, for really needy students. Large allotments to the local chamber are proving to be a boomerang to the merchants since some faculty members are thereby induced to shift their purchases to Dallas and Fort Worth. Judging by the size of our contribution to the local chamber, I would say that our institution of higher learning is not an institution with a soul, but merely a business enterprise.

At all events, with the cost of living already increased by ten to twenty per cent and still advancing, with the rate of discount on our checks raised from one to one and a half per cent, and with federal taxes increased by 300 to 400 per cent and still advancing upward without any prospect of a salary adjustment for two years, I respectfully urge our committee to economize with a view to a lower rate next year. As a contributor to this fund, I also request a statement of last year's allotments and current proposals.

> Very cordially yours,
> Amos L. Herold

Within three days I received the following response from President Hubbard, our omniscient judge:

Dr. Amos L. Herold   November 13, 1941
T. S. C. W.

Dear Dr. Herold:

Thank you for sending us the schedule of donations which the Teachers College is proposing to make from its faculty community fund for 1941-42. Our fund is not all expended for charitable purposes. Its purpose is to meet calls on the faculty for every sort of contribution, thereby relieving the individual of the necessity of considering such payments.

Some of your statements seem to me intemperate and I do not agree with them. In the case of contributions to the Chamber of Commerce, I consider our contribution justified. I feel that every faculty member should be interested in the work of the Chamber and willing to contribute to its maintenance. The Denton Chamber of Commerce has done much to assist our College.

A statement of the expenditures of the funds for the past year will be sent to the contributing members when we have had time to prepare it.

> Yours very truly,
> L. H. Hubbard, President

Though this letter showed a definite intention to be calm and rational, his promise to report on the fund to the faculty seemed to involve him in embarrassments, which perhaps he did not foresee. Inadvertently, my request as a contributor for a report on the allotments for the preceding year led to Dr. Hubbard's revelation of the facts regarding the fund. In September he had reported over his signature that the faculty was contributing to 13 agencies without specifying the amounts to each. When in early December he listed over his signature 25 agencies, 12 more than in September and not previously reported, his chagrin must have been disconcerting, since he always tried to be goody-goody and increased his reputation for saintliness by sometimes serving as a lay preacher. The December report indicated the amounts to each activitiy, and included $125 for the National Democratic Fund and $135 for Legislative Expenses, which could not be classified as charities.

A Second Assessment

About the time this report was made, Dr. Hubbard levied a supplementary Red Cross assessment. Soon after receiving my copy of this second assessment, I happened to meet him in the men's toilet room and offered to help raise the Red Cross addition on a voluntary basis. Right then and there Hubbard's pent-up rage exploded like a small bomb filled with abuse for me for interfering with his plans, so he declared. Perhaps, he had not planned to make an itemized report to the faculty and to give documentary evidence of his irregular practice in reporting on the fund. He had not planned to disconcert himself! Never have I known a college administrator to lose control of himself so completely and utter such abuse in his efforts to muddy the waters and shield himself! The monarch had trapped himself and was overcome with rage!

It seems that Hubbard had originally intended to dismiss me for protesting the arbitrary assessments enforced by veiled threats of losing positions, but Dr. Ellison warned him that such a charge would draw the fire of the American Association of University Professors. Instead, still unaware of my written commission (See page 180) to expand American Literature, Ellison suggested that my zeal to develop American Literature and disinclination to follow his plans would be more tenable or effective or something of the sort. This piece of evidence I got from a friend who was close to me and close to Ellison. By this time the president may have forgotten the exact terms of my employment or did not care what they were.

My Resignation Demanded

At all events, under date of December 12, 1941, Mr. Hub-

bard, following up the explosion in the toilet room, wrote me
an ugly letter bristling with mistaken claims about my efforts
to expand American Literature, ignoring his explicit commission
to me, and concluding with this paragraph so typical of monarchs:

"I will, therefore, await your resignation with the understanding that failing to receive it I will recommend to the Board
of Regents that your connection with the College terminate at
the end of the summer school, and with the further understanding that if, in the mean time, you should attempt to cause any
disturbance that would embarrass the College, especially within
the Deparment, you will be asked to leave the College at once.
Yours very truly, L. H. Hubbard, President."

Whether this part of his letter was courteous or discourteous,
worthy or unworthy of a college president, I will let the reader
decide. Since, however, its implications were discreditable to
me, I wish to counteract this impression by quoting Dean White's
testimonial on my behavior and competence:

"Dr. Herold is studious, energetic, and despite a heavy teaching schedule has found time for a great amount of scholarly
research in unexplored corners of American Literature. I com-
mend him as a competent, thorough, capable, and resourceful
teacher of college English.

"E. V. White, Dean of the Texas State College for Women."

Well, I did not plead guilty to Mr. Hubbard's allegations and
run away as some timid souls might have done; nor did I have
any intention of acting the part of a rowdy in the English Department or anywhere else, though I did intend to stand by my
guns. In the mean time I wrote him two or more letters, reminding him of my original contract and commission to expand
American Literature, the difficulties encountered, and at least a
very considerable success in doing what he had called for. True
to his threat, though camouflaged by seemingly friendly New
Year greetings, Hubbard did return to the Board with the business in January, 1942, and a month later he wrote me the following letter, which shows how shamefully he had mishandled my
employment without fully informing the Board of the terms of
my contract.

Dear Dr. Herold:

In regard to the correspondence that we had before
Christmas, I am writing to notify you that at the last meeting [January 16] of the Board of Regents the Board was

apprised of the trouble that you had caused in the department since you joined the faculty, of your lack of co-operation with Dr. Ellison in working out his plans for the department, and of your attempts to disregard him in expanding the work in American Literature, and I made the statement to the Board that in view of this continued friction I had been forced to recommend that your services be discontinued at the end of your term of summer teaching this year. This recommendation was unanimously approved.

Yours very truly,
L. H. Hubbard, President

A pungent satirist, reading this misleading letter on the report to the Board of Regents and evaluting it correctly, might well say in allegorical form: "Well done, thou good and faithful servant. Enter thou into thy reward with thy brethren!"

Two Summarizing Letters

But after a month of troubled meditation I wrote the two following letters to President Hubbard about the misadventure of my employment under his leadership, to which he did not reply. I quote them, because they put the matter just as I saw it then and I think now that I evaluated it correctly.

Box 3883 TSCW.,
Denton, Texas,
March 18, 1942.

Dear Dr. Hubbard:

At your early convenience, I urge you to read Dr. Floyd Stovall's article on "Place of American Literature" in the January number of the *Texas Outlook*. Based upon a number of questionnaires and recent college catalogs, his study is most helpful in clarifying an issue now before college English departments for adjustment. The recent development of American Literature in college and the demand for it by students and progressive educators raise the question as to its place in the curriculum. The general tendency is clear though the variety of opinions is not easy to explain. The friction you refer to is not between any two instructors anywhere, but between British and American literature, the first receding somewhat as the second gets its proper place.

It is chiefly owing to your foresight and planning that

a fairly satisfactory adjustment has been secured in this college. In commissioning me seven years ago to try to secure expansion, you were taking the right step though it soon became evident to me that you and the department head were not in agreement. You desired some expansion, but the department head did not, and showed his opposition to your wish by hazing and harassing the instructor of American literature, who was sincerely and loyally trying to carry out your wish and meet the needs of the students. That tangle between the President and the English head directly affected me adversely and is the source of an undeserved misfortune unless the President uses his power to set things right. Though I accepted the commission in good faith and carried it out in good faith, yet in the end I find myself persecuted and deprived of employment for doing the very thing that I was specially engaged to do at the beginning. I urge you to remove the tangle and give me a chance to function without touching any one's special and zealously guarded prerogatives.

That instructors in American literature should be thus hazed, harassed, and persecuted is to me incredible; but the records show that Bliss Perry at Harvard encountered the same difficulty when he introduced a course in Emerson, and in his autobiography, as I remember, Perry implies that some of the prima-donna, reactionary professors would have turned him out but for President Eliot's consistent support. J. Frank Dobie had a similar experience with Literature of the Southwest at the University of Texas. Then, there is the classic example of John A. Lomax's experience in collecting cowboy ballads; scoffed at in Texas; honored at Harvard; and finally nationally famous for his fine work in preserving our literature. Is it possible that a progressive and enlightened administration here is going to permit such shortsighted, irrational practice to prevail at the Texas State College for Women? Is it a crime at this college to teach literature in a way that students enjoy it and seek one's classes? Are the happiness and security of faithful teachers and scholars of no concern to the administrators of the college?

I raise questions that are of vital concern to teachers everywhere and that may not be tossed aside lightly.

Very cordially yours,
Amos L. Herold

Supplementary Letter

March 20, 1942

President L. H. Hubbard,
T. S. C. W.,
Denton, Texas

Dear Dr. Hubbard:

On March 18, I wrote you a note, referring you to an article by Dr. Stovall, and pointing out that there is a certain element of clash between British and American literature in all our colleges, with students, teachers, and progressive educators asking for more American literature, and reminding you that there was and still is disagreement between the President and Head of the English department over its proper expansion, which affected me adversely. Let me add that every change made here was approved by the department head and that no progress could be made without his approval so that he should be fully satisfied with the little progress made.

In accepting an appointment here, I did so with a tacit and implied understanding that, in return for good and faithful service, I would always be dealt with fairly and justly; that just as I was expected to promote the best interests of the college, so I might hope to have my personal interests promoted and safeguarded. That was a mutual understanding. Moreover, in 1938, I was given strong, written reason for expecting continued employment till the age of retirement under Texas regulations.

Since in 1935 the President gave me a commission to seek the expansion of American literature in spite of the department head's negative and thus gave me an exceedingly difficult assignment, I now request the President to exercise the same degree of authority in order to clear away the tangle which his action then initiated. To aid in this clarificaton, I request that my letter of March 18, 1942 be read to the Board of Trustees with such explanations as the President may wish to make. This letter covers the essential facts in brief form and courteous manner. In this way, I earnestly request the President to take the initiative in completely clearing my record and reputation as a teacher and a scholar, as they deserve to be cleared, in order that I may not have a deepseated and justifiable cause of grievance against this college and administration.

In the past I have had many reasons and occasions for feeling grateful to you and to this college. I sincerely hope that you will give me a greater reason than ever before for feeling gratitude and thankfulness, and I believe you will.

Very cordially yours,
Amos L. Herold

Appeal to Board of Regents

In the month of May, 1942, in accordance with the By-Laws of the College Regents, I requested an opportunity to appear before the board at its next meeting and drafted a six-page letter to send to the Governor of the state, the President of the college, and to each of the nine-member Board, in which I reviewed the case in some detail as in this narrative, stressing the terms of my employment, the mismanagement of the Activities Fund, and calling upon the Board to investigate these conditions at the college. For expository purposes I quote my opening and two closing paragraphs:

As a veteran of the First World War to save democracy and as a patriotic American and teacher, deeply interested in preserving our free institutions and our personal rights and privileges, I hereby register this protest against the misrule that oppresses the Texas State College for Women. In accepting a position here in the English department seven years ago, I did not agree to surrender any of the privileges usually enjoyed by college teachers nor any of the personal rights of American citizens. Yet, as I will show, these personal rights and faculty rights have been repeatedly infringed or wantonly invaded.

I do not believe that the good people of Texas established and maintain this college at great expense in order that anyone should luxuriate here in misrule. Moreover, if administrators instill in teachers and students a spirit of subjection and passive obedience, we can not hope to preserve our democratic faith, traditions, and practices. Suppression of democracy in college government is an insidious and dangerous evil.

For these reasons and for these malpractices, the Regents of the college should investigate conditions here thoroughly to determine whether President Hubbard should retain leadership at the Texas State College for Women.

Very truly yours,
Amos L. Herold,
Associate Professor of English.

On June 1, I appeared before the Board to speak in support of my letter and to show the members a few of the most important documents in the case. At my request, one woman member checked and read to the other members my letter of employment, two or three papers pertaining to the Activities Fund, and the documentary evidence of lying. I did not mince matters. Mr. Hubbard was not present, but, while I was before the Board, he sent cold drinks to the members to keep them cool and considerate. The questions of one or two women members showed that they were minded to look into the business, but the Board as a unit shut its eyes and stopped its ears and let matters drift. It took no constructive action, being itself under the thumb of the president and afraid to act. One of my college mates on the Board made excuses and stayed away! The next day I addressed this letter to the President:

Dear Sir:

For the reasons given in my letter to Mr. J. K. Brim, President of the T. S. C. W. Board of Regents, Sulphur Springs, Texas, dated May 28, 1942, of which you have a copy, and for other good and sufficient reasons, I hereby resign my position in the Texas State College for Women for the remainder of this year, effective today. There is neither satisfaction nor honor in being connected with this college under the conditions that your personal leadership has created in the past year especially.

Very truly yours,
Amos L. Herold
Associate Professor of English

Owing to conflicting and confusing stories in the press regarding my appearance before the Board of Regents, I issued a factual statement covering the business, showing that no question regarding my scholarship, teaching ability, or character was involved and that I had excellent testimonials from the college officials (secured several months before I began to show my fighting intentions and equipment). Under the date of July 4, 1942, I also had a sheet printed for circulation among my friends and students and addressed to them, in which a central paragraph was the following:

The termination of my service here comes perhaps from such an academic question as definitions. What does democracy mean as applied on a college campus? For me, it means freedom of discussion as a means of mental and spiritual growth: it means tolerance for the views and practices of other people in religion, in politics, in industry, in education, and in everything else vitally connected with our life and our nation. It means freedom to protest without penalty as a safeguard against abuse and oppression. It seems to me that a college or any school without perfect freedom of debate and of friendly discussion in the classes and in faculty and committee meetings is out of step with progressive Americanism. For me, democracy means parliamentary procedures for groups of people working together, and it means the privilege to be heard either directly or through representatives. In short, democracy means democracy.

In the course of my long teaching and reading experience, I have observed that dictators appear to have four common traits of character, which reveal a species of moral obliquity. These traits are: 1. An excessive love of power over other people. 2. A callous disregard for the rights of other people. 3. A contempt for truth leading to prevarication. 4. A hypocritical show of religion to cloak and conceal evil motives and evil conduct.

I CHOSE TEACHING
Part VI. Seeing the United States

CHAPTER 21

The Southwest and California

O NE of my earliest wishes was to see beyond the hilltops and to learn what was there. Since I spent my boyhood among Virginian hills and mountains, my curiosity led to many climbing expeditions, including Paddy's Knob, and many years later the high Alps and Rockies. Once in my early teaching, with a schoolboy, I ascended to the top of nearby Michael Mountain for the distant views, and, to improve them, I climbed into a treetop near a precipice! Though my native valleys and mountains were lovely and impressive, as I grew older, I felt shut in, restricted, or even imprisoned, like a wild turkey in a coop, with a wish to escape and to see the rest of the world. Sometimes this feeling came to me strongly as I walked home over the hills on Friday afternoon from my teaching. When at the age of ten or twelve with an Uncle I first visited Staunton, a small city, I was not satisfied, for I longed to see the national capital. Somehow, a few years later, I got funds for this trip and spent a full day and night there. Though I ran short of money and for my last meal I had only a bowl of soup, I was happy from my sightseeing in the beautiful and impressive city of Washington, D. C.

Early Journeys

While I was a boy, my parents traveled back and forth frequently between Virginia and West Virginia, visiting our relatives and enjoying new scenes and associations. A favorite trip was the 75 miles across the Allegheny, Back Creek, and Shenandoah Mountains to the Ruckman home on Long Glade north of Staunton. In a carriage that was then a three-day journey each

way with marvelous valley and mountain scenes, villages for
night stops, and a few toll gates to block the roads. In an automobile one can now make this round trip in a single day with
several hours for shopping or visiting. How the motor car and
improved highways have revolutionized travel and transportation! Living through this marvelous change, I passed from the
horse-and-buggy age to the automobile and airplane era.

Since I was an ardent admirer of the character, scholarship,
and political aims of Woodrow Wilson, I attended his first inauguration on March 4, 1913, which was a memorable and
momentous occasion. The following September I journeyed
into the cotton South for two years while teaching in North
Carolina. Besides repeated trips to New York, I was in Missouri
on a courting adventure in 1914 and in Kansas and Oklahoma
to visit my Herold relatives. On my return to North Carolina I
passed through six southern states. At the Fort Sheridan training
camp in 1918 a group of us sought diversion by spending a day
in Milwaukee, Wisconsin. While I was teaching at Bucknell and
researching on Paulding, I traveled in July, 1922, by boat from
New York City to Fall River, Massachusetts, and thence by train
to Plymouth, Boston, and Concord, sightseeing and visiting several libraries. It seemed to me that the land around Plymouth
was so poor and rocky as to force the first settlers to fishing for a
livelihood and to make their survival as a colony all the more
remarkable, since they succeeded chiefly because of their character and their courage. Next, during my teaching in Oklahoma,
I vacationed once in Colorado and journeyed several times into
North Texas. Thus, at different times I became acquainted
with all of the eastern states except Maine, Vermont, New Hamp-
shire, and Florida, and all of the midwestern except Iowa, Minnesota, Nebraska, and the two Dakotas. My two long automobile
trips later included all the far western states except Nevada, Oregon, and Washington.

After my long and expensive trip to Europe in 1926, after
my investment in Tulsa real estate in 1927, and during a ten-
year depression, my zeal for traveling was either satisfied for
the time or prohibited by financial necessity. Though short on
vacation funds, I did return to New York for the Columbia
Summer School of 1931 and for the New York Exposition of
1939. Yet, during a period of nineteen years, apart from business
and professional errands, my traveling was so restricted and my
gypsy instincts became so clamorous as to require three long
automobile excursions to quiet them. These were to California

in 1945, to Yellowstone Park in 1948, and to the Virginias in 1950.

Trip to California

In May, 1945, while temporarily living and teaching in Lexington, Missouri, I sold the last of my lots in Tulsa for $7,600 in cash, which added to my other funds gave me a comfortable surplus. Since by September, 1945, I had not secured a desirable college position, I decided that I could afford to use my leisure for traveling to the Far West. Though gasoline was no longer subject to war-time rationing, new automobile tires were, but one could buy recapped tires without much difficulty. To my set of five, I added two recapped extras, making three spares for my ten-year-old Chevrolet car, which had been two years in storage.

On September 29, 1945, with this expeditionary outfit, three suitcases, two light overcoats, and my portable Remington typewriter and letter file, Mrs. Herold and I left Missouri for California, getting on the Santa Fe Trail at Independence and following near it to Wichita, Kansas, where we visited two aging Herold relatives, Aunt Lula Miller and Aunt Nina Dean; then Uncle Penic the banker at Anthony, Kansas, and Uncle Bedford the farmer and stockman at Byron, Oklahoma, Thence we crossed Oklahoma to Amarillo in northwest Texas, where we detoured south a hundred miles to Lubbock to see my friend, Dr. J. M. Gordon, dean of Texas Technological College.

Since with two long detours we would travel 2,000 miles from Missouri to California, my chief concern was whether my old tires would carry us there. If necessary, I was prepared to store the car and continue our journey by train. However, I resolved to drive carefully and to conserve my tires zealously. With my own gauge I frequently checked the air pressure in them and watched them like precious jewels. I would tolerate no speeding or unnecessary side-trips, and over rough roads I would pick my way like a tender-footed cat, because the success of our trip depended upon the endurance of my seven veteran tires! Near the Continental Divide on Highway 66, I detected a rear tire losing pressure abnormally. At a nearby filling station we checked it to expose a subversive nail plotting to delay or terminate our pursuit of happiness! For a fee of one dollar the nail was seized and extricated and the tire mended and replaced on the wheel so that we could proceed. At night I parked in safe places, fearing my tires might be stolen, and sometimes I had visions of double blowouts in remote places such as I once had in Oklahoma!

Two Similar States

New Mexico and Arizona are notable in history for having been explored by the Spanish in the 1540's, including the Grand Canyon, and for being the last states admitted to the Union in 1912. They are also alike in aridity, each receiving only 8 to 15 inches of annual rainfall in contrast with 30 to 60 inches in most of the states. So, they are arid or semi-arid, best fitted for grazing sheep and cattle, for mining and lumbering, and irrigation projects. New Mexico has large quantities of uranium, gypsum, coal, natural gas, and petroleum. Its mild, sunny climate, large forests, high mountains, and its evidences of an Indian civilization antedating that of the Spanish, which is three hundred years old, annually attract many artists and thousands of travelers. The elevation of the state, ranging from 3,000 feet in the south to 7,000 in the north, mounts up to 13,000 feet in the Rocky Mountains north of Las Vegas and Santa Fe, which are centers of the tourist trade.

Seven National Forests and four Indian Reservations (chiefly Apache and Navajo) occupy about fifteen per cent of New Mexico's area. I was surprised to observe that seven lava beds with a few volcanic holes or craters spread over several hundred square miles, recording violent actions of the remote past. East of the Rio Grande and about 100 miles north of El Paso is a barren, sandy, lava region of about 6,000 square miles, internationally famous as the location of the first atomic explosions in 1945. Since then, the state has been the scene of tremendous nuclear laboratories and aircraft developments, accompanied by a large increase of the population.

But the unique wonder of the state, discovered in 1901, is the three-tier, limestone Carlsbad Caverns in the southeast corner. On my return from California I veered northeast from El Paso to be fully convinced of their impressive size and spectacular beauty in a cool underworld with an all-year temperature of 56 degrees. The Big Room is nearly 4,000 feet long with a maximum width of 600 feet and a maximum height of 350 feet, where the limestone decorations are richly varied and superbly beautiful. Some of the stalagmites resemble snow-banked forests. The cactus vegetation on the surface and nature's fairyland below are the two chief attractions of the Carlsbad Caverns National Park.

After detouring from Amarillo to Lubbock for one night,

we returned through Clovis and Fort Sumner to Santa Rosa, New Mexico, for a second night stop. The next day on our chosen route, Highway 66, we regretfully passed fifty miles south of Santa Fe and across the Rio Grande at Albuquerque. Ascending at an easy grade the 100-mile stretch toward the Continental Divide, we drove through Laguna Indian Reservation and across two lava fields, where I picked up a few specimens for trophies. Continuing slowly upward with a small mountain to the north and then another to the south, we crossed an almost level summit, near Thoreau, at an elevation of 7,268 feet. Though we were at such an elevation on the high plateau, I could scarcely realize that we were at the Continental Divide. Thirty minutes later we halted for the night at Gallup, which is a commercial center, near the Navajo Indians, famous for their colorful rugs and handmade silver ornaments.

In extensive area, rapidly increasing population, Indian reservations, aircraft factories, and irrigation projects as well as in climate and historical associations, Arizona resembles New Mexico, though Arizona Indians are more numerous and perhaps wilder, and remote places are less accessible. One dirt road in the southwest is called the Devil's Highway! Though there are few high mountains and though the southwest border is near sea level, yet the northern half of the state is an elevated plateau of 5,000 to 7,000 feet, through which the Colorado River cut the superlative American wonder, the Grand Canyon. Other features of special interest in Arizona are petrified forests, a meteor crater, two monument areas of giant cacti, and Boulder Dam in the northwest corner.

Natural Wonders in Arizona

Leaving Gallup early one morning over Highway 66, we soon arrived at the Petrified Forests at the edge of the Painted Desert. In a monument area of 92,000 acres are six forests of petrified tree trunks, some 250 feet long, relics of a remote past. Here, too, is a freakish natural bridge of great width. At Holbrook we came to the Little Colorado River, which flows 200 miles northwest into the main river above the Canyon. Continuing past Winslow on the southwest side of the Little Colorado, we felt constrained to detour five miles south over a rough road to Meteor Crater, which is about 600 feet deep and one mile in diameter with a ridge of earth and broken rocks all around the rim. Meteoric fragments found there have led to the plausible conclusion that some thousands of years ago a meteor crashed into the earth and left the crater.

From this point onward past Flagstaff and north to the Grand Canyon for 150 miles, we had on our right a marvelous view of the Painted Desert all the afternoon when the sunlight was most effective in revealing the phenomenal play of vivid colors on the bare eastern hills and terraces. Even while crossing over the Devil's Canyon just west of the Crater, we could reassure ourselves and gain spiritual strength by watching the celestial glory on the eastern horizon, where earth and heaven seemed to meet. Similar mineral combinations continue the varied play of rich colors in the Canyon.

In the late afternoon at Navajo and Grandview Points on the south bank of the Colorado River, we got our first thrilling views of the mighty depths and pinnacled heights and variegated coloring of the Grand Canyon of the Colorado. Parking our car for a while, we drank in the wonderful, awe-inspiring beauty of the marvelous scenes, the handiwork of the ages. Spending the night at a Canyon hotel, we were abroad early the next morning for a walk at the edge of the Canyon and dizzying views of the precipitous banks and the mighty river far below. As the reader probably knows, the Grand Canyon, nature's unique masterpiece, which awed Theodore Roosevelt and inspired John Muir to adoration, is one mile deep, 4 to 18 miles wide at the top, and 217 miles long. Through this Canyon for countless ages have roared the waters of many co-operating rivers, draining an area of perhaps 250,000 square miles on the west slope of the Rocky Mountains from western Wyoming to eastern Arizona. J. W. Powell, who first explored the river, declared, "A hundred roaring rivers unite to form the Colorado, a mad, turbulent stream". In the last fifty years, however, several big dams on the Colorado River and its tributaries have tamed them and converted their water power into electrical plants and irrigation projects.

California Contrasts and Marvels

Driving 60 miles south to Williams, we completed our detour of 150 miles to the Grand Canyon, and continued westward through Seligman and Kingman, Arizona, and across the Colorado River to Needles, California, for the night. Still nursing my tires, we then headed west toward the 150-mile desert of bare hills, dry lakes, and lava beds, with a few filling stations along the way. Since Mrs. Herold thought she smelt something burning as we emerged from the Colorado River Valley at Dead Mountain, we stopped at a filling station to investigate. After a few minutes the operator and I found a smouldering, handsize fire in the floor packing under the rear seat, caused by a broken exhaust pipe, which had been spouting hot fumes from the engine against the metal flooring. Repairs being impossible there, the attendant bent the broken pipe downward so that we could drive the car safely. We then passed through the hot, monotonous desert to Barstow on the Mohave River and Desert; thence south to San Bernardino among irrigated vineyards and orange groves, and west into the magic city of Los Angeles, our immediate destination. Including two long detours, we had traveled 2,000 miles in a week without a single flat tire!

In Los Angeles we visited my Aunt Margie and Uncle Arthur Cook, a retired college professor, and Mrs. Herold's sister, Mrs. Mary Green, whose home was our headquarters for two months. We enjoyed the refreshing autumn climate and the picturesque palm trees, and we became acquainted with the attractions of the city and the innumerable wonders of California, which has about every cultivated product and natural marvel that one can desire or imagine. Los Angeles County is unequaled for the variety and value of its agricultural products. The state has our deepest depression, Death Valley, and within fifty miles of it our highest mountain, Mount Whitney, respectively, 280 feet below sea level and 14,495 feet above. It has not only lava beds as in New Mexico but an active, smoking Lassen Volcano. In height and beauty its Sierra Nevada Mountains are a match for the Rockies or Alps, and like Arizona the state has its own painted deserts. The harbor of San Francisco easily equals that of proud New York City, and its ocean shore line is unsurpassed for length and beauty. Its forests of giant redwood and sequoia trees containing the earth's tallest, largest, and oldest are likewise matchless. Besides much traveling and sightseeing in Los Angeles, which is about twenty miles square, we sidetripped to Pomona, Santa Anna, and Long Beach. Though Beverly Hills, Hollywood, and Pasadena, snow-capped mountains, orange groves, and vineyards had attractions, the two chief centers of interest for me were the Los Angeles County Museum and the Huntington Library. Since they were unique and educational, I visited them several times.

Museum and Library.

Besides extensive art galleries and records of Indian culture, the County Museum exhibits a remarkable collection of animal and plant fossils obtained from the tar or asphalt deposits of Rancho La Brea, about 23 acres of which are now a city park. In the dim past many thousand years ago, petroleum escaping to the surface there formed tar pits or pools, which became death traps for all sorts of creatures then living and an almost perfect preservative of their bones, representing thousands of individuals. Many of the animals still exist, but some have disappeared or been modified. Among the extinct animals I found fascinating the imperial mammoth, mastodon, giant sloth, camel, saber-tooth tiger and a lionlike cat, both felines of large size and fierce killing power.

The supposition is that the tar pits frequently looked like or contained water, to which both birds and animals were lured, got stuck, and became living or dead bait for predatory creatures that frequented the deceptive tar pools. In 1792 the Spanish explorer, J. L. Martinez, reported near Los Angeles "twenty springs of liquid petroleum, pitch, etc" — "a great lake of pitch with many pools". — "In hot weather animals have been seen to sink in it and when they tried to escape they were unable to do so, because their feet were stuck, and the lake swallowed them." This Spaniard also collected specimen bones "as if petrified". From the pits most productive of fossils, 15 to 25 feet deep, in the last 50 years many scientists have assembled the bones, studied and reconstructed them, and published their conclusions on the significance of this unparalleled fossil depository. (See Chester Stock's *Rancho La Brea, A Record of Pleistocene Life in California*, Revised, 1942.)

The second unique attraction was the Henry E. Huntington (1850-1927) Library, Art Gallery, and Botanical Gardens at San Marino, Pasadena. Here Mr. Huntington, after accumulating a fortune in railroads and other business enterprises, retired and invested much of his wealth in fine books, choice paintings, Americana, globes, tapestries, and rare or prized plants. Among the paintings are Stuart's "Washington", Reynold's "Sarah Siddons", and Gainsborough's "Blue Boy". Among the prized books are an Egyptian "Book of the Dead" on papyrus of 1200 B. C., the Ellesmere Chaucer on vellum, and the earliest printed Bibles in Latin and English.

Mr. Huntington sought to collect and to leave to the public and scholars, under the control of trustees, a library of the history and literature of the English-speaking peoples, rich in manuscripts and rare editions. Expending several million dollars for choice items and collections already made, he assembled about 150,000 rare books and a million manuscripts and documents — all stored in two vaults best fitted to preserve them. Though the Library of Congress and many public and college libraries have similar collections, the donor left the nation an endowed, educational institution with unique treasures, a free museum, an art gallery, and a botanical garden of 75,000 specimens.

Yosemite National Park

Early in November on a four-day excursion, we traveled a thousand miles through central California to San Francisco and then down the coast to Los Angeles. Passing through Bakersfield, we planned to visit Sequoia National Park, but, finding accommodations very scarce in that section, we spent a night at Selma, and early the next morning from Fresno we ascended the foothills of the Sierra Nevada Mountains to the southwest corner of Yosemite National Park. As we entered the reservation, it began to sleet and when we reached the nearby Mariposa Grove of Big Trees, including Old Grizzly, the earth was white with snow. Truly impressive and majestic were the great trees whether standing straight and handsome in defiance of time or lying huge and fallen on the earth. In spite of Mrs. Herold's warning against bears, I got out of the car and paid my reverential respects to the tree Old Grizzly by walking around it with bared head and adoring eyes and mind. Such tenacious longevity, such serene majesty, and ancient uprightness I had not hitherto observed. This Grizzly Giant, 27 feet in diameter, 209 feet high with top missing, and more than 3,000 years old!

Returning by the park entrance and accompanied by flying snowflakes, we began a 25-mile drive over a winding road across the timbered, mountainous park to Yosemite Falls. Soon the snow was falling so thick and fast that my windshield wiper would stall and I could scarcely see to drive. By this time Mrs. Herold was delighted by the fairyland scenes made by the snow on the evergreens and hillsides while I was altogether concerned with keeping in the road as we passed by treetops near the roadside, indicating that we were near precipices! Stopping a few times to clear my windshield, I was thinking of turning back at the first opportunity to the entrance. When we met a stalled car on a hillside, I pulled off to the side against a bank, stopped and securely applied my brakes. By this time the snow was about five inches deep and still falling. Behind the stalled car, a truck came up, fortunately driven by a park employee. I conferred with him as to what we had better do. To my surprise, he advised, since we were past the worst part and the snow was slackening, that we should proceed ahead, but leave the park by following down the valley of the Merced River, which would be free of snow. Then he helped the stalled car to start, and, with many thanks for his timely appearance and advice, we renewed the drive. On the way, however, I observed that the filling stations and summer resorts had closed for the season though the park is open the year round.

Passing through a long tunnel near the Merced River, we came out at Bridal Veil Falls, El Capitan, Yosemite Falls, and the other wonders of this remarkable and celebrated park. We spent an hour or more in the museum, lunched, and chatted with other visitors. With snow still hanging on the heights and my recollections of a fatal snow storm in the Sierras described in Harte's "The Outcasts of Poker Flat," we did not tarry long but carefully picked our way down the Merced Canyon for twenty miles and then up and out by Mariposa to the town of Merced for our second night. Here we found a room after much enquiring, because everybody seemed to be traveling.

The next day from Oakland we drove out to Berkeley for a glimpse of the University of California. Thence we crossed the long Bay Bridge into San Francisco and then south to Stanford University at Palo Alto. At San Jose we made two short friendly calls and then proceeded down the coast to Salinas for our third night. The next day we continued our return trip, stopping at Santa Barbara to see the mission and college, and then back to Los Angeles in time to enjoy a full night's rest from four days of strenuous sightseeing.

My Return to Texas

After three more weeks of visiting and dodging the multitudinous automobiles of Los Angeles, I decided to return to Texas alone, since Mrs. Herold wished to stay longer with her sister. On December 3, I came by Riverside to Indio for my first night, where I could scarcely find a place to sleep. Thence, through Blythe, California, I reached Phoenix, Arizona, a bustling, ambitious city, in an irrigated desert with dark, bare, cheerless mountains on the horizon. The next day I stopped to view the prehistoric ruins, four stories high with stone walls four feet thick at the base, in the Casa Grande National Monument, on my way to Tucson, where I visited the University of Arizona and spent a restful night. The next day I broke one of my traveling rules by picking up two stranded sailor boys, whose papers I checked carefully, and who entertained me with their naval experiences on our way across the Continental Divide to the Rio Grande and down to El Paso for the night.

That evening I boarded a street car and crossed the Rio Grande to Juarez, Mexico, for a glimpse of that country, getting off for a few steps on Mexican soil and returning to El Paso on the same car. The next morning I left an hour before daylight in order to arrive at the Carlsbad Caverns in time to join the day's party into that fairyland, on the way passing Guadalupe Peak, 8,571 feet, the highest point in Texas. Emerging from the Caverns, I drove through the town of Carlsbad and by Texas cattle ranches to Pecos for the night. The next day I passed more cattle ranches, the West Texas oil fields, Midland, San Angelo, and Brady to Fredericksburg for the night in a German settlement. The next day I arrived in San Antonio, where a filling-station attendant warned me that one of my tires needed air, nearly down, but not quite! Not flat yet!

My tires were all safe and intact! At an expense of $600 for two months I had traveled 5,000 miles on old tires without a single blowout and no complete flat! Just threatened twice! I was elated to have accomplished what seemed to be almost impossible when we started the trip in Missouri.

After visiting colleges in San Marcos and Houston in search of work, I stopped in Austin, where because of its mild climate, excellent libraries, and investment opportunities I was thinking of buying property. For some time past in Missouri, Oklahoma, and Texas I had been looking for a property that would provide some income and a retirement home. Late in January, 1946, I found what I was looking for in Austin, a small apartment house where I now live, which I bought, paying cash so that there would be no mortgage around my neck. That spring and summer I taught in the University of Texas, but in the fall I accepted a more attractive position at Monticello, Arkansas, and later another for five years in Arkansas College at Batesville during the presidency of Dr. John D. Spragins.

CHAPTER 22

Texas to Yellowstone Park

WHETHER rightly or not, Texans have a widespread reputation for boasting about their big Lone Star State of 267,000 square miles with California a poor second of 158 thousand in area. To enclose its "wide open spaces," Texas has 4,100 miles of boundaries, or it would form a square with 517-mile sides. In this vast area live about eight million people, whose state flower is the lovely bluebonnet and state bird the matchless mockingbird. Actually, Texas leads the states of the Union not only in area but also in the value of mineral products (chiefly oil, gas, and sulphur), in cotton, in live stock, and probably in paved highways with 45,000 miles. One of the tall tales relates that a Texan wore out a new automobile by one trip across the state! A comical map shows Texas pushing all the other states into smaller spaces so that it occupies a third of the nation!

Putting jokes aside, however, if one will place a map of Texas on the eastern half of the United States, with uniform scale, so that El Paso is at St. Louis and Texarkana at Washington, D.C., he will find that Brownsville at the mouth of the Rio Grande is near Savannah, Georgia, and that the border of East Texas parallels the Carolina coast and crosses Virginia near Norfolk. The Panhandle of North Texas will occupy Michigan south of Lansing and include both Detroit and Toledo. Virtually all of Kentucky, Virginia, and West Virginia, most of the Carolinas, Tennessee, Maryland, Ohio, and Indiana, and big slices of Georgia, Illinois, Michigan, and Pennsylvania will fall within the boundaries of Texas.

John Erskine in his autobiography, *The Memory of Certain Persons,* praised the tall, muscular, deep-voiced, steady-eyed men of Texas and called them heroic like those carved by Phidias. This observation and another on the huge size of the state, made on lecture tours, are correct, but Erskine's further statement that they hold human life cheaply and still tote hidden pistols is only an echo of former practices and cowboy fiction which the author mistakenly attributed to a modern, law-abiding generation. During a 12-year residence in Texas the only gun-toters I have seen were policemen, state rangers, and hunters. To be sure, loving the outdoors in a sunny land and breathing the air that won independence from Mexico, Texans do manifest the independent spirit of pioneer Americans. They remember proudly that their state was once an independent nation that voluntarily joined the Union and later seceded. Much of this former spirit and status carries over to the living generation in various ways, especially in politics. The people are interesting, because they are still independent and unpredictable.

Mountains in Texas

Most strangers, I think, consider both Texas and Oklahoma as uniformly flat or level. When I came to Oklahoma in 1923, I was much surprised to find that the south and east sections of the state had handsome, timbered hills and mountains of creditable elevation and diversity — the Arbuckle and Kiamichi Mountains. Likewise in Texas, it was surprising to learn that the Big State had two mountainous areas. The first is Edwards Plateau, or Hill Country, a rugged, cedared region, well fitted for deer and panthers, or goats and cattle, extending west from Austin and San Antonio and having an area as large as West Virginia with an elevation of 600 to 2,500 feet. Through this hilly terrain, the Colorado River flowing southeast has cut a wide and deep bed for 75 miles or more by its snaky curves, making possible the construction of six dams 90 to 270 feet high for water supply, electric power, or flood control at a total cost of 62 million dollars, financed successfully by the Lower Colorado River Authority, which was created by the Texas Legislature in 1934. Here is a brilliant example of a state developing its own resources for its people. This lakelike region with nearly 120 square miles of water surface, popular for hunting, fishing, and boating, is called the Highland Lakes and Hill Country of Texas. Austin, the state capital and seat of the University of Texas, a city of 170,000 people, stands at the point where this Colorado River of Texas emerges from the hills. The second mountain area of 30,000 square miles with two towns a mile high and peaks up to 8,000 feet lies in the southwest corner east of El Paso and includes the Big Bend National Park with a notable canyon and a varied list of wild plants and animals.

Journey to Colorado

With this explanation of the magnitude and terrain of Texas, the reader will more readily believe my statement that from Austin, which is 100 miles southeast of the state's center, I was two days getting out of Texas to the northwest on an automobile trip to Colorado and Yellowstone Park in the summer of 1948. Still driving my repaired Chevrolet car and untroubled by rationed tires, Mrs. Herold and I left Austin on July 30, spending our first night at Sweetwater and second at Dalhart, Texas, near the New Mexico boundary in the Texas Panhandle, 600 miles from Austin. The next day we crossed the high, peaky, cattle region of northeast New Mexico, where rise the Canadian and Cimarron Rivers of Oklahoma. Entering Colorado through Raton Pass at 7,800 feet, we passed by Trinidad with a fine view of the Spanish Peaks, about 13,000 feet high, to our left in the Rocky Mountains. At Pueblo we crossed the Arkansas River, which from its source in the highest Rockies tumbles down the Royal Gorge at Canon City on its long journey through Kansas, Oklahoma, and Arkansas to the Mississippi River. After driving

278 miles, we spent the afternoon and night at Colorado Springs near Pike's Peak, which I had visited in 1925.

Since one of my aims in making this trip was to get my eyes and mind full of the Rocky Mountains, I planned to drive to Denver the next morning, where I would turn West across the Rockies, up the Colorado River to Milner Pass, and return through the Rocky Mountain National Park to Estes Park or Loveland. Arriving in Denver about 11 A. M. (too late for this wild drive), we headed straight into the Rockies at Idaho Springs and then up Clear Creek until we began to ascend the mountain in the Arapaho National Forest. Up and up we circled and climbed till we reached the Continental Divide at Berthoud Pass, where we halted. Not fully satisfied with the elevation of 11,314 feet of the Pass, I parked my car near a refreshment stand, and on foot we began to climb to a higher point. Since Mrs. Herold soon found the ascent too strenuous, she turned back to the Pass while I continued upward. Sometimes holding to rocks or bushes, I climbed up and up till I was above the timber line, where the peak rounded off in a mass of age-old granite. Though I was nearly out of breath and the wind almost snatched my hat away, I got a grand view in all directions and rested there a few minutes, feeling refreshed and victorious. As a memento of my climb to the top, I found a paper-weight piece of granite, weathered on three sides and freshly broken on the fourth, where shone the reddish-gray natural color. So, on my desk I now have this piece of the mighty Rocky Mountains.

Snow in August!

Then, back in our car, we passed a winter sports area and down the beautiful Fraser River to Granby, where we left Highway 40 and turned north on Highway 34 beside the Colorado River for nearly 40 miles. Then, turning east, we wound and twisted up a steep ascent to Milner Pass at 10,759 feet on the Continental Divide, where we were surprised to find a little lake. But the highest and most exciting was yet to come! Driving onward and upward along the side of a vast, steep mountain, bare of trees, we came thrillingly to Fall River Pass at 11,797 feet, a thousand feet above the Continental Divide! There, above the timber line and the snow line, I could park my car with dubious safety!

We got out of the car and looked around at the stupendous, snow-capped mountains. We picked a crust of snow from an August bank and rested a little. But not long because snow began to fall and I decided that it was wise to proceed at once.

So, I steered along the mountain top in a slushy, August snow with the road looking none too wide and high above deep abysses where one could easily plunge to destruction. At an elevation of 12,000 feet, we hugged the Trail Ridge Road for three or four miles with Forest Canyon on our right and Fall River on our left. Far ahead to the right was Long's Peak with boxlike top and on our far left the wonderful Mummy Mountains. In the depths below were little lakes and glaciers, but I could scarcely glance at them though Mrs. Herold was ecstatic with the views. Not until we again reached the tree line did I feel easy and relaxed. The unexpected fall of wet snow, which I mistakenly feared might freeze and make driving a car truly hazardous, was exciting but detrimental to my comfort and delight in wild, natural beauty.

Passing through much-publicised Estes Park, which is a summer resort with facilities for riding or climbing to the lakes, glaciers, and mountain heights, we entered Thompson River Canyon, which we viewed with delight for 30 miles on our way to Loveland for the night after an exciting day along the sides and on top of the Rocky Mountains. I had realized my ambition to fill my eyes and mind with the Rockies!

On the morning of August 3, we drove north to Cheyenne, capital of Wyoming, and in the pioneer days of 1867 a tent and shanty town called "Hell on Wheels," then the western terminus of the Union Pacific Railway. It is still a central point for this railroad and for transcontinental airlines. After visiting the capitol and the interesting pioneer museum, we drove west to Laramie and then northwest beside the railway with the Medicine Bow National Forest to our far left. At Como Bluff we stopped to view some of the dinosaur fossils discovered there in 1877 and renowned as geological evidence from an incredibly ancient era before the Hebrew God had even thought of creation! At Rawlins we spent the night in a town crowded with vacationists from the Upper Mississippi Valley, as shown by the car tags.

The next morning over an almost level surface we crossed the Continental Divide at an elevation of 7,178 feet, about 70 miles southeast of the historically famous South Pass, where Whitman's party, the Mormons, and their followers found easy passage from the Sweetwater River to the Green River. Here the Rocky Mountains disappear in the Great Divide Basin, which south of the Sweetwater contains a Red Desert, Sand Dunes, and Alkali Flats. Since Wyoming and Montana have an annual precipitation of only 12 to 15 inches, they are semi-arid and thinly populated. Both states are famous for cattle and sheep, timber, minerals, colorful characters like Buffalo Bill Cody, wild animals, and gigantic mountains.

Forests and Grand Teton Mountains

At Rock Springs we turned northwest across the pioneer trails toward the Grand Teton and Yellowstone National Parks. Soon after crossing the headwaters of Green River, we passed through cool, beautiful Bridger and Teton National Forests to Jackson on the Snake River for the night of August 4. By stopping early, we got a room easily though during the night other travelers arrived from Yellowstone, vainly looking for quarters.

Early the next morning, looking across lovely, placid Jenny Lake, we rejoiced in the Alpine beauty of the snowy, rock-spired, 13,000-foot Grand Teton Mountains, from which we could hear refreshing snow-water pouring down to the lake. Farther north at the larger Jackson Lake a picturesque scene showed flowers and evergreens in the foreground and then the still, blue lake reflecting the marvelous, upstanding beauty of the snow-capped Grand Tetons. Unforgettable lakes and unforgettable mountains, unsurpassed by the Alps, the Rockies, or the Sierras! I should love to spend a week there among the fresh forests, the clear lakes, and the fascinating mountains. In Jackson we visited the shop of a painter who was reproducing the thrilling beauties of that entrancing region.

Yellowstone National Park

Advised in Jackson by tourists returning from Yellowstone Park, we headed straight for the hotels at Old Faithful Geyser and by ten A. M. I was standing in line for rooms being vacated. Fortunately we were in time to get a cabin, which we held for three nights at $4 a day. How convenient and comfortable that cabin was while we were viewing the astonishing attractions of Yellowstone Park — fascinating geysers, wild animals, birds, and trees native to the region, and American visitors from everywhere! That afternoon we drove through the chief geyser basins and across the park to Yellowstone Falls for a first view, almost running out of gasoline on our return and coasting on every down grade. The next day we made the circle tour by serene Yellowstone Lake with 100-mile shore-line lying at an elevation of 7,730 feet, the Upper and Lower Falls totaling 417 feet, the Yellowstone Canyon with its rich coloring, Mammoth Hot

Springs, the Norris Museum, and back to our cabin for the night. The third day we rested or rambled among the nearby geysers. From time to time we saw deer, antelope, elk, moose, and buffalo. Of special interest were the black and grizzly bears, which sometimes loitered along the roads. Most of the trees were small evergreens — pine, fir, and spruce. More than 200 species of birds live naturally in the park.

The famous Geyser Old Faithful is so nearly regular, operating every 50 to 70 minutes, that bulletin clocks announce when she will next perform. As a result hundreds of spectators may congregate to witness her act of spouting a stream of hot water and steam for a few minutes about 150 feet high. Other geysers have shorter or longer or more fitful schedules of performance, and a few have become inactive. I observed that Riverside Geyser was clocked to act every eight hours. Since her act is highly dramatic and accompanied by thunderous rumbling and earth tremors, we succeeded in seeing and hearing her perform three times. The last was early on August 8, my birthday, when we were leaving the park. The evening before I made a date with her, so to speak. Though we were hard pressed to arrive on time, she was dependably prompt in keeping the engagement! As we drove up, she was already celebrating my birthday and saying farewell to her ardent admirers, emitting a large volume of water and steam at an angle of 45 degrees with the earth.

But more astonishing and astounding than either geysers or wild animals is the geological and historical record of the Yellowstone region. A basic fact is that the geyser basins are the tops of dying volcanoes, whose activity long ages ago was terrific, spreading lava or volcanic ash and debris over an area 200 or 300 miles in diameter. Twenty petrified forests at different levels in the debris show that long periods of plant growth were intermittently terminated by volcanic action, which could recur in our time. Besides, since most of the ancient rock strata are exposed there and since evidences of later volcanism and glaciation are abundant, Yellowstone is a geologist's paradise. John Colter, a member of the Lewis and Clark expedition, was the first white man to report on the geysers. Incredulous hearers of his tales called the region "Colter's Hell." For more than half a century the truth about Yellowstone was ridiculed as myths or tall tales! Hence, for the information of visitors and students, two excellent pamphlets present the historical and geological records, namely: Dr. Arthur D. Howard's *Yellowstone through the Ages* (Columbia University Press, 1938) and geologist C. M. Bauer's *Yellowstone — its Underworld* (Univ. of New Mexico Press, 1948).

Lake Bonneville

Leaving the park by the West Entrance and crossing a corner of Montana and the Rockies at Targhee Pass, we descended the spectacular valley of Snake River west of the Grand Tetons through Idaho Falls to Pocatello for two nights, where I wished to learn more of the ancient outlet of pleistocene Lake Bonneville, predecessor of Great Salt Lake. In an ancient era of glaciers that covered Canada and northern United States, both Yellowstone and Bonneville Lakes drained into the Snake-Columbia River system. Though in the 19th century the depth of Great Salt Lake varied 13 feet, its predecessor Bonneville, a fresh-water lake, in the pleistocene or glacial era was 1,000 feet deeper and had an area ten times larger than Great Salt Lake, as shown by the ancient shore lines on the mountain east of Salt Lake City. Since the present levels of Great Salt Lake and the nearest points on the Snake River are about the same, a 1,000-foot increase in depth enabled Lake Bonneville to overflow through a well-marked valley to the Snake River. Through this ancient outlet runs a railroad so nearly level at the watershed as to make the pass scarcely discernible. My interest in this ancient Lake Bonneville, as geologists name it, and its outlet to the Snake River was so consuming that Mrs. Herold thought I was daffy on the subject. Frequently I pointed to the ancient shore lines along the mountain and imagined a fresh-water lake that would submerge Salt Lake City and extend into Idaho and Nevada! This fascinating revelation of ancient history was made by the seeing and knowing eyes of geologists, who show both knowledge and imagination in reconstructing earth's ancient status.

Since our important mail was forwarded to us at Ogden, Utah, we next drove there for one night, observing on the way evidences of Mormon industry and ingenious irrigation. The next day in Salt Lake City we visited the headquarters, temple site, and university of the Latter Day Saints, who maintain ten institutions of higher learning. The handsome State Capitol, overlooking the city, is a symbol of Utah's agricultural and commercial industry and mineral wealth. Like Moses, Brigham Young led his followers to a Promised Land. We also visited the salt works on the lake and the hotel and business center of the city, attractive and prosperous, where before the Mormons came there was no civilization. They proved that they could originate and establish a new faith here in the United States with all the energy and accoutrements of other religions, including the Book of Mormon reputedly entrusted to Joseph Smith by an angel, so the faithful believe or pretend to believe!

Home Again

Spending the night of August 11 at Provo, seat of Brigham Young University, on Utah Lake, we then followed Highway 50 across the Wasatch Range with its coal mines and through a dry hot region at Green River to Grand Junction on the Colorado River and on to Delta for the night of August 12. The next day we climbed across the Rockies again on the same highway and down the Arkansas River Gorge to Pueblo for the night. At this point our homeward route crossed our outward route, which together formed an oblong figure 8 made by starting from Austin at the bottom in this order: first, a left curve through Texas and New Mexico to Pueblo; then, a right curve through Denver and Cheyenne to Yellowstone Park; next, a left curve through Salt Lake City and Grand Junction to Pueblo; and finally, a right curve through Kansas and Oklahoma to the starting point.

In 18 days on this trip we traveled 4,000 miles in nine states for the following items of expense: gasoline at 23 to 33 cents a gallon, $63; lodging rooms, $58; car gear repairs in Kansas, $55; meals for two persons, $96; miscellaneous items excluding Mrs. Herold's outlay, $12.50. Starting with $300 in cash and traveler's checks, I had $15.00 left upon returning to Austin. With two days off for rest our average daily journey was 250 miles. The longest was 374 miles from Sweetwater to Dalhart, Texas, and the most exciting was 357 miles from Colorado Springs to Loveland, Colorado — twice across the Rockies and on the Trail Ridge Road through the Rocky Mountain National Park!

CHAPTER 23

Arkansas to the Virginias

DURING a six-year residence in Arkansas I had ample opportunity to become acquainted with its natural features and its friendly, contented people. Settled mostly by hardy pioneers from Kentucky and Tennessee, whose ancestors had come from the Carolinas and Virginia, Arkansas is a southern, Anglo-Saxon state, of which Little Rock is the chief and central city and the political, commercial, and cultural capital. Besides the winding Mississippi on its eastern border, three notable rivers cross the state: the Red River in the southwest, the Arkansas through the center from west to southeast, and the White in the northern and central sections. If one drives west up the Arkansas River from Little Rock, he will see and enjoy the Ozark Mountains and National Forest on his right and on his left the Ouachita Mountains and National Forest with elevations of 1,000 to 3,000 feet. In 1953 the two forests produced timber worth $2,500,000. Famous Hot Springs in the Ouachitas, Fayetteville with the state university in the Ozarks, and Fort Smith near the Oklahoma border are popular vacation resorts. On the White River above Batesville in the Ozarks are two big dams impounding Lake Norfork and Bull Shoals Lake, prized sources of electric power and recreational facilities. Veterans hospitals at Hot Springs and Fayetteville proclaim them as fitting places to find rest and restoration.

A striking characteristic of the mountains in Arkansas as in the eastern states is that they are restful and refreshing whereas the Rockies and Sierras are sometimes overpowering and somewhat disconcerting to a spectator. I love the Grand Tetons and the adjoining lakes of western Wyoming, because somehow they combine these contradictory qualities — the mountains emanating grandeur and majesty and the lakes instilling peace and repose.

Reasons for this Trip

After living in the Southwest for 25 years and seeing California, the Colorado Rockies, and the Yellowstone region, I became eager to revisit the scenes of my youth in the Virginias more thoroughly than had been possible on incidental or hurried trips there. I wished to see my relatives and old friends while they lived and I could travel easily. So, from my teaching at Arkansas College, I arranged to be away the second term of the 1950 summer school for a month's vacation. Since in September, 1948, my Chevrolet car and I had been knocked out near the college in an automobile collision, which sent me unconscious from a fractured skull to a nearby hospital for a week and the crumpled car to a shop for extensive repairs and sale, we had ceased to be traveling companions, however pleasant my recollections of its former faithful performances. The next year when my driving courage revived, I bought a nearly new Nash sedan, which I drove East.

Leaving Batesville on July 24, Mrs. Herold and I stopped one day in Memphis to consult medical specialists — one to examine and advise my wife and one to examine and prescribe for my right eye, slightly injured in the collision and out of focus with my left. Though I can drive a car and see with both eyes at a distance, I still read best with one eye blocked off by a shield, recommended and supplied to me by the Memphis specialist, who advised against tampering with the eye muscles affected. For two years I had been doing all my reading with one eye voluntarily closed, hoping in vain that nature would make an adjustment.

We then motored through the pleasant cotton, grain, and pasture lands of west Tennessee and across the Tennessee River, now Kentucky Lake, at the Fort Donelson Military Park and Cemetery to Springfield, where for a day we visited Mrs. Herold's cousins, Mr. and Mrs. Russell Stone. We next turned south to Nashville, the state capital and seat of the Peabody Teachers College, Vanderbilt and Fisk Universities, and a reproduction of the Greek Parthenon. Nearby we visited Andrew Jackson's domicile, the Hermitage, emblem of an era long since past. Up, down, around, or beside green hills and by rolling farmlands, we passed through Lebanon, Cookville, and Crossville on our pleasant way to Knoxville, seat of the University of Tennessee. Here we were in sight of the Great Smoky Mountains to the southeast with several 6,000-foot peaks higher than any point in the Virginias, and all around us were artificial lakes with a total area of about 900 square miles.

TVA and AEC

In this region the Tennessee Valley Authority in an extraordinary soil-conservation and hydro-electric development and the Atomic Energy Commission in the Oak Ridge Atomic Plant expended several billion dollars, which have transformed the economy of the state. Thirty miles north of Knoxville is the much-publicised Norris Dam, named for Senator George W. Norris, and twenty miles northwest is the internationally famous Oak Ridge Plant, which is the birthplace of the atomic bomb. Here in quiet, peaceful, green, beautiful Tennessee we were near the source of earth-rocking and terrifying developments of the Atomic Age. In contrast to this troubled world of the 1950's both Arkansas and Tennessee with annual precipitations of 47 inches are naturally peaceful and peace-loving, agricultural and stock-raising states with much lumber and its products, though in recent years many new factories have helped to diversify and balance their industries.

Still among the dams and lakes at Morristown, Tennessee, we spent a pleasant and restful week-end with my cousin sweetheart of long ago, once widowed and a graduate nurse, Mrs. Her-

bert S. Walters, and her second husband, who is a businessman
with diversified interests including long service as Democratic
National Committeeman from Tennessee. While in their spacious
home, where my Aunt Lillian Ruckman was visiting, we were
driven to nearby Greenville to view the log-cabin tailor shop
and museum of President Andrew Johnson of Civil War fame.

Back to Virginia

Driving thence into southwest Virginia, we passed near Mt.
Rogers, 5,700 feet, Virginia's highest peak, then along and across
the New River, which through the ages has so stubbornly evaded
its natural destination, the Atlantic Ocean, for a long, wild-
goose chase or flight over the Allegheny Mountain to the Ohio
and Mississippi Rivers and the Gulf of Mexico! If the great
Colorado River has shown tenacious, destructive power in the
Grand Canyon of Arizona, then the New River, rising in western
North Carolina, has shown shameless perversity as well as power
in flowing 2,500 miles when about 250 would have sufficed! I
am tempted to name it one of our Natural Wonders!

Crossing the Blue Ridge at the Meadows of Dan, we visited
my sisterly cousin, Annah Ruckman MacCorkle, wife of the
Presbyterian pastor at Stuart, Virginia, who is related to former
Governor MacCorkle of West Virginia. Annah and her husband
Fred have a son and a daughter and two grandchildren, of
whom they are rightly proud. Annah, always fond of study and
writing, like her ancestor, Samuel Ruckman, has overcome her
shyness to become a leader among women. She and Mrs. Herold
had been schoolmates at Mary Baldwin Seminary in Staunton
when I was attending Washington and Lee.

Friends and Relatives

Then, for adventure, we traveled along the Blue Ridge Parkway on the top of this mountain, beautiful and free of dangerous
abysses and August snowfalls and, coming down at Roanoke, we
passed over the commercialized Natural Bridge, and up to Lexington for a day at my *alma mater* with friends and schoolmates. I
took Mrs. Herold to see Major Houston's residence, where I
lived my first year in college. Though Major and his daughter
Mary were long since dead, a sister and her editor husband still
live there and greeted us warmly. We had so much to see and
talk about that we could scarcely get back to our hotel, where
my classmate, Earl Paxton, called to greet us with a world of
news. All of our professors were dead except Dr. L. W. Smith,

our professor of mathematics, then a feeble old man. My friend, James S. Moffatt, was away teaching in a summer school, and others were on vacation.

The next morning we returned by Buena Vista to the Blue Ridge Parkway for a 40-mile drive at an elevation of 2,500 feet to the highway between Staunton and Charlottesville, where we descended to the farm home of my brother Henry and his wife Reba at Ivy, a few miles west of Charlottesville. With two grown children, a son Van Meter and a daughter Katie Howard, both married, Katie living in Florida and Van and his wife with his parents, they now have two small grandchildren. An excellent farmer, owning farm machinery worth $10,000, Henry successfully combines agriculture and dairying. With two silos he keeps a fine herd of milk cows, using machines instead of hand-power to extract the milk from gentle and well-trained animals, with no kicking Lizzies such as he and I used to deal with on Knapp's Creek. Though somewhat crippled from the after effects of a case of typhoid fever in 1914, he is still strong and active, the same good, dependable citizen he has always been, happy and contented with his model family at their country estate called Holcomb. While my chief interest in life has been education and scholarship, which are sometimes precarious means of independent living, his ambition and work have found expression in agriculture, dairying, and devotion to his family and many friends.

While visiting here, Mrs. Herold and I spent one day in Charlottesville — she to look up distant relatives and I to visit James Monroe's Ash Lawn home and museum. Besides President Monroe's carriage, some furniture, and household utensils, I saw his Norway pine tree, planted by himself and now nearly three feet in diameter, and his odorous box-hedge, both still green and thriving. An admission charge of 75 cents helps to keep up the property. On my return past familiar Monticello, I stopped at the Michie Tavern, once owned by Patrick Henry's father, a favorite resort of revolutionary patriots and statesmen, restored in 1927 and refurnished as of two centuries ago. Here James Monroe entertained Marquis de Lafayette, and the old-timers chatted, danced, and drank their toddies and juleps.

Virgina's Tourist Attractions

The most remarkable development in Virginia in the last 40 years has been the widespread recognition, symbolized by Rockefeller's restoration of Williamsburg, of what Virginia calls Historic Shrines, Scenic Attractions, and Natural Wonders of the Old Dominion. The state-highway map devotes one side to geography and highways and the reverse side to places of special interest all over Virginia. One finds such wellnigh unmatchable items as the birthplaces of eight presidents and the Lees; the sites of notable events or decisive battles in the Revolution and Civil War; three venerable universities; a dozen intriguing caverns and the Natural Bridge in the Valley of Virginia; the Blue Ridge popularized by the lower Parkway and the upper Skyline Drive in the Shenandoah National Park, totaling nearly 200 miles of fascinating, top-mountain, scenic roads, overlooking the Valley and the Piedmont; and excellent tourist facilities at Natural Bridge, Staunton, Charlottesville, and elsewhere along the paved roads, low and high. Skyline Drive claims a million visitors annually. The only comparable southeastern attractions are the Tennessee lakes and the Great Smoky Mountains National Park.

On Saturday, August 5, we crossed the Blue Ridge to Staunton, birthplace of Woodrow Wilson and the central city in the Valley of Virginia, hoping to see my cousin, Dr. Glen Campbell, and his mother, my Aunt Lollie, but they too were on short vacations. Sunday morning we drove north to the former Herring-Ruckman property on Long Glade and to Mossy Creek in time for the Presbyterian service, after which we visited the family burial site in the cemetery. Returning to Staunton, we looked up and conversed at length with my old friend and schoolmate in high school and college, Harold Houston Leach, and his wife, who was Miss Moomau from Pocahontas County. They have a handsome son, then on leave from military service, who met and directed us to his father's comfortable home, where they live in retirement from long service in the Presbyterian Church. Surely, he is one of the best and sincerest men I have ever known, whose clear blue eyes reflect the uprightness and purity of the man. Like myself, but ten years older, he secured an education by overcoming many difficulties. At the age of 75, he looked somewhat thin and frail but healthy and cheerful. I was gratified to learn that his physician is my cousin, Dr. Campbell.

To Highland and Pocahontas

Late in the afternoon we drove 44 miles across the Shenandoah and two smaller mountains to Monterey, high on a divide between river heads, to see Uncle Edwin Wade, his children, and other relatives. Uncle Ed was then 86 years old, entirely blind, confined to his bed and room, and lovingly cared for by his devoted sons and daughters. Though he was hard of hearing and consequently loud talking, we conversed with him for about twenty minutes. His sense of humor was still active. Taking my wife by the arm, he examined it to her shoulder and then declared, "Why, you are a big woman!" Though he was a truly good and venerable man, our visit was for all of us somewhat melancholy since he had not long to live.

The next afternoon we drove by the neglected burial place of Samuel Ruckman, whose two-by-four-foot flat tombstone was standing erect like the man memorialized though he was almost forgotten. We also took a kodak picture of the stalwart Ruckman home at Mill Gap, where I was born 65 years ago. Late in the afternoon on a well-graded, paved road we crossed the Allegheny Mountain in the Happy Hunting Ground to Knapp's Creek for a short call at my old farm home and then down the valley to the Alpine Hotel in Marlinton, to see a half-sister, Mrs. Pollyanna Varner, the young mother of a little girl.

While there, on behalf of the Herold family, I let a contract for placing, over five graves in the burial plot on the former Wise Herold farm, five cement blocks each 6 by 10 feet and 6 inches thick, with the gravestones imbedded flat in the cement except my sister Margie's square monument, which stands firmly upright in the cement like a sentinel on guard. An original plan to erect a rock or cement fence around the graves we abandoned as, in the long run, vulnerable to the ravages of time, and impractical. There rest my Herold grandparents, my mother, one sister, and a little half-brother under the whispering young pine trees, eternally safe from aging care and worldly strife.

After two days of visiting old friends and relatives in Marlinton and on Knapp's Creek — the remaining Herolds, Harpers, Moores, Devers, Prices, and others, and a farewell to the last resting place of the pioneers, Christopher and Elizabeth Herold — we were ready to resume our homeward journey. At Mill Point we turned west for a lovely wild drive across Yew Mountain and by the Richwood lumbering center to Summersville in Nicholas County, where for a few minutes I chatted with Porter Herold, a distant cousin and local merchant, living in the county where my great-grandfather, Henry S. Herold, achieved the age of ninety years. Then, after passing over rugged hills and deep valleys, we picked our way through the heavy traffic above, in, and below Charleston, the state capital and industrial center. We had a restful night in Huntington and the next morning a good talk with my first cousin, Roy Campbell, a rising young businessman of rare good nature and personal charm, whose wife and children were then visiting in Pocahontas County.

My Sisters in Cincinnati

In the afternoon we crossed the Ohio River and traveled down the north side to Cincinnati for a four-day visit with my teacher sister, Reta Lillian, and my nurse sister, Lula Bryan. Though Reta for good and sufficient causes had divorced two husbands, Lula was then planning to try her luck in the matrimonial gamble. Her prince charming was an elderly printer, journalist, and minor politician, William O'Brien, who after their marriage secured an appointment for his wife to the Ohio State Board of Nurse Examiners. Since I had seen little of my sisters for several years, we had many long and satisfying conversations and good meals together in their comfortable apartment. Our talks finally veered around to the ownership of mother's ancestral, mahogany furniture — a four-poster bed, a bureau, a table, chairs, and so on. We boys had long ago agreed that our sisters should have them, but Reta, Lula, and Elizabeth had not been able to reach an amicable division or settlement. Though I advised them, I otherwise sidestepped this spirited sisterly rumpus with charges and countercharges!

Since the time when they were teenage girls, I had advised and helped them with their schooling and the achievement of financial independence. Reta and Lula had received college degrees, and were each able to earn three to five thousand dollars a year — Reta by teaching in the grades and Lula by nursing or supervising hospitals. With fine executive ability and the knack of getting the job done in first-class style, Lula is well fitted to manage a hospital and supervise or train nurses. My sister Elizabeth also fitted herself to teach and practiced the art till she met and married another teacher, George H. Denny, Jr., a nephew of my old friend, President George H. Denny. Their only child, a son, is making a splendid record as a scholar at Johns Hopkins University, entirely worthy of his name, George H. Denny III.

We called at the University of Cincinnati, then much expanded, and at our former places of residence in the Clifton area north of the campus. From Professor Clyde W. Park, I learned that he himself, Dr. Hubertis M. Cummings, and others had retired, and that former President Dabney and Dean Chandler were dead, as I had probably already heard. Thirty years ago I had there joined the benedicts and served a three-year apprenticeship in the English Department of the University of Cincinnati.

Thence to Missouri

On August 15, we arose early and after sisterly farewells we were off to Missouri over Highway 50. In leaving the hilly, widespread city, we missed our way once and police turned us back once to bypass a fire so that we were a full hour in escaping the clutches of Cincinnati. Though we were slowed by rain and wet paving, we chanced to stop for the night in Salem, Illinois, which was the birthplace of my early hero, William Jennings Bryan, whose later record in science and religion I could not regard as either worthy or heroic.

The next morning, after being slowed down for three or four hours by thick and treacherous fog on the highway, we happily by-passed the city of St. Louis and its traffic problems. Later in the day, when my speedometer went noisily haywire, I had a mechanic disconnect it and from there home I estimated my speed without untoward incident. In the Daniel Boone Hotel at Columbia, Missouri, we had a delicious lunch, but at the town of Booneville on the Missouri River we were delayed for half an hour by a spectacular parade in honor of Boone, staged by a Kiwanis Club, I thought, as a publicity stunt. Being trapped at a bridge over the river, we could neither go ahead nor turn aside. Two long lines of automobiles on the highway were thus stopped and delayed, quite unnecessarily, it seemed to me. In retaliation, I refused to stop there for either oil or gasoline! In true Scriptural fashion I shook the dust from my tires and went my way!

Arriving in Marshall, Mrs. Herold's native place, we visited her sister, Mrs. Tate Sweeney, and her brother, Charles G. Smith, and their families. Mr. Sweeney is a traveling commercial agent and Charles is a farmer and for successive terms assessor of Saline County. Both are genial and prosperous, and blessed with children to help them carry on. One day we drove to Alma in Lafayette County to check on Mrs. Herold's farm economy and thence to Lexington for the night with some of our friends. Meditating here upon my observations in crossing four states, I decided that in a single sentence I would characterize Ohio, Indiana, Illinois, and Missouri as typical, productive, prosperous, and progressive American states in which our democratic and republican principles of government and economy have achieved a brilliant success for their citizens and the nation.

Home Once More

On August 20, we traveled south from Marshall to Fayetteville, Arkansas, to see my dear old cousin poet, Mrs. Mary E. Overholt, and her family. Though mentally alert and fresh of memory at the age of 91, she was thin, frail, and blind, barely able to distinguish day from night. Though I did not then expect this heroic woman to live another year, she observed her 95th birthday on August 3, 1954. Truly she is a remarkable woman, the oldest member of my family now or in the past. However, she was frank to observe quietly that she had lived too long! She died on April 6, 1956, at the age of 96 years, 8 months, and 3 days. The next day south over Boston Mountain, down the valley of the Arkansas River, and up the White River to Batesville, we completed a round trip of 2,200 miles to the scenes of my birth and youth.

CHAPTER 24

Our Seven Chief Natural Wonders

THE Seven Wonders of the ancient world, all works of art made by man before the Christian era began, were in the chronological order of their creation the following: The Pyramids of Egypt, giant tombs of the Pharaohs, erected from 3,000 to 1,800 B. C., the largest covering nearly 13 acres and originally 481 feet high; the Hanging Gardens of Babylon, erected by Nebuchadnezzar about 600 B. C. to please his queen; the Statue of Zeus, made of marble and decorated with ivory and gold by Phidias about 430 B. C.; the Tomb of Mausolus, a king in Asia Minor, erected by his widow about 325 B. C.; the Colossus of Rhodes, supposed to be a bronze statue of Apollo 100 feet high on the island of Rhodes near Asia Minor, built about 280 B. C.; a Lighthouse at Alexandria, Egypt, built by a Ptolemy about 200 B. C. and destroyed by an earthquake in 1375 A. D.; and the Temple of Diana at Ephesus, a large, pagan shrine with 127 marble columns each 60 feet high, built about 5 B. C., where the Apostle Paul enraged a crowd of people by challenging pagan worship. Ancient writers show some variations in the list.

In concluding Part VI on "Seeing the United States," I will list what I regard as the Seven Chief Natural Wonders of our country, which were all made by natural forces, chiefly running water. Man's delight in natural beauty and wonder is of fairly recent origin. Each marvel is distinctive and outstanding of its kind. Arranged in an approximate order of distinction and importance, my list includes:

1. First and foremost is the Grand Canyon of the Colorado River in northern Arizona, which for grandeur and beauty probably has no rival on our earth.

2. A close second is the collection of Geysers in the Yellowstone National Park of northwest Wyoming, surpassing in number, variety, and glamor all other terrestrial geysers.

3. The Giant Redwood and Sequoia Trees of California including the world's tallest, largest, and oldest merit a high rating. Several of these majestic and venerable trees are said to be older than the oldest of the Pyramids. Thousands of them were living when Christ was born and are still thriving. John Muir, the brilliant naturalist and author, called them "nature's forest masterpiece."

4. Of our many celebrated waterfalls first place belongs to Niagara Falls. Though Yosemite and Yellowstone Falls are higher and very beautiful, they have not the grand power and compelling distinction of historic Niagara Falls.

5. Among our natural bridges none quite equals the famous Natural Bridge in the Valley of Virginia, over which a real highway has long passed. Return of the site to state or federal ownership and control would be a boon to all lovers of our natural wonders.

6. Because of its size, uniqueness, and beauty, the Crater Lake of Oregon deserves a place among our Seven Wonders. Without direct inlet or outlet, this marvel is a deep, fresh-water lake in the top of a volcanic mountain 35 miles in circumference, surrounded by hemlock, fir, and pine forests where wild flowers and animals are abundant.

7. For the last place in our list, one may choose either Carlsbad Caverns in New Mexico or Mammoth Cave in Kentucky. These Caverns are true rivals. Though Carlsbad is novel and unmarred by trophy hunters who defaced delicate decorations in Mammoth Cave in the 19th century, still Carlsbad has no underground river with eyeless fish where one may go boating nor a pre-Columbian mummy, found in 1935 three miles from an entrance in Mammoth Cave and preserved there in an air-tight glass case. Besides, in 1938 four cavern guides looking for eyeless fish found new sections of amazingly beautiful limestone caverns with miles of main avenues, unsurpassed gypsum flowers, and marvelous onyx formations, which replace the former defacements and add novel glamor to Mammoth Cave.

Our mountains for grandeur and beauty I would rate in this order: first, the Rocky Mountains; second, the Sierra Nevada or Grand Teton Mountains; and third, the Great Smoky Mountains between North Carolina and Tennessee. It is fortunate that these mountains and our natural wonders, including those not listed here, are so well distributed as to be within driving range of large portions of the American people. If Niagara Falls is a long way from Oregon, Yosemite and the Big Trees are nearby; and if the Yellowstone Geysers are distant from Alabama, the Great Smokies are fairly close. Most Americans are happily near one or more of our Natural Wonders and at least one of our delectable mountains.

I CHOSE TEACHING
Part VII. Terminus

CHAPTER 25

Retrospect and College Reforms

IN THE 70-year period from 1885 to 1955, I witnessed many remarkable innovations. The wireless telegraph led the way to the radio and television. Silent movies became talking pictures in true colors. The motor car and airplane revolutionized travel and transportation. Electricity was hitched to scores of useful machines and gadgets. Gunpowder, dynamite, and TNT were surpassed by atomic bombs. The names of Edison, Marconi, Ford, the Wright brothers, and Einstein frequently headlined the news of their inventions or leadership.

In American education I observed the rapid development of free high schools for all youngsters, colleges for those who may wish to attend them, and improved facilities for adult education. In social service the halt, maimed, blind, deaf, aged, unemployed, and insane received more attention and benefits. The medical arts curbed diseases and lengthened the span of human life nearly fifty per cent. In the United States a new day dawned for underprivileged groups and neglected races. After many years of effort and distress, labor unions acquired power comparable to that of their employers. Passing through two bloody World Wars, I witnessed several attempts to establish a world organization to settle international disputes and to preserve the peace. As the former world leaders, England and France, lost power and prestige, the United States and Russia gained them and became rival leaders of different political and social systems.

But much progress and gain have been offset by losses. For example, though the American Indians were formerly denounced and hated for the indiscriminate slaughter of old men, women,

245

and children, so-called respectable, Christian people have acquiesced in the deliberate destruction of cities as a war measure! This fact points to a weakening or perversion of the moral sense and to a loss of normal human sympathy. Some churches stress quantity rather than quality in membership, seeking power and display rather than virtue and truth. In a world professing faith in the rights and rule of the people, I have seen democracies languish and dictatorships rise and fall and rise again. In some nations new and horrible tortures have been devised and practiced upon many dissidents.

In college education and elsewhere two distressing problems still call for adjustment. These are obsolete systems of old-age retirement and obsolete college governments. The retirement problem arises from a nearly fifty-percent increase in the average age of Americans within the last fifty-five years. The second stems from an outmoded denial of self-government to many college faculties.

Age and Retirement

In the last half century no change in the United States has been more astonishing than the phenomenal increase in human longevity as conclusive evidence of medical progress in the prevention, treatment, and cure of many human ills and diseases. In 1900, as shown by the U. S. Public Health Service, the average age of Americans was 47 years. By 1920 it had increased to 54 years. By 1930 it had risen to nearly 60 years. By 1950 it was nearly 69 and still rising. That is, in about fifty years and in spite of two World Wars and influenza and polio epidemics, the average life span increased 22 or 23 years. In the same period infant mortality was reduced about eighty per cent, and every other age group showed a notable reduction in the death rate. In 1955 about two-thirds of the people were living past their 65th birthdays.

These plain facts make obsolete and unjust virtually all of the retirement systems based upon an average age of 60 years or less. In 1935, when Congress enacted the first Social-Security legislation, the data then available indicated an average age of 60 years, but in 1955 the average was known to be about 70 years — an increase of ten years in one generation! Yet, though many million Americans are sooner or later adversely affected, retirement policies and hiring practices have not been correspondingly modified and adjusted. The result is that in the course of years several million employable persons aged 40 to 70 are continued or forced into unemployment, penalized, and cruelly punished, because on an average they live ten years longer than their elders.

If retirement at the age of 65 was ever fair and equitable when the average age was 60 in 1930, then by the same standard an average age of 70 in 1955 calls for a retirement age of 72 to 75, which would likewise be past the average age. However, instead of an arbitrary and uniform age for retirement, the system should be flexible and adjusted to the physiological aging, health, wishes, and working capacity of the persons concerned, because some are as unfit for work at 55 as others at 75 or 80. Chronological age is only one of several factors to be considered in determining the need for retirement.

In 1954 many active and outstanding leaders were near or past the age of 80. On the international scene were Winston Churchill of England, Konrad Adenauer of Germany, Syngman Rhee of Korea, Chiang Kaishek of China, the Pope of Rome, and Herbert Hoover, Alben W. Barkley, and Bertrand Russell in the United States. Several members of the United Senate varied in age from Senator Guy M. Gillette's 75 to Senator Theodore F. Green's 87. Benjamin Franklin was past 80 when he helped to frame the Constitution of the United States, and his greatest service to this country was rendered between the ages of 70 and 84. Truly, with fullness of years comes wisdom.

My Experience with Retirement

In 1948, when I was 63 years old, I accepted employment at Arkansas College at a modest salary, chiefly because the college permitted and encouraged its teachers to work as long as they could give worthy service. As a potent inducement to me to join the faculty, President John D. Spragins named two professors on the staff, then about 75 (one of them previously retired elsewhere), who were still teaching and who served well and acceptably till about 80 years of age. So long as this Christian gentleman, Dr. Spragins, was president of Arkansas College, these just and generous retirement practices of the college continued, and several of us already 65 were able to qualify for social-security benefits though we wished to work as long as we could function well. But in 1952, after ten years of excellent service in building goodwill and democracy in the college, he was pressured into resigning and accepting other employment.

Unfortunately for the college and the faculty, President Spragins was succeeded by a callow, inexperienced fellow from Georgia, who at once began overturning the college self-government and setting up a one-man rule for the most part. To accomplish his personal aims, he asked the Board of Trustees for power to assume the functions of any professor or other employee and for a retirement age of 65 except as a favor from him. For previous employment arrangements, for the rights of faculty members, and the longer life span, this fellow had no regard. He acted as if he had legal permission to ignore the just claims of the faculty. When it suited his ruthless purposes and hot temper, he could be insulting to members of the staff.

Feeling his power and stalking the campus, he dismissed a competent widowed teacher with four dependent children under circumstances that caused her to lose $2,000 in a forced sale of her home. Probably foreseeing from my remarks in faculty meetings and one of my published articles that I would probably not welcome his regime, he appears to have marked me for early dismissal under the smoke-screen of retirement. Though I had promptly and faithfully performed all of my duties to the college, this novice, while seeming to be my friend, was at the same time preparing to hit me a double blow in a single letter — first, a belated announcement of his retirement program at 65, and second, its immediate application to me.

Below is the cruelest letter that I ever received and that left me dazed and sleepless for a day or two as if thugs had struck me on the head and left me unconscious. It also reeks with subterfuge and sarcasm. The principal actor was not the Board but the president trying to shield himself behind the Board. Though this letter was dated March 31, 1953, I did not receive it till a week later.

Dear Dr. Herold:

At the recent winter meeting [January 15] of the Board of Trustees, the Board inaugurated a retirement program in which all employees become subject to retirement upon reaching the age of 65. Under this policy the Board has directed me to notify you of your retirement at the end of the current academic year.

The members of the Board have asked me to express their appreciation for your services to the college. Although I have been at the college only a few months, I am aware of the important contributions you have made, and I want to thank you personally for your interest and efforts towards raising the academic standards of the college. We shall miss you on our faculty next year.

I shall be happy to talk with you about your plans for

the future and your benefits under the Social Security program.

With best wishes, I am
Cordially yours,
Paul M. McCain

This letter was the first word that I received of any change in the retirement plans of the college. I was being retired or dismissed by a system of which I knew nothing. Mr. McCain had concealed his blackjack weapons for three months. Though I was frequently from January to April in his office on special assignments for him, he spoke not a word to me about any retirement system or my retirement. My first action was to call at his office and ask for a copy of the new retirement system. He tried to satisfy me with a verbal statement, but I insisted on having a written copy of it, which I received the next day. Already I had been engaged to teach in the summer school at a low salary of $300 for a term of five weeks — just the usual verbal agreement. Then, after regaining my senses, I composed the following letter dated April 12, 1953, to President McCain.

Dear Dr. McCain:

In response to your letter of March 31 (delivered April 8) and the copy of Arkansas College Retirement Plan of 1953, let me say that this plan does not apply to me, because I accepted appointment here and have worked for the past five years under the policies and practices on employment and retirement then in effect and established through the years by such leaders as Dr. W. S. Lacy, the two Longs, and Dr. John D. Spragins. Moreover, let me say that if the Retirement Plan of 1953 had been in effect in 1948, I should certainly not have sought or accepted employment in Arkansas College.

When I was first visiting the college with a view to employment, President Spragins carefully and thoroughly explained the policies and practices of the college on employment and retirement, which I regarded as wise and humane. The main feature was that no age year was set as a time for retirement. Not age but capacity to do work was the basis of determining employment and retirement. The President referred to two professors who were then in their seventies and who worked till almost 80, I think, as concrete examples or cases showing how the system worked. Several others have continued to work efficiently up to and into the seventies, and are still on the faculty.

The experience of Arkansas College shows that an age limit of 65 for retirement is antiquated and unresponsive to the greatly increased longevity of people because of the marvels performed by modern medical science in all its aspects.

Therefore, I wish earnestly to request and insist that my service as Professor and Head of the English Department be continued on the basis of employment and retirement policies in the Spragins administration as explained in 1948 and in effect since then, and that my salary conform to the latest scale for professors.

No college has any moral or legal right to pass rules and regulations affecting the faculty and make them retroactive to some earlier date, nor has it any right to shirk the responsibilities assumed by college officials in the legitimate performance of their functions in engaging instructors and conducting the college business.

Since this matter of my employment and the rest of the faculty has been exceedingly late in the year, I ask that my request be acted upon favorably on or before April 30, 1953.

If I can furnish additional information, I shall be glad to do so, and I am sure that Dr. Spragins will be glad to explain more fully his policies.

Professors on tenure are universally allowed one year or more notice before retirement can become fair, just, and effective.

Very cordially yours,
Amos L. Herold
Professor of English

The next day Mr. McCain replied making the astonishing claim that the college had no system of retirement prior to the one he had initiated. As a matter of fact, Dr. Spragins had arranged for two or three retirements since my coming, one for ill health and one for age. Then Mr. McCain threatened to break my engagement to teach in the summer school, because, as he said, I was not in sympathy with the college program! He did not propose to pay any attention to my vigorous protest, which an attorney alumnus of the college advised me to carry to the Personnel Committee of the Board of Trustees.

Toward the end of April, my physician supplied me with the following statement regarding my health and capacity for work:

To Whom It May Concern:

This Statement is to Certify that I have examined Amos L. Herold and found his physical condition to be good except for mild enlargement of the Prostate. It is not necessary for surgery to be done at this time to correct the enlargement.

It is my opinion that this 67-year-old man will be able to work for at least seven or eight years longer.

Respectfully,
Paul Gray, M. D.

When some of my best students heard of the administrative program, they offered to aid me in any way they could. One brilliant young woman went straight to the president to register her emphatic personal protest, and the President of the Student Body, Doin Hicks, wrote for me on May 21 the best testimonial I ever received. Here it is:

To Whom It May Concern:

My impression of the English Department of Arkansas College is one of high regard. I have thoroughly enjoyed my work in the department. Being an English minor and having had both general and specialized courses in American and British Literature as well as the required freshman course, I feel qualified to pass judgment upon the department. As a basis for expressing my feelings I would set up the following criteria: selection of material, presentation of material, and the effect upon the student. I would say that the department ranks very high on all three counts. Professor Herold has done an excellent job in selecting texts for the various courses and also, when necessary, selecting material to supplement certain texts. The material is presented in a very enlightening manner. The student is given a chance to formulate his own opinion and to give his interpretation of the material. Dr. Herold draws upon his vast store of knowledge and experiences to help bring the material into the scope of the students' understanding, and to give it further and deeper meaning. Concerning the English Department's effect upon me, as a student, it has strengthened my appreciation of the fine art, helped me learn to express myself both orally and in writing, and has helped me achieve a richer and fuller understanding of life for which I am very grateful.

Doin Hicks
President of the Student Body
Arkansas College

On May 8, I wrote Mr. McCain a supplementary letter naming the three persons whose retirements were handled in whole or part by his predecessor, Dr. Spragins, and covering other minor matters. On May 19, Mr. McCain wrote me of the red tape I must follow to be heard by the Board, but, since I was seeking to meet with the Personnel Committee, I paid no attention to his letter. On May 21, he telephoned me to come to his office about an unspecified matter, probably the red tape referred to in his letter. Since he had been wholly unresponsive in a previous conference and to my letters, I declined to go. This refusal he used as an excuse for breaking the engagement to teach in the summer school, though there was no real connection between this engagement and my protest against the premature retirement. Dodging the main business, the dictator looked for some penalty to impose.

Making many excuses of one kind or another, the Personnel Committee of the Board did not meet with me until Commencement Day and then for only about fifteen minutes. It then made some kind of perfunctory report to the Board, which took no further action. However, I notified Mr. McCain that unless he kept his agreement with me for summer work, I intended to bring suit for the compensation. At the summer registration I appeared and reported to the dean and president of my willingness and readiness to keep the agreement, but another instructor was pushed into my place. Then, I engaged an attorney and brought suit in the Municipal Court of Batesville for $300. This action put Mr. McCain on a hot spot. Programs listing me as a summer instructor for two named courses had been circulated in April and May, which were documentary evidence of my engagement.

In the trial, however, on July 9, 1953, after I had testified fully, Mr. McCain on the witness stand took an oath to tell the truth and then denied my basic allegations. He claimed that he had made no agreement with me to teach in the summer school and that the announcements were unauthorized. The fact was that my engagement had gone regularly through the dean's office for the two courses and through the president's for the compensation. Both he and one board member also swore that the president had no authority to engage summer instructors. Documentary evidence from the records of the board, discovered later, showed this claim to be untrue. Though my attorney and I lost the suit, we had the satisfaction of unmasking the president of the college. At one time the college had offered to pay one-half of the $300, but I refused to let pass an opportunity to bring

Mr. McCain to the witness stand. My attorney and I then decided that the small amount in controversy would not justify me in appealing to a higher court.

Thus, at the age of 68 I was not only denied a bit of summer work but also deprived of my right to work at my profession. Regardless of the lengthened life span, the age of 65 at Arkansas College had in effect been made a crime punishable with unemployment, though this cruel fact is concealed by the honeyed words "subject to or eligible for retirement." My indignation was hot then and it is still hot against this infamous crime of forcing experienced teachers capable of much good service into the barren lot of the unemployed.

I vowed then and I still vow to do something about this wicked, cruel, and inhuman practice, even though I am personally able to live comfortably whether or not I work. All men and women have an inalienable right to work, if they wish, as long as they can render efficient service. The act of willfully and needlessly forcing unemployment on the capable and competent is a crime that should be severely punished. Under Arkansas law for the public schools, the age for compulsory retirement is 72, which almost conforms to the lengthened life span at the middle of the 20th century.

On Reforming College Government

This criticism of obsolete systems of retirement leads naturally to a demand for discarding obsolete college governments, which are partial or complete dictatorships. In my article of 1943 on "Democratizing the Colleges," I had asserted that nowhere is the need greater for democratic attitudes and habits than in our schools and colleges, for, if they degenerate into dictatorships, the spirit of democracy will languish and die in the youth of America. In so-called democratic America, is it not incredible that the majority of the American colleges and universities should be legally organized on an autocratic basis? With many intellectual centers in the United States emulating Caesarism or Hitlerism, how can we hope to nurture and inculcate in youth effectively the democratic faith, traditions, and practices? Is there a more insidious or dangerous evil than the suppression of democracy in our schools and colleges?

Usually boards of trustees are composed of busy men of affairs — bankers, manufacturers, lawyers, politicians, physicians, and clergymen. Seldom does the board have a representative of the teaching profession, or scientific research, or industrial workers. Such a board may understand a business corporation organized to make profits, but, apart from endowment and budgets, it knows little of educational institutions organized for training youth and extending the bounds of knowledge. Having neither the knowledge nor the time to examine and evaluate delicate matters of educational policy, it delegates its functions and powers to the president, who then often proceeds to set up a personal dictatorship.

Consequently, two fundamental changes should be made in college government. The first change, already begun in a few colleges, is that one-third of the college board should be chosen by the sponsoring organization or state, one-third by the college alumni, and one-third by the college faculty, all for three-year terms when fully organized. These alumni and faculty representatives should be experienced educators, either active or retired, or possibly members of some other faculty. Enjoying all the powers and privileges of other board members. they would bring to the board an element of academic intelligence and experience now most apparent by its absence. They would share the responsibility of the president and be an aid in initiating and carrying on the policies and business of the college or university.

At Oxford and Cambridge Universities the scholars and scientists are their own boards of trustees and manage the educational institutions just as in America experienced bankers operate and direct our banks and experienced railroad men operate and direct the railways. At the University of Manchester, England, the public, the alumni, and the faculty participate in the government of the institution. For many years the rule of the faculty has been maintained at Cornell University. In 1912, President Jacob G. Schurman of that institution gave this significant advice:

"What is needed in American universities today is a new application of the principle of representative government. The faculty is essentially the university; yet in the governing boards of American universities the faculty is without representation. The only ultimately satisfactory solution of the problem of the government of American universities is the concession to the professoriate of representation in the board of trustees or regents and these representatives of the intellectual, which is the real life of the university, must not be mere ornamental figures; they should be granted an active share in the routine administration of the institution." (J. M. Cattell, *University Control*, p. 476.)

The second fundamental change needed in college government, if there is to be any real democracy in college, is that all